City Comp

CITY COMP

Identities, Spaces, Practices

Edited by

BRUCE McCOMISKEY

and

CYNTHIA RYAN

STATE UNIVERSITY OF NEW YORK PRESS

Published by
STATE UNIVERSITY OF NEW YORK PRESS
ALBANY

© 2003 State University of New York

For information, address
State University of New York Press,
90 State Street, Suite 700, Albany, NY 12207

Production by Kelli M. Williams
Marketing by Fran Keneston

Library of Congress Cataloging-in-Publication Data

City comp : identities, spaces, practices / edited by Bruce McComiskey and Cynthia Ryan.
    p. cm.
Includes bibliographical references and index.
ISBN 0-7914-5549-1 (alk. paper) — ISBN 0-7914-5550-5 (pbk. : alk. paper)
    1. Education, Urban—Social aspects—United States—Case studies. 2. English
language—Rhetoric—Study and teaching (Higher)—Social aspects—United States—Case
studies. 3. Urban universities and colleges—United States—Sociological aspects—Case
studies. I. McComiskey, Bruce, 1963– II. Ryan, Cynthia.

I.C5131 .C52 2003
370'.9173'2—dc21

                                                                2002191119

10 9 8 7 6 5 4 3 2 1

For our parents

Mary Ann and Gerald Ryan
and
Eleanor and Thomas McComiskey

CONTENTS

PART II
Composing Spaces

PART III
Redefining Practices

FOREWORD

Linda Flower

A rhetoric of real places (were we to develop one) would describe how writing is not merely situated in and shaped by its time and place, but how the writer's sense of that time and place is the source of meanings, motivations, and identities. It would also be the source of contradictory and conflicting forces—of ideologies, intentions, and values. A rhetoric of real places would reveal not only the influence of place and its multiple meaning-making voices, but would take us into the ways writers must negotiate these forces as they interpret the world around them in their own literate acts.

City Comp: Identities, Spaces, Practices takes an imaginative step in the direction of a rhetoric of real places. Yet it also takes on another challenge. It shows us how this constructive, situated meaning making and its energetic negotiation with conflict and context can emerge not only in the writing of urban planners, theorists, administrators, and their ilk, but also in the work of urban students. These portraits of urban students, their teachers, and their institutions reveal the drama of contested meaning making.

Rhetorics typically function as both descriptions of literate practices and as heuristic guides to literate action. The essays collected here suggest that a rhetoric of real places is not just the production of tourist travelogues. It is a rhetoric that describes and guides the processes of encounter, inquiry, and intervention.

An encounter with an urban space is an encounter with its multiple, heterogeneous discourses, its competing languages. Each space comes loaded with cultural and social histories that write the meaning of cities in its own concepts and values. One place where we encounter this melee of voices is in

the urban planning of cities and the strategic plans of universities—both trying to write identities into being. Birmingham seeks to redefine its image; a
downtown Wilmington community college seeks to give itself a history, while
its neighboring university seeks prestige; and Georgia State remakes itself into
a "metropolitan university." As the rhetoric of identity making changes, so do
programs, priorities, and the support services schools offer or eliminate.
Throughout these chapters, students become aware of rhetorical processes
swirling around them and of the stake they have in their outcomes.

But encounter does not stop at words on a page. DePaul students,
engaging in this rhetoric, find themselves changing trains on the Chicago
"el," as they are immersed in a week's journey into "the sprawling, cos-
mopolitan, increasingly multi-ethnic-racial-religious character of metropolitan Chicago" where they find ideas linked to real places and where the flesh
and blood "leaders" and the authorities students talk with do not agree (Jolliffe, this volume).

In a rhetoric of real places, such encounters with conflict are generative.
They pose open questions. They open the door to inquiry; and in urban
spaces, they call us with particular force into an intercultural inquiry.

The philosophical grounding for each chapter here differs, of course, yet
they also collectively reflect John Dewey's "experimental way of knowing"
and Cornel West's prophetic pragmatism, which underlie what my colleagues and I have called a "*strong* rival hypothesis stance" (Flower, Long,
and Higgins). This stance is an approach to inquiry that sees the meaning
of ideas in their consequences, that recognizes our understanding (even our
strongest beliefs) to be our best current hypotheses about the consequential
meaning of those ideas. From that understanding, such a stance calls us
actively to seek good "rivals"—alternative, complementary, and competing
readings of the world. The special challenge of the "strong" version of the
rival hypothesis stance is that it requires us to cross lines of racial and cultural differences, to acknowledge the agency, and to seek the rival readings
of the powerless, the marginalized, the silenced. We are asked to seek meaning in discourses that do not talk the language of the academy, the urban
planner, or the social engineer and to build a broader, more negotiated
understanding with it. The authors of these chapters, and the students represented in them, often find themselves taking the "strong stance" of intercultural inquiry.

In San Francisco's Tenderloin, intercultural inquiry takes us to a skills
center that has revamped its programs to support "get-ahead" literacy skills.
This means replacing personal writing activities with training in the formal
conventions required to get that "legitimizing" GED. But the "rival reading"
of this learning process—the interpretations offered by students such as
Renee, Ellie, and Moses—is an account of loss. These adults discover that

their initial positive sense of identity as writers, based on self-expression, has no apparent connection to learning. For them the "meaning" of GED instruction is in part the dismissal of that identity and the active erosion of their fragile sense of self-efficacy in writing.

The experience of Birmingham students is wrapped up in the claims, hype, racial history, and new identity making of their city and its institutions. They stand within the "tension between the mythologized city of Birmingham and the evolving promotional image of UAB" (Baker, Jolly, McComiskey, and Ryan, this volume). But not everyone is represented in this discussion, and a composition class becomes a place of inquiry that seeks out some of the "alternative myths" that live in this city. In doing so, invisible urban students find a way to claim their own identities in the classroom.

In Pittsburgh, students actively seek out the "critical incident" stories of food service workers to contrast to their own middle-class work histories. In writing classrooms in Detroit, Atlanta, Pittsburgh, and Chicago, composition courses allow students not only to talk back to myths and critique versions of their identities, but also to seek out voices that are not their own. And these voices, too, become part of their story.

Finally, the rhetoric of real places is, in the best tradition of rhetoric, an art of intervention. If the mission of higher education is the production of knowledge, this rhetoric defines the knowledge we need as "learning how to respond to societal issues ethically and collaboratively" (Feldman, this volume). It supports the literate action of an "engaged university" that asks why Atlanta public transportation does not extend to the counties where urban commuter students live—doing what Tom Deans describes as service learning projects that write "about" and "for" the community. Or it may lead to what he calls writing "with" the community—to community problem-solving dialogues on urban issues such as risk, respect, and police curfew that create a public, literate forum for marginalized voices, or to dialogues on health care or workplace performance that redefine patients and low-wage workers as partners in solving shared problems (Flower). In this study of city comp, in Deans's study of service learning, in the student writing you can see emerging in urban classrooms, newsletters, and on websites (e.g., see Carnegie Mellon's site on *Intercultural Inquiry* and the *Neighborhood Writing Alliance* page on NCTE's site for the *Journal of Ordinary Thought*), we can see the power of a rhetorically situated approach to writing. Whether the goal is a letter to the editor or a highly engaged intercultural dialogue, a rhetoric of real places moves us toward civic participation. And if the projects that fill this book are like Hull-House—if they "cannot remake Chicago," and if their own agendas must live with internal contradictions—they affirm that writing *can* affect real lives "and for the rest it is a guide to the imagination" (Hillard, this volume).

WORKS CITED

Deans, Thomas. *Writing Partnerships: Service-Learning in Composition.* Urbana: NCTE, 2000.

Dewey, John. *The Quest for Certainty.* Vol. 4 (1929). *The Later Works of John Dewey, 1925–1953.* Ed. Jo Ann Boydston. Carbondale: Southern Illinois UP, 1988.

Flower, Linda. *Problem-Solving Strategies for Writing in College and Community.* Ft. Worth, TX: Harcourt Brace, 1998.

———, Elenore Long, and Lorraine Higgins. *Learning to Rival: A Literate Practice for Intercultural Inquiry.* Mahwah, NJ: Lawrence Erlbaum, 2000.

Intercultural Inquiry. Research Briefs and Student Writing on Intercultural Inquiry. 20 May 2001. <http://english.cmu.edu/inquiry>.

Neighborhood Writing Alliance. Service-Learning in Composition. *Journal of Ordinary Thought.* Chicago, IL. 20 May 2001. <http://www.ncte.org/service>.

West, Cornel. *The American Evasion of Philosophy: A Genealogy of Pragmatism.* Madison: U of Wisconsin P, 1989.

INTRODUCTION

Bruce McComiskey and Cynthia Ryan

Cultural theorists Henry Lefebvre and Michel de Certeau both describe cities not as "places" that contain people, but as "situations" in which people act, and, as such, each particular urban context becomes a text that is written by its inhabitants. In *Writings on Cities*, Lefebvre makes an important distinction between "the *city*, a present and immediate reality, a practico-material and architectural fact, and the *urban*, a social reality made up of relations which are to be conceived of, constructed or reconstructed by thought" (103). However, while "the city" and "the urban" may be distinct, they are also perpetually in contact, dialectically, for there can be no urban social experience without the fact of the city, and cities do not exist unless people think of them as such. Urban/city contexts, then, are negotiated, not given; they both construct, and are constructed by, their inhabitants. Michel de Certeau offers "walking" as a metaphor for the kind of dialectic Lefebvre describes. In *The Practice of Everyday Life*, de Certeau writes, "The ordinary practitioners of the city . . . are walkers, whose bodies follow the thicks and thins of an urban 'text' they write without being able to read it" (93), and the "act of walking is to the urban system what the speech act is to language or to the statement uttered" (97). de Certeau explains that the "walking of passers-by offers a series of turns and detours that can be compared to 'turns of phrase' or 'stylistic figures.' There is a rhetoric of walking. The art of 'turning' phrases finds an equivalent in an art of composing a path" (100). These paths/texts that de Certeau's urban inhabitants walk/compose are in part constrained by the material geography of cities (we cannot walk through walls); yet, within certain undeniable limits, inhabitants construct, whether communally or individually, the paths/texts of their own design.

1

In this Introduction's first section, "Moving to Birmingham," we discuss the urban paths/texts that we composed (and that were composed for us) upon accepting positions at the University of Alabama at Birmingham in 1998. In the remaining sections, we detail the complicated history of urban universities in the context of higher education generally, discuss the important role that rhetoric and composition plays in urban education, and plot out the organizing principles behind the essays that comprise *City Comp: Identities, Spaces, Practices.* All of the contributors to this collection have composed their own paths through the thicks and thins of the cities in which they live and teach, and we hope that as our readers follow these diverse paths, new ways will emerge to compose alternative paths through the thicks and thins of these and other cities.

MOVING TO BIRMINGHAM

We were both educated at large Midwestern universities that got their start in the nineteenth century as normal ("teacher-training") colleges and land-grant universities. Our first post-TA jobs were at a rural branch campus in the North Carolina State University (land-grant) system. Needless to say, when we got a call from the chair of the English department at the University of Alabama at Birmingham (UAB) offering us both tenure-track jobs teaching composition and professional writing, we experienced a mix of excitement and anxiety. The details of the jobs sounded great, but "Birmingham?" we muttered to ourselves. Immediately, black and white media images of guard dogs and water cannons filled our minds. After sixteen years of education and teaching in rural universities oriented toward education, engineering, and agriculture, how would we deal with this new environment, this urban space that, we imagined, was rife with social ills? Despite both of our having lived in or near Chicago for many years, we still had negative associations with urban universities and commuter campuses: "urban" equals congestion at best, and violence, racism, and poverty at worst.

We accepted the jobs. When we arrived in Birmingham during the summer of 1998, we were initially skeptical to say the least. The Humanities Building (HB), where the English department is housed, had four floors, with walkways around the outside of the building, classrooms that were accessible only from these external walkways, and small professors' offices connected to an H-shaped hallway on the inside. We were told that HB was constructed during the early 1970s and designed specifically to prevent large numbers of student protesters from gaining a stronghold inside the building. It wasn't until a week into our first term of teaching that we noticed HB's cornerstone:

BUILDING THREE
UNIVERSITY OF ALABAMA
IN BIRMINGHAM
1972
GEORGE C. WALLACE
GOVERNOR

George Wallace? Wasn't he the governor who was elected on a platform promising strict segregation "yesterday, today, and forever"? Hadn't he blocked two African American students from rightfully entering a classroom building at the University of Alabama in Tuscaloosa?

Later, as we drove down University Boulevard, the main artery that bisects UAB into two halves, we saw the state of the art medical school on the left and what those in the medical school call the "academic division" (or "the rest of the university") on the right. The buildings on the left side of University Boulevard, we noticed, were brand new, made of bright red brick and shiny mirrored windows. The buildings on the right were old, made of gray cement and few, if any, windows. We had unwittingly become implicated in a deeply entrenched class system, and we were at the bottom of the ladder.

Clear class divisions, both inside and outside the university, and in-your-face reminders of a racist past—these were our initial experiences at UAB. But what we saw at first was only part of the story. As we got into the first quarter of teaching, our interactions with UAB's students began to turn our attitudes around. These students were (and are, switching now to present tense) keenly aware of these damaging class divisions, and they understand the lasting effects of Birmingham's vexed history. Students in Birmingham are not only aware of these problems, but also openly willing to discuss and try to solve them. Our composition students write often about issues of race, ethnicity, class, sexuality, and gender differences partly because they *live* with these issues as integral aspects of everyday life in Birmingham.

The students we had taught at normal and land-grant universities were shy about such difficult topics, happiest to play in the safe zone of freewriting and formal essay structures despite our urging to the contrary. But our urban students seemed positively predisposed toward "socially" oriented writing pedagogies right from the very beginning. Cultural studies, critical discourse analysis, and feminist media studies have proven to be fertile ground in which our students can explore issues of cultural identity and how the social "space" (both geographical and conceptual) of the city itself promotes and legitimizes certain identities over others. Our urban students are not content to play in the safe zone; they want to accomplish real social goals through their writing, goals that embody visions of a better Birmingham.

During the past few years, we have recognized important differences between our experiences teaching at an urban university versus teaching in normal and land-grant universities, yet these differences were initially only anecdotal. Thus, we began to seek explanations that would move beyond the level of anecdote, and we began our more formal search in the very nature and function of urban universities. In order to understand urban universities fully, we must consider their genesis in the historical context of higher education generally.

CITY UNIVERSITIES

During the early nineteenth century, higher education consisted mostly of private liberal arts and teacher training colleges catering to local, elite populations, and these colleges were situated, quite intentionally, in rural (not urban) contexts. According to Carol Severino, "Prejudice against the corrupt city and in favor of the supposedly pure and innocent country has pervaded American thinking since the early days of the republic and influenced the development of American colleges, often founded in small country towns" (293). By mid-century, however, there was growing sentiment in the United States federal government that these small and elite institutions were not serving the most basic, pragmatic needs of each state and its citizenry. In 1862, Congress passed the First Morrill Act providing each state with the financial resources it would need to establish its own "land-grant" college(s). These land-grant colleges, free of tuition and open to the general public, focused on the pragmatic subjects that would most benefit each state, including engineering, mining, and especially agriculture. The Second Morrill Act, passed by Congress in 1890, granted each new state college an agriculture research lab, further focusing the efforts of these institutions on agrarian issues.

By the turn of the twentieth century, and partly the result of industrialization and the rise of mass transportation following the Civil War, America's population centers experienced a period of rapid growth. In fact, according to Howard P. Chudacoff, "Between 1860 and 1920 the number of people living in American cities of 8,000 or more inhabitants mushroomed from 6.2 million to 54.3 million" (101), totaling more than half of the nation's population for the first time in its history. The fundamental problem during this period of rapid growth was that the cities of 1860 were not designed or built to accommodate the population densities of 1920, resulting inevitably in congested streets and neighborhoods, unemployment or degrading employment, housing shortages and slums, inadequate waste and sewage disposal, few opportunities for quality education, and deteriorating roadways and buildings. Further, many of these new urban residents were ethnic immigrants or descendants of freed slaves. In 1910, for example, thirteen of the largest six-teen cities in the United States (in descending order of total size: New York, Chicago, Philadelphia, Boston, Cleveland, Pittsburgh, Detroit, Buffalo, San Francisco, Milwaukee, Newark, New Orleans, and Washington) had popula-tions in which more than 30 percent were immigrants or African Americans (Chudacoff 102). Thus, the brutal realities of urban life after the turn of the century, combined with cultural differences among neighborhood groups in close proximity, contributed to the rise of (stereo)typically "urban" social prob-lems, including violent crime, poverty, and ethnic conflict. The stock market crash and subsequent Great Depression of the 1930s exacerbated all of these material and social problems that had become endemic to urban existence, laying waste to any reforms that might have eased the problems in the earli-est stages of their development.

While land-grant institutions continued with their mission to serve each state through engineering, mining, and agricultural research (despite the fact that most states' populations were fleeing rural America for its burgeoning cities), America's urban centers, replete with their own unique problems and needs, were being left behind. Land-grant curricula and research agendas had little, if anything, to do with city planning and urban development. Thus, in this context of urban growth during the late nineteenth century, a new kind of university emerged, the "municipal" university. Just as the early land-grant universities served the states that supported them, municipal universities, too, acted upon their own mission to serve the cities (municipalities) that sup-ported them. William S. Carlson writes, "a municipal university is an institu-tion of higher learning supported in part by local taxation and administered by a local governing board to bring the services of higher education to the community" (1). Part of this mission to serve the community through higher education involved preparing graduates to live productive public and private lives within the boundaries of the municipality itself. As Carlson notes, "To grow and prosper a city must have engineers, business leaders, and lawyers. To be a better place to live it must have school teachers and citizens who assume the responsibility for community leadership" (38–39). And all of these future professionals must learn their disciplines in the unique context of urban life rather than rural life, a task that the liberal arts, teacher training, and land-grant universities of the early twentieth century were neither prepared nor willing to undertake.

On November 9 and 10, 1914, twenty-five representatives from Amer-ica's most prominent urban universities met in Washington, D.C., to discuss the future of this unique institution and establish the Association of Urban Universities (AUU). The proceedings of this meeting were published by the United States Bureau of Education under the title *The University and the Municipality*. In his contribution to the volume, Charles William Dabney, then President of the University of Cincinnati and newly elected first President of the AUU, underscores the importance of focusing the nation's efforts on improving higher education in its *urban* centers: "Originally a confederation of states, America is fast becoming a republic of cities" (8), and state universities are not fulfilling the needs of these rapidly gowing urban centers. Dabney laments, "We are training [citizens] to-day for nearly all the services except [those] of the municipality" (9). Thus, Dabney concludes,

> The training [the municipal university] gives is parallel to that of the State university, but will be different as the work of the city is different. No matter how efficiently organized the private institution may be, the municipal university is more intimately bound up with its community. No matter how large and complete a State university may be, it can not educate all the people of the cities. The municipal university, by the very conditions of its existence, is inseparably united to the life of the people of the city. It differs from the university in the city in that its relation to the city is one of participation in the life of which it is a vital part, rather than cooperation with a life of which it is independent. A part of the city society, the municipal university is a vital organ of the body politic. (14)

In his own contribution to *The University and the Municipality*, P. P. Claxton, then United States Commissioner of Education, reinforces the idea that state universities are unable to serve the needs of America's growing cities: "The State University, located in the village or small town away from any large center of population, and having no direct connection with municipal affairs, will hardly become conscious of the opportunity and the need of this kind of service" to cities (19).

Today, only a handful of universities exist that can truly be called "municipal." As the costs and methods of transportation improved throughout the early part of the twentieth century, municipal universities drew more and more students from outside their own city boundaries, calling into question the mission (as well as the financial practicality, since students from outlying counties could be charged much higher tuition rates) of strictly serving local populations. Indeed, forecasting their demise, Carlson argues that most municipal universities "will hope to retain their identity, both for sentimental and practical reasons, but the changes sure to come may necessitate either a redefinition of the term 'municipal university,' or perhaps even lead to its disappearance as one of the categories in higher education" (100). The subsequent history of municipal universities shows that, in fact, both of Carlson's predictions (disappearance and redefinition) have been realized. On the one hand, throughout most of the twentieth century, municipal universities *disappeared*, being absorbed into existing state university systems or endowed with private funds. On the other hand, during the late 1980s a "new" academic movement toward local urban accountability and community service has resuscitated and *redefined* the idea of an "urban" mission, characteristic of the early municipal universities, as a "metropolitan" mission. We will discuss metropolitan universities more in a moment; let us first turn to the characteristics of urban universities following the demise of the failed municipal ideal.

By the mid-twentieth century, it appeared that administrators had not heeded Claxton's 1914 warning that urban universities are "no place for cloistered seclusion and dreams that do not take hold on life" (23); the demise of the municipal university in particular was accompanied by an equal demise in the civic missions of many urban universities. The municipal universities that were revived by private endowments most often adopted liberal arts orientations, emphasizing studies in the humanities as a way of cultivating compassion, morality, and understanding. And many of the municipal universities that were absorbed into existing state university systems adopted the German model of higher education, emphasizing theory, research, and publishing at the expense of praxis and application. Further, inaugurated by the exigencies of Cold War politics, the federal government made millions of dollars in grant funding available to universities whose faculty would engage in military and scientific research. Urban universities, seeking national reputations in their own right, competed for these funds as vigorously as did other universities. There arose during this period a kind of ambivalence between urban universities and their local communities; neither seemed to be completely aware of, or to care much about, the other.

In the late 1950s, however, not only were urban universities detached from their city contexts, but many also began to expand geographically into poor surrounding neighborhoods, turning urban communities' ambivalence toward their universities into outright disdain. In 1959, Congress passed Section 112 of the National Housing Act. According to Maurice Berube,

> Under the terms of that provision, universities would receive three dollars of federal urban-renewal assistance for every dollar spent on "acquisition of land, buildings or structures within, adjacent to or in the immediate vicinity of, an urban renewal project, for demolition . . . for relocation of occupants and for rehabilitation of buildings" used for educational purposes. The urban university was given carte blanche to clean up its slums, solve its land problems, and make a nice profit in the bargain. (50)

The problem, of course, is that urban universities, previously viewed as detached, were now being viewed as aggressive, destroying communities and lives in the process. Berube concludes, "In retrospect, the urban university's problems with neighboring communities in expansion were a result of federal urban-renewal policies. Had these policies been more mindful of repercussions, they could have played a beneficial role in creating greater harmony between the university and the city" (61–62). The unfortunate reality, however, is that these policies were definitely not mindful of their repercussions, and instead of harmony between universities and cities they created antagonism.

During the 1960s and 1970s, in addition to the crises urban universities were causing for their own neighbors, these institutions experienced two crises of their own, and these crises, though painful, proved to be fertile ground for important changes. First, significant government cutbacks in spending on education limited urban universities' abilities to compete at a national level. Second, local student and community protests called into question the very identity and function of urban universities, rightly accusing them of being irrelevant and uninvolved (or, worse yet, aggressively dominant) in the context of city affairs (Berube 4). Further, much of the research with which urban universities had been engaged targeted developing technologies of war and weapons of mass destruction, and in the context of the antiwar movement, especially among the nation's college students, urban universities became *the* social problem rather than serving as a vehicle for the development of viable solutions.

The sentiment that arose out of the 1960s and 1970s was a new awareness of the "situatedness" of the urban university. Urban universities had to be reformed; they had to recognize and act upon their responsibility to meet the needs of urban contexts. Berube describes the new urban university that resulted from these crises as one that is "able to develop something comparable to the agricultural experimentation idea—centers of research and practical know-how serving city government, helping to supply city personnel, and encouraging them to develop new approaches to city problems" (15); there would be a renewed "dedication to social change and the improvement of city living" (16). One of the changes that came out of this new awareness of urban universities' contextual situatedness was the development of urban studies institutes, departments, programs, and courses devoted to promoting urban research and communication with city governments and community groups. At many urban universities, in its earliest manifestations, urban studies was little more than an appendage to elitist institutions that continued to be aloof and, at times, aggressive in their treatment of neighboring communities. Yet as this new discipline evolved over time, its positive influences were felt not only in the city, but in the university as well.

During the 1980s, based partly on the critical cultural theory of Jürgen Habermas, Pierre Bourdieu, Michel Foucault, and Clifford Geertz (among others), urban studies and, in particular, the practice of urban planning experienced a "social turn." Patsy Healy, for example, describes postmodern urban planners as focusing their efforts, not on the individualist invention of "ideal" public spaces, but instead on intersubjective debate and collaborative planning of functional and democratic spaces. Progressive urban planners such as

Healy urge other urban planners to think of cities as contexts for communication and action rather than as freestanding objects. This "social turn" (also called the "communicative" or "rhetorical" turn) in urban studies and urban planning has resulted in more egalitarian city geographies in which the very physical structure of the built environment fosters intercultural communication and productive public debate. Yet even in its best manifestations, urban studies remains but a small part of most academic institutions, leaving poorly funded and often marginalized urban studies departments to do the difficult and important work of community engagement for their entire universities. Further, urban studies departments were most often limited in their research and outreach efforts to inner city cores. Yet in the United States, it has been true for decades that the greatest increases in population and economic development have occurred in suburbs and outlying neighborhoods beyond inner city boundaries.

During the 1990s, a new movement in higher education arose that challenged the urban studies model of academic/community engagement. The urban universities that led this movement renamed themselves "metropolitan universities" and dedicated themselves (every department, every faculty member) to community service in both inner city cores and greater metropolitan areas. In "Metropolitan Universities: Models for the Twenty-First Century," Charles E. Hathaway, Paige E. Mulholland, and Karen A. White explain, "The term urban . . . refers in the minds of many of our constituents only to the core or central city. . . . The metropolitan university must address the challenges presented by the inner city as one facet of its overall responsibility, but those challenges do not exist in isolation from the whole metropolitan area, nor can they be addressed successfully in isolation" (13). Administrators at metropolitan universities have attempted, with varying degrees of success, to restructure the very foundations of their institutions in an effort to create total universities that, in every way, including criteria for tenure and promotion, reflect an expanded urban mission. These newly *re*-fashioned urban institutions view service to the city as a central priority, redefining in the process the goals and strategies of the failed "municipal" universities of the early twentieth century.

Throughout the pages of *City Comp: Identities, Spaces, Practices,* diverse universities come into focus, each with its own place in the history of urban higher education. Many of the universities represented in this collection were founded during the late nineteenth and early twentieth centuries and have enacted urban missions from the very beginning (e.g., Georgia State, DePaul, and Wayne State). Other universities began with clear urban missions, but have since distanced themselves from the negative qualities many Americans associate with urban environments (e.g., the University of Alabama at Birmingham and the University of Illinois at Chicago, which recently removed the

word "urban" from its mission statement). And still other universities represented in this collection have historically been identified as research institutions but have also developed strong service learning and community outreach
programs (e.g., Carnegie Mellon and the University of Minnesota). Interestingly, many of the service learning and community outreach programs in these
and other city universities across the country have their origins in rhetoric and
composition studies, where writers (students and teachers alike) negotiate
urban identities, compose urban spaces, and redefine urban pedagogical practices—all through acts of *writing* that require engagement with city contexts
beyond university walls. In the next section of this Introduction, we explore
the role that rhetoric and composition can play in urban rhetorical education
and writing instruction.

RHETORIC, COMPOSITION,
AND URBAN UNIVERSITY CONTEXTS

There is an emerging commonplace in rhetoric and composition studies, a
phrase that is often repeated, with little or no need for argument, in conference hallways, composition committee meetings, and writing classrooms. The
phrase, *"writing does not happen in a social vacuum,"* has become a kind of
mantra for many compositionists at least since the 1980s when, as John Trimbur and Lester Faigley point out, the discipline experienced a "social turn." Yet
it is not sufficient simply to say, "writing does not happen in a social vacuum,"
for if it does not happen there, then it must happen somewhere, and that
"somewhere" must be (and has been) explored and problematized. From the
ancient doctrine of *kairos* (the "right time" or "opportune moment") to twentieth-century theories about rhetorical situations and discourse communities,
the context of communication has been a productive object of study for
rhetoric and composition. Yet throughout this rich scholarship on contexts of
communication, specifically *urban* contexts have not yet been described and
interrogated with the rigor that they deserve. The unifying thesis of *City
Comp: Identities, Spaces, Practices* is that practitioners of rhetoric and composition who learn and write and teach in urban spaces must understand both the
common and the unique qualities of city contexts, responding in productive
ways to the special exigencies, both opportunities and obstacles, presented to
them in their own universities.

Why publish a book on "city comp," considering *urban* environments as
"different" contexts for teaching writing and administering writing programs?
We argue that there are many reasons, and our response to this question also
explains the organization of the book—that is, approaching "city comp"
through issues of *identities, spaces,* and *practices.*

First, we argue that in city contexts, the identities that students carry with them into the composition classroom are particularly varied and complex. In part, this complexity stems from the fact that cities, themselves, take on identities of their own, and individuals who live in cities learn to accommodate, resist, and negotiate these identities as they play out their particular roles as urban citizens. Residents of Birmingham, Alabama, for example, continually face representations of their city as racist, backward, and tumultuous; citizens of New York are assumed to live in a contradictory environment of social inequities and artistic progress; those who live in Las Vegas are often perceived as risk takers, night lifers, transients. Further, these identities (labels, generalizations, misconceptions) that have been created for cities and the people who inhabit them are continually reinforced through media representations in which sensationalist stereotypes sell. Many of the authors in this book, in fact, argue that the perceived identities of their particular cities must be revisited and reevaluated before readers can begin to understand the context in which composition, broadly conceived, takes place.

Just as citizens of a city must cope with the identities imposed upon their surroundings, students must also negotiate the institutional identities that urban universities construct in response to the people, places, and politics that exist outside their walls. In an examination of web sites for a group of schools known as the Great Cities Universities (GCU), we found that the identities, goals, and practices of many of these institutions are inextricably tied to the environmental and social settings that distinguish them. In its mission statement, for example, the University of Massachusetts Boston outlines six components that address the unique intersection between the academy and the city: access, excellence, public service, innovation, economic development, and quality of life. In each of these components, UMass Boston emphasizes the connection between superior work in teaching and research in the academy and progress and development in the Boston area. Matthew Goldstein, Chancellor of The City University of New York (CUNY), articulates the enduring urban mission of CUNY, which was first founded in 1847: "Open the doors to all—let the children of the rich and poor take seats together and know of no distinction save that of industry, good conduct and intellect." Temple University also boasts of the unique relationships it has formed with members of the Philadelphia community:

> While many universities struggle to find points of entry into partnerships with their surrounding communities, Temple and North Philadelphia have an unbroken and robust history in integrating community and university needs. Temple grew out of a partnership between its founder and the community. Today Temple not only continues its Conwellian mission of educational opportunity, but as a university we are constantly investigating how "academics" and "community" can not be mutually exclusive terms but mutually beneficial categories in education.

While we can locate similar statements on each of the web sites for GSU institutions, as well as for other city universities not included in this organization, our point is that many urban universities define themselves according to their unique and highly recognizable contexts. And students who attend city universities, and the faculty who teach these students, are often "called" to join these institutions through the very mission statements and promotional materials that emphasize the integral connection between the university and the city.

Of course, many of the contexts in which "city comp" takes place exist outside of the university, so the identities of these nonacademic institutions also need to be addressed. Throughout this collection, readers will encounter opportunities for, and problems with, composing urban identities at alternative city sites, such as literacy centers, street newspapers, community centers, and urban planning meetings. Other essays examine how histories, events, and institutions outside of academia affect how urban students see themselves as members of particular academic communities.

A second justification for merging "city" and "comp" centers on the importance of urban spaces, emphasizing the ways in which universities, teachers, and students define their roles in connection to the material and social geographies of their cities. Historically, urban universities (and other institutions as well) have struggled over how best to respond to questions of space. How does (or should) location within a city influence the work that academics do? To what extent should academic work be disseminated to nonacademic urban institutions? In the metropolitan universities movement, for example, many institutions have reconsidered the spatial boundaries that determine which populations should be served and which issues should be brought to the forefront in research and teaching. Space has also figured prominently in rhetoric and composition studies during the past two decades. In *Rhetorics, Poetics, and Cultures,* James Berlin argues that rhetoric and writing always reflect power struggles between groups situated in particular social spaces, and, more generally, social composition pedagogies take into account the roles and values created and enforced by dominant institutions such as the media, which are defined not only by the discourses they promote, but also by the spatial configurations that reinforce these discourses.

City spaces, then, are rich material and ideological resources for composition students who are attempting to situate important personal and social issues in context. Specifically, students can look at city spaces as rhetorical constructs that offer ample opportunities to engage in dialogues with histories (i.e., how has the past been represented through city museums or monuments, and whose narratives have been omitted from these representations?), citizens (i.e., what spaces have been appropriated for community interaction and private reflection?), and issues (i.e., what physical structures and urban plans have resulted from local debates and controversies?). Urban spaces, then, are texts (recall de Certeau); and through composition pedagogies that incorporate vital city environments into classroom discourses, students learn to compose urban spaces, either accommodating, resisting, or negotiating existing narratives that give meaning to their cities.

A final reason to merge "city" and "comp" is that urban contexts force composition and literacy teachers and administrators to redefine their practices in response to the exigencies of their own cities and urban universities. As compositionists, we view ourselves as practitioners of writing, as members of academic and nonacademic institutions whose main goal is to strengthen the textual strategies and skills of students/readers/writers, thus enabling them to better contribute to and shape the discourses that impact them within their own home and work communities. And as compositionists situated in urban contexts, we, along with the contributors to this collection, find ourselves continually challenged by the unique "mission" of our institution to serve both the students we encounter in the classroom and a broader population of urban citizens. Thus, those of us who ply our trade in urban teaching institutions must negotiate between varied, and oftentimes conflicting, expectations brought about through issues of identity, space, and text.

Several of the essays in this collection present the hands-on work that urban compositionists (both as teachers in the classroom and as administrators who devise curricula appropriate to their unique urban settings) must do to accomplish the practical goal of improving students' writing. They illustrate, for instance, the effect of one's immediate surroundings on the expectations (both false and fulfilled) of teachers and learners; the tensions between student needs, institutional goals, and varied urban agendas that writing program administrators, other university administrators, and composition teachers must confront in producing course content and procedures; and the constantly changing dynamic between academic writing communities and communities situated outside academia. These essays highlight the importance of following through with theories about how writing should be taught in urban settings to create programs and assignments that work in particular city classrooms.

ORGANIZATION OF CITY COMP

The fourteen essays that comprise *City Comp: Identities, Spaces, Practices* address each of the concepts discussed above, exploring, first, how urban composition students negotiate their *identities* in relation to existing urban narratives (Part I), second, how the *spaces* in which city comp takes place influence the writing that occurs there (Part II), and, third, how composition *practices* are redefined in order to address issues of urban identity and space in the teaching of writing (Part III). In the remaining pages of this Introduction, we briefly discuss the interplay of essays in each of the three parts of the collection.

Part I, "Negotiating Identities," highlights the importance of how urban composition students perceive themselves (as readers and writers) and their universities (as institutions) specifically within their own city contexts. Each contributor to this section addresses the unique social, economic, and political conditions (both historical and present) of a particular city context, highlighting the effects that these histories and conditions have on the identities of local composition students. In "Myth, Identity, and Composition: Teaching Writing in Birmingham, Alabama," Tracey Baker, Peggy Jolly, Bruce McComiskey, and Cynthia Ryan describe the media "baggage" that students in Birmingham carry into the classroom as an integral part of their identities, and the authors offer three pedagogical principles that guided the construction of UAB's writing program in response to these students' identities. In "Writing Against Time: Students Composing 'Legacies' in a History Conscious City," Elizabeth Ervin and Dan Collins demonstrate the importance of historical identity at their respective institutions in Wilmington, North Carolina. Both the University of North Carolina at Wilmington and Cape Fear Community College erected memorial clocks in an effort to give their campuses the appearance of a "historical" identity where there is, in fact, little history at all. Susan Swan addresses the issue of unemployment in the Pittsburgh area, and she illustrates how her composition pedagogy challenges Carnegie Mellon students' own identities and engages them with members of a local population of food service workers facing difficult socioeconomic realities.

Other essays included in this section consider the identities of language learners located in urban institutions outside of academia. In "A Paragraph Ain't Nothin' But a Sandwich: The Effects of the GED on Four Urban Writers and Their Writing," Krista Hiser demonstrates the gradual disillusionment of individuals enrolled in a writing class for homeless/low-income citizens of San Francisco. As these students learn the required GED formula for paragraphing, Hiser describes the self-doubt that occurs among students both in reference to themselves as writers and to the texts they are encouraged to compose. In "'Not Your Mama's Bus Tour': A Case for 'Radically Insufficient' Writing," Paula Mathieu discusses her work at *StreetWise*, a Chicago street newspaper written, produced, and sold by local homeless and low-income individuals. In response to the overwhelming forces (prison records, debt histories) that continually diminish the personal accomplishments of individuals at *StreetWise*, the population about which Mathieu writes takes to the streets, composing and presenting their real-life stories through a theatrical bus tour of Chicago. While both Hiser and Mathieu acknowledge the value of institutionalized programs that attempt to address the needs of marginalized citizens, they also point to the inadequacies of these programs, especially as they purport to mainstream the values and goals of diverse populations or ignore the insurmountable obstacles that they face.

In Part II, "Composing Spaces," readers encounter diverse city spaces where urban issues play out in unique and often problematic material (geo-rhetorical) configurations. Each of the essays in this section, despite obvious differences among their city contexts, points to the importance of urban space as a focal point for teaching and writing. In "Simulated Destinations in the Desert: The Southern Nevada Writing Project," Ed Nagelhout and Marilyn McKinney describe Las Vegas as a "simulated destination," a space with no originary point of reference, and they discuss the specific challenges they have encountered in their involvement with the Southern Nevada Writing Project as a result of this view of simulated space. In "A Place in the City: Hull-House and the Architecture of Civility," Van Hillard writes about a historical urban space, Hull-House, exploring the ways in which this site was more or less consonant with the trajectory of critical literacy education in American cities during the late nineteenth and early twentieth centuries. In "The Written City: Urban Planning, Computer Networks, and Civic Literacies," Jeffrey Grabill describes a project that involves a group of Georgia State University's technical writing students in an urban planning project in Mechanicsville, an underdeveloped area of Atlanta. This essay illustrates alternative ways for teachers of professional communication (as well as composition, by extension) to engage students in the ethical distribution of urban space. Through the Mechanicsville community planning project, Grabill's students see how decisions about urban spaces affect actual citizens, and they are also taught how to intervene in the process of allocating these spaces. And in "Speaking of the City and Literacies of Place Making in Composition Studies," Richard Marback discusses the Heidelberg Project in inner city Detroit, a spatial "urban art" text that challenges many dominant ideological messages about city space. This aesthetic configuration of graffiti and trash occupies more than a block in an inner city Detroit housing district, and, Marback concludes, has important implications for teaching composition students about the rhetorical functions of city spaces.

Part III, "Redefining Practices," extends many of the issues raised in the first two sections. Practices, the contributors to this section argue, are pedagogical and administrative ways of responding to the identities constructed for and by students and the urban institutions where they learn as well as to the city spaces that greatly influence how students perceive and understand textual practices inside and outside the composition classroom. David Jolliffe identifies in "Composition by Immersion: Writing Your Way into a Mission-Driven University" the need to reconsider composition pedagogies that pit students against the institutions within which they learn, and he describes two courses at DePaul University in Chicago that help students to understand and adopt the roles they need in order to succeed in an urban university with a Jesuit mission of tolerance and community outreach. Lynee Lewis Gaillet, the writing program administrator at Georgia State University, describes a hybrid ethnographic writing course that helps establish and reinforce her institution's identity as a "metropolitan university." In "Urban Literacies and the Ethnographic Process: Composing Communities at the Center for Worker Education," Barbara Gleason argues that ethnographic writing pedagogies enable urban students to retain their own communal literacies while also developing the academic literacies they seek to acquire. Ann Feldman focuses on one aspect of the metropolitan mission of the University of Illinois at Chicago, specifically the call to "partnership" with communities located in the city, and she reveals how the development of the Great Cities Initiative at UIC has led to greater local engagement with (versus distanced service for) urban institutions that also have much to teach the academically trained composition instructor about the value and production of texts. Finally, Patrick Bruch writes in "Moving to the City: Redefining Literacy in the Post–Civil Rights Era" about the racial politics of Minneapolis and the focus on literacy as a means of "upward mobility" in the General College curriculum at the University of Minnesota, Twin Cities.

Together, the essays collected in *City Comp: Identities, Spaces, Practices* demonstrate the complex ways in which cities are identified, how these representations are played out in everyday living and learning spaces, and the crucial role writing teachers and administrators play in devising practices that meet the needs and peculiarities of unique city contexts.

WORKS CITED

Berlin, James. *Rhetorics, Poetics, and Cultures.* Urbana: NCTE, 1996.

Berube, Maurice. *The Urban University in America.* Westport, CT: Greenwood, 1978.

Carlson, William S. *The Municipal University.* New York: Center for Applied Research in Education, 1962.

Chudacoff, Howard P. *The Evolution of American Urban Society.* Englewood Cliffs, NJ: Prentice-Hall, 1981.

City University of New York. 22 March 2001. <http://www.cuny.edu>.

Claxton, P. P. "Cooperative Methods in Education." *The University and the Municipality.* Bulletin of the United States Bureau of Education, Number 38. Washington, DC: Government Printing Office, 1915. 18–25.

Dabney, Charles W. "The Municipal University." *The University and the Municipality.* Bulletin of the United States Bureau of Education, Number 38. Washington, DC: Government Printing Office, 1915. 7–15.

de Certeau, Michel. *The Practice of Everyday Life*. Trans. Steven Rendall. Berkeley: U of California P, 1984.

Faigley, Lester. *Fragments of Rationality: Postmodernity and the Subject of Composition*. Pittsburgh: U of Pittsburgh P, 1992.

Hathaway, Charles E., Paige E. Mulholland, and Karen A. White. "Metropolitan Universities: Models for the Twenty-First Century." *Metropolitan Universities* 1 (1990): 10–20.

Healey, Patsy. "Planning through Debate: The Communicative Turn in Planning Theory." *Readings in Planning Theory*. Ed. Scott Campbell and Susan S. Fainstein. Cambridge, MA: Blackwell, 1996. 234–57.

Lefebvre, Henry. *Writings on Cities*. Trans. Eleonore Kofman and Elizabeth Lebas. Cambridge, MA: Blackwell, 1996.

Severino, Carol. "The Idea of an Urban University: A History and Rhetoric of Ambivalence and Ambiguity." *Urban Education* 31 (1996): 291–313.

Temple University. 22 March 2001. <http://www.temple.edu>.

Trimbur, John. "Taking the Social Turn: Teaching Writing Post-Process." *College Composition and Communication* 45 (1994): 108–18.

University of Massachusetts Boston. 22 March 2001. <http://www.umb.edu>.

PART I

NEGOTIATING IDENTITIES

CHAPTER ONE

Myth, Identity, and Composition
Teaching Writing in Birmingham, Alabama

Tracey Baker, Peggy Jolly,
Bruce McComiskey, and Cynthia Ryan

The process of writing about our urban university and the teaching we do in this space has reinforced what we always knew—that there is no single Birmingham, no "reality" that we could all isolate and describe, no starting point on which we could all agree. This realization in itself was no surprise as we each have traveled diverse paths through the city. Peggy Jolly grew up just outside of Birmingham; Tracey Baker moved to the city more than sixteen years ago and has since married a native Alabamian and raised a child here; Bruce McComiskey and Cynthia Ryan have lived in Birmingham for just a few years, neither having stepped foot in Alabama before coming to the city. Our widely varied impressions of and histories with the place echo what urban and literary theorists have long told us, that cities are more about the people who live in them and the practices in which they engage than the physical structures that surround them (Calvino, de Certeau, Lefebvre). Each of us has widely different understandings of our city, each a kind of mythologized Birmingham, a representation that can never hope to be "true" beyond the limits of our own experiences. There are no true representations of cities; there are only urban myths. Drawing from these assumptions, we have three primary goals for this essay: first, to illustrate certain complex and competing myths that surround representations of Birmingham; second, to critique the ways in which the University of Alabama at Birmingham has constructed its institutional identity in

response to these myths; and, finally, to describe certain aspects of the program in rhetoric and composition that we have developed, negotiating our
own curricular identity in response to these same myths.

URBAN MYTHS: BIRMINGHAM, ALABAMA

Birmingham is a complicated city, and its residents and institutions often
exhibit a certain anxiety or paranoia regarding perceptions and representations
of its past, present, and future. Even the publication that the Birmingham
Chamber of Commerce sends to new residents, the *Guide to Birmingham for
Newcomers and Natives Alike,* exhibits this anxiety. The first few sentences of
the very first article, "Introduction: Birmingham Explained," by Dale Short,
begins in a predictably defensive way:

> "Where are you from?"
> "Birmingham."
> For decades now, as I've traveled other parts of the country and of the
> world, I watch the eyes of strangers as they take in this information, and
> I try to peer into their minds . . . to see how they're picturing the place I
> call home. . . .
> [Most] often, I see them thumbing their mental file cabinet for first
> impressions: the concept "Deep South" or "Bible Belt," some grainy black-
> and-white news-reel footage from a generation ago, and maybe the image of
> a steel mill spraying a corona of orange sparks toward the stars. (20)

Of course, the remaining pages of Short's article, and the three hundred more
pages of articles and advertisements in the *Guide,* are devoted to debunking
these "myths" of Birmingham. But why the anxiety, the paranoia, the defensiveness? Some of the many possible answers to this question, we believe, lie
in the social nature and function of urban myths, particularly the myths of
Birmingham as a Southern, industrial, and racist city.

Although Birmingham lies nestled within the heart of Alabama, one of
the Deep South's most "Southern" states, Birmingham itself has never really
been a Deep South city. All of the traditional symbols of the Deep South
(agrarian economy, slave workforce, and devotion to the Confederacy) were
never really formative aspects of Birmingham's history, as they were in other
Southern cities such as Atlanta, Charleston, and Montgomery, Alabama's
infamous capitol city. As Paul Hemphill argues in *Leaving Birmingham: Notes
of a Native Son,*

> Never for a moment in its brief and tortured life has Birmingham been a
> genuinely "southern" city. . . . Even southerners know that on the one hand

there are Memphis and Charleston and Mobile and Natchez, old cities truly tied to the agrarian South, that gossamer myth of *Gone with the Wind*, and then there is Birmingham. No, Birmingham isn't southern except by geography. It was conceived as a gawky stepchild, more northern than southern, and was nurtured by outsiders to become the only industrial giant that ever developed below the Mason-Dixon line. . . . The word "southern" implies a past, a connection to slavery and cotton and the Civil War, but Birmingham never had that past. Indeed, the city didn't even exist when Union general William Tecumseh Sherman razed Atlanta on his march to the sea. (15–16)

Until the Civil War, what would later become Birmingham was sparsely populated by pioneer sharecroppers who were unable to grow profitable crops in the rocky, undulating, red-clay soil, yet they were still required to pay property owners for the privilege of using their land. So, Hemphill continues, "when the call to arms was sounded, when the time came for Alabama to secede from the Union, the slaves and the [white] dirt farmers were much more interested in killing planters than in killing Yankees" (16). Following the Civil War, economic devastation throughout the South made industrialization difficult, since Birmingham's coal, iron, and steel industries required capital to begin and maintain operations. Yet as the process of reconstruction continued, the need for iron and steel became increasingly urgent. As a direct result of this postwar urgency, Birmingham began to flourish, going from three to thirty-three metal working shops in the 1880s alone (McKiven 7).

But during the late nineteenth century, Alabama's (but not Birmingham's) Deep South, agrarian attitude created numerous difficulties for the new iron and steel manufacturers and mining companies establishing themselves throughout Birmingham, and many of these difficulties led to racial tensions. According to Henry McKiven, white residents of north-central Alabama had, for well over a century, constructed their identities around a white/land-owner versus black/slave-laborer economic system that maintained clear social and political divisions between the races. When the new industrial movement hit Birmingham, owners of the iron and steel manufacturers and mining companies sought skilled white laborers, fearing that black workers would work only if forced and could perform only the most menial tasks. These "skilled" jobs, however, were wage labor only, which, in the context of Alabama's Deep South, agrarian values, was insulting. And the sheer numbers of new manufacturers opening shops in Birmingham each year led to terrible labor shortages. As a way of dealing with the shortage of white skilled laborers, many owners of Birmingham's mining and manufacturing companies began to train promising black workers for semi-skilled positions, and, later, for even more difficult skilled labor jobs (23–55). The white skilled workers who were then employed in the mining and manufacturing industries began to resent the presence of black workers in "white" jobs, causing racial tensions in Birmingham to escalate by the early 1900s and continue for another two-thirds of a century.

Although it was certainly replete with social failings, Birmingham developed into a thriving industrial center, mining some of the highest quality coking coal and producing some of the best iron and steel in the country. Throughout the first half of the twentieth century, Birmingham continued to produce iron and steel for both industry and military interests, maintaining the racial divisions, in terms of both social class and physical segregation, for which Birmingham was becoming notorious.

The second half of the twentieth century was a terrible yet formative period in Birmingham's history, in which its residents witnessed a number of economic, political, and social transitions. One important transition rocked the economic foundation as well as the very identity of the city—the transition from a purely industrial society to a largely postindustrial society. In his landmark *The Coming of the Post-Industrial Age*, Daniel Bell argues that the transition from industrial to postindustrial is not just an economic one—it is also a social transition in which the very political and cultural values of a particular society change along with the economic structure. Bell writes, "If an industrial society is defined by the quantity of goods as marking a standard of living, the post-industrial society is defined by the quality of life as measured by the services and amenities—health, education, recreation, and the arts— which are now deemed desirable and possible for everyone" (127). Although some of Birmingham's manufacturers still produce iron and steel even today, the city's primary economic base now (and since the late 1950s) lies in finance, health, education, and communication industries, with the University of Alabama at Birmingham tipping the scales as Alabama's largest employer. In many ways, however, this transition in Birmingham's economic and social structure only served to fuel the racial tensions that were already raging: black residents in Birmingham, who had found satisfying skilled work in the gutted labor markets of the first half of the twentieth century, suddenly found themselves unemployed, victims of a shifting interest from iron and steel toward health and education. During the 1960s, many of the riots with which Birmingham is now associated grew out of these tensions that had been brewing throughout Birmingham's short and tumultuous history.

Although racism still exists in Birmingham, certain political reforms of the 1970s led to the election of our first African American Mayor, Richard Arington, who served five consecutive terms from 1980 to 2000. The early 1960s saw the establishment of the Birmingham Community Affairs Committee, a local government-sponsored group dedicated to "changing the city's racial climate from one of confrontation to one of cooperation—no small task for a city that faced the 1960s torn by racial strife as the nation looked on" (*Operation New Birmingham* 8). But then Mayor Boutwell's opposition to the integrationist recommendations of the Community Affairs Committee resulted in its ultimate failure (Connerly 341–42). Continued pressure from national government agencies, however, saw the establishment of another local government-sponsored program targeting racial inequities, the Citizen Participation Plan, which was more successful in achieving its integrationist goals than was the Community Affairs Committee. Established in 1974, the Citizen Participation Plan was a network of local neighborhood organizations that were given direct political access to Birmingham's city government, empowering—as they had never been empowered before—citizens who lived in traditionally lower income or racially segregated communities (Connerly 349–58; Seibels). While the Citizen Participation Plan has had a tremendous impact on Birmingham's racial politics during the past few decades, it is important to recognize, as the Alabama Advisory Committee reported in 1988, that "we have come a long way, but we still have a long way to go" (2). Yet, as of the year 2000, Birmingham boasted a black mayor, a black-majority city council, and a black superintendent of the public schools.

Some of these social and political reforms have led to other problems with which Birmingham has had to contend in more recent years. Despite its very *un*-Southern origins, Birmingham is, nevertheless, located in the South, and some of its residents have come to Birmingham from outlying Alabama communities with Deep South values firmly embedded in their social fabric. Wealthy white (and, for some, formerly agrarian) families that had migrated to Birmingham during the 1950s, '60s, and '70s to take advantage of its postindustrial opportunities and amenities, and the white *nouveau riche* who had made their fortunes in Birmingham's industrial economy, were largely opposed to the new integrationist movement that required local Birmingham government agencies to put an end to the Jim Crow laws that had defined the city for almost a century. As a result of this white opposition to the new integrationist ideology, Birmingham experienced a process that some urban theorists call "gentrification," or suburban "white flight." White residents, who (because of the movement toward integration in the city) fled from Birmingham into certain outlying neighborhoods, continued the process of racial segregation both directly, since integrationist laws did not apply or were not enforced outside metropolitan boundaries, and also indirectly, hiking local taxes, property values, and goods prices to a level that lower-income blacks could generally not afford (Wilson 147–67). And in suburbs such as Mountain Brook, Homewood, and Vestavia Hills, upper-class white residents were able to develop and maintain a kind of superficial "Deep South" culture (values tied to class-specific neighborhoods, rather than farmable acreage; values tied to Southern gentility, rather than devotion to a Confederate ideology; and values tied to the "voluntary" economic separation of the races, rather than supporting enforced segregation), despite Birmingham's lack of "Deep South" history.

It should be clear from the preceding discussion that Birmingham is a complicated city, rife with contradictions: Southern, but not; industrial, but not; racist, but not. Yet outside media representations of Birmingham focus almost exclusively on the infamous (and marketable) aspects of the city's history, thus telling only a narrow version of Birmingham's complicated story. Media representations portraying Birmingham as a Deep South, industrial, and racist city are partial truths and simplifications—they are "myths." Myths, Roland Barthes tells us, are the products of associations that have been emptied of their meaning. Mythic representations are simplifications that can never hope to fully capture the complexities of the "real" Birmingham (precisely because no "real" Birmingham exists). Yet these empty, mythic (though certainly not *entirely* false) associations still persist in media representations, despite the city's significant transitions during the past few decades.

It is easy to see why current Birmingham residents exhibit a certain paranoia and defensiveness when faced with mythologized representations of their city. And in the media produced *in* Birmingham, *about* Birmingham, and intended for audiences *outside* of Birmingham, authors (individual or institutional) often show symptoms of what Harold Bloom calls the "anxiety of influence." For Bloom, the anxiety of influence, the desire to be different from one's predecessors, controls literary production more than purely creative thought. In a similar way, many of Birmingham's own media productions, including the *Guide* discussed above, focus more on distinguishing the city from its mythologized identity (as Southern, industrial, and racist) than focusing exclusively on the city's more apparent characteristics.

This anxiety, this paranoia, this defensiveness has resulted in *counter-myths*, representations of a "new Birmingham" that describe a city that has undergone a sudden and radical transformation leading it away from its Deep South, industrial, and racist "roots" to a more "likable" New South, postindustrial, and fully integrated city of the future. These counter-myths, however, are also based on associations that are, at least in part, simplifications, partial truths, and ultimately empty of meaning (except, of course, for their rhetorical function of combating the empty meanings of other myths); they are based on an idealized, utopian conception of Birmingham, a conception that can never hope to be "true" in any real sense.

INSTITUTIONAL IDENTITIES:
UNIVERSITY OF ALABAMA AT BIRMINGHAM

In this section, we address some of the ways in which the University of Alabama at Birmingham (UAB) has responded to the competing myths of the city. We draw on two sets of recruitment materials (one set used until 1998, and the other set used after 1998) to illustrate the images and ideals that UAB associates with its students, faculty, and institutional programs, as well as with the city in which it is situated.

Prior to 1998, UAB distributed recruitment materials that feature the university's city context as a primary attraction. Appearing repeatedly throughout these documents (including flyers, pamphlets, and viewbooks), the slogans "adding life to learning" and "a university for real life" emphasize the importance of the city itself to UAB students' educational experiences. Cityscape photographs are prominent throughout the materials, and accompanying words highlight urban lifestyles: "All the energy, excitement, and advantages of a large, vibrant city are right at your doorstep," and "Our campus is rich with different faces, cultures, ages, and backgrounds." In these early recruitment materials, UAB capitalizes on the one thing that no other large university in Alabama could offer—the educational, economic, and social opportunities of urban life. Emphasizing UAB's city context was a logical marketing strategy given the institution's annual enrollment statistics: each year, about 94 percent of UAB's students come from Alabama (and many from the immediate Birmingham area), while only 3 percent come from other states and 3 percent from other countries. Since Alabama residents tend not to fall victim to the media-induced myths of a Southern, industrial, and racist Birmingham, these early recruitment materials do not exhibit the sort of anxieties characteristic of documents intended for audiences outside of Alabama.

During the early 1990s, however, UAB began a campaign to re-make its image from a local urban university into a national (and international) research institution, and one aspect of this campaign was a revision and expansion of UAB's recruitment materials (now including flyers, pamphlets, viewbooks, videos, CD-ROMs, Web pages, and even postcards). First distributed in 1998, UAB's new recruitment materials target potential students from across the country (and world), raising the difficult issue of Birmingham's mythologized identity outside of the city and state. The most obvious new rhetorical strategy used in these revised materials is to disavow UAB's urban context, since, first, urban universities are often associated with serving local, working populations, and second, urban environments are often associated with violence and xenophobia. The pages of these new recruitment materials are filled with a kaleidoscope of glossy visuals that capture the smiling faces of young men and women at athletic events, cheering the Blazers to victory, or in comfortable classrooms, their studious expressions focused on a professor's explanation or demonstration (a kind of land-grant dream). Intermingled with these images are candid views of the campus, which comes alive in lovely photos of buildings and lush lawns dotted with sculptures and water fountains. Opulent interiors contain an extensive array of technology—computerized classrooms, science labs, broadcast studios—as well as more traditional scenes of book-lined shelves, spacious dormitory rooms, and cavernous performing arts spaces filled with appreciative patrons. The city itself, the few times it is even represented, is seen only in muted tones: a dusk cityscape with lit offices contrasted against a mauve background; a daytime cityscape tinted with calming shades of pale blue and sepia, more closely invoking memory than reality. "Change Your Mind. Change Your World." "The future is here." These slogans are central to UAB's most recent recruitment materials because they provide potential students with positive images (counter-myths) of the school, and they emphasize a broader scope than did the previous materials: "world," not city; "future," not present.

Once UAB's association with its urban context is broken, the new recruitment materials further address (directly and indirectly) the myths about Birmingham proper that are perpetuated in outside media representations of the city. Throughout these documents there are numerous cues, both visual and verbal, that reveal UAB's anxiety about Birmingham's identity as a Southern, industrial, and racist city. Information about the city itself in these documents revolves around two key phrases: "small town friendliness" and "lively urban neighborhood." The specifically urban and industrial qualities of Birmingham are directly countered here with the words "friendliness" and "neighborhood," ideas that contradict the mythologized identity of Birmingham as a harsh industrial center. While Birmingham may not be an entirely industrial city anymore, UAB's counter-myth describing the city as a friendly neighborhood is merely a partial truth at best.

There are also hints throughout the new recruitment materials of UAB's discomfort with Birmingham's enduring mythologized reputation for racial injustice. The myth that Birmingham is a racist city is dispelled visually in these documents through the hundreds of pictures of student life portraying a diverse student body studying and playing together. These depictions show a race-friendly place, one that shares little with the city's segregated and violent past, both factual and mythic. Further, UAB's recruitment materials subtly recall the city's past by invoking phrases that were in common use during the civil rights movement: After "waiting years," now is the time for students to make "the decision" for a "better tomorrow" and "realize [their] dreams," all language evoking the ideals of Martin Luther King Jr.

The central theme of the new recruitment materials, "The future is here," is a counter-myth specifically addressing UAB's anxiety about being identified with the Deep South, with a culture that cannot move beyond a glorified (and certainly mythologized) past. Consistently, the recent recruiting materials displace UAB outside of the South by highlighting quotes from successful out-of-state alumni and from faculty involved in research projects with NASA "on other planets," "across Europe," and in Ethiopia, Russia, Thailand, Antarctica, and Costa Rica. These documents boast that UAB's medical school is "world-renowned"; the university has made "international headlines"; it ranks with "prestigious institutions including Duke and Harvard"; its faculty are "visionaries and problem-solvers"; its alumni "are shaping the future in all 50 states and 31 countries"; and "UAB's discoveries and innovations make international headlines."

STUDENTS COMPOSING IDENTITIES:
UAB'S WRITING PROGRAM IN CONTEXT

As composition and rhetoric faculty committed to empowering the students we teach, we wish to move beyond the myths about Birmingham that are promoted in outside media representations of the city and in UAB's new recruitment materials. It is our hope that students will not only succeed in an academic setting, but that they will also learn strategies for addressing some of the local "truths" that have been authorized by dominant institutional discourses. This hope relies on our ability to teach students how to recognize and validate alternative responses to the myths we have explored in this chapter, in addition to many others that they individually and collectively bring to the composition classroom. In the final section of this chapter, we illustrate three ways in which we devised our composition program to help students locate their own understandings of the city in which they live and work, as well as determine how they wish to participate in the shaping of Birmingham's past, present, and future identities. Our discussion takes the form of "principles" that we believe encourage students to become active makers of their own identities and contributors to the conversations within and about their urban communities.

Principle 1: Strengthen Students' Identities
within the Urban Academic Setting

Many of the urban students who enter UAB are ill-equipped for the rigors of college life and hence uncomfortable in the classroom. Unlike the images presented in UAB's new recruitment materials, many of the students here are products of a poorly funded state educational system that was ranked forty-sixth in the nation for 2001 (up two places from its 2000 ranking). Some of our students feel great anxiety about their first-year composition courses (a required two-course sequence) because they know that they are not prepared for rigorous academic writing, while others are defensive about the "good grades" they received in their local high school English classes.

Across the country, required first-year composition courses are viewed by students simultaneously as obstacles to be overcome and as a means to gain confidence in their writing skills. But when students come to first-year composition carrying the additional baggage of debilitating myths about their own identities and the identities of their home cities, success seems even more difficult to achieve. In a recent survey of UAB composition students, respondents revealed not only their knowledge of how Birmingham has been perceived in the media, but also the importance they place on succeeding in this thoroughly mythologized urban university (Baker). One student writes, "[Birmingham is often shown] as a city that is behind economically, but I often hear [about] UAB as highly preferred." Another offers, "They [the media] seem to think that Birmingham is the same city of the past, which is not true. They only seem to say anything when it is negative. . . . [At UAB], I strive to make a good name for myself as I do in my own community." And a third states, "Many people view Birmingham, Alabama as a racist, behind the times place. And people who live here don't see it that way." In each of these quotes, students' identities are split between what others think of their city and what opportunities they know exist in Birmingham and at UAB. In defining themselves, students speak first of the "bad rap" they and their city have received; and succeeding educationally, economically, and socially is one way to prove that such perceptions are wrong and unfair.

Our response to UAB students' anxieties has been to address them head-on, emphasizing a pedagogy that will help retain these students within the university system so that they have the time and opportunity to learn academic discourse and thus establish identities that counter those the media might impose on them. UAB students are required to complete two first-year composition courses, yet students who enter the university without the necessary skills for this sequence begin with a basic reading/writing class to improve their chances of succeeding. In the Writing Skills Center, located near English department faculty offices and classrooms, students can receive additional help with their writing as it develops, and experts in each level of composition are available for tutoring. While this program may sound familiar to most compositionists who work in university settings, we want to emphasize the importance of this "building block" approach to teaching writing at UAB. If students who view themselves as academically underprepared do not get a "boost" at the point of entering the university, they are unlikely to thrive at more advanced academic levels. Further, situated in an urban environment, many of our students spend most of their days off-campus, working to pay their way through school and spending time in their local communities. It is vital, then, that our composition program be accessible to students and address the textual issues with which they are struggling.

Principle 2: Enable Students Actively
to Construct Their Urban Communities

In addition to strengthening students' academic identities through providing opportunities to develop confidence in their writing, students must also be granted the authority in composition courses to speak for themselves and their communities. It would be wrong to assume that our students all share a common history with the city of Birmingham. In fact, Birmingham, Alabama, like all cities, is comprised of multiple communities, and the individuals who enter our classes have varying experiences with the area and attitudes toward outsiders' perspectives on the place.

In a sophomore-level course called Writing in Birmingham, students have the opportunity to "talk back" to the city and those who represent it locally, nationally, and globally. Rather than accommodating the mythologized identities of Birmingham, whether represented in outside media representations or UAB's new recruitment materials, students are asked to study competing representations of the city and to write themselves into these dynamic discussions. Course assignments include reflection essays, in which students describe their personal impressions about this complicated city; historical essays, in which students conduct primary, secondary, and archival research on some aspect of Birmingham's troubled past; and controversial issue essays, in which students take a stand on a current problem in Birmingham that has no clear solution. Such assignments encourage students to view their city as more than a material space; it is also a rhetorical space from which they can draw ideas and contribute their own.

The historical essay assignment provides one example of how students learn to engage in complex rhetorical processes within the city context. As with all assignments in the course, students are given the freedom to choose their topic of interest, further reinforcing that "the" city experience is unique for each individual. Students' essays may be either synchronic (presenting a timeless "slice of life") or diachronic (providing a record of "change over time"), and they might address such topics as the transformation of a Birmingham building, changes in the life of a long-time Birmingham resident, personal responses to a historical site in the city, or an examination of past political leadership in Birmingham. While students are required to complete "formal" research in learning about their topics (e.g., interviews, archival research, newspaper searches, etc.), a central goal of the assignment is to uncover students' own reactions to the city's past. What places, people, or events do students perceive as significant in the making of Birmingham? And how might stories about the place be retold or re-framed, revealing divergent historical accounts?

One student, Anna, focused in this assignment on the Farmer's Market (officially named the Jefferson County Truck Growers Association), begun in 1921 in downtown Birmingham. In "A Scrapbook from Home," Anna presents the factual history of the place alongside colorful photos of the produce stands that line the market and the farmers who come each week to sell their goods. While this layout is captivating in itself, Anna effectively intersperses her own history with the Farmer's Market, showing how the discourse that takes place there both reflects her particular urban/rural identity and distinguishes her from others who might visit the site.

Anna comes from an Alabama farming family. On the first page of "A Scrapbook from Home," she refers to this legacy: "I have heard my grandfather, now eighty-six, talk about selling produce to Mr. Bruno [the founder of one of the largest grocery chains in the South] there before World War II." The sights and smells of the Market take Anna back to familiar images of her life growing up on the farm:

> The smell of woody wheat straw mingles with memories of my family. I am again fifteen, with arms as tight and shaped as any man. It is just after sunup in June. My father, grandfather, brother, ten or so field hands and I walk beside a wagon, cutting and pitching Sugar Baby watermelons, ten to twenty pounds each, to quick catching hands on the wagon. Before sundown, two of us will pull through the gate of the Farmer's Market with those same watermelons.

The Market not only reminds Anna of her family home in south Alabama, but it also becomes another kind of home filled with people and conversations she can understand. She writes,

> I can freely speak a language of farming at the Market, unlike any other place in Birmingham. Stoop-labor, physically stooping to pick vegetables from plants growing below your knees is understood here, not in my upper class white neighborhood. My neighbors do not know or understand the determination that comes from being a fifth generation farm family.
> Market talk pays respect to the people who turn seed and dirt into food. Farm language speaks of a delicate ongoing dance between hope and faith and fate. Farmers plant seeds by faith, and hope, often pray to make a crop that will not be destroyed by the whims of drought, flood or storm.

In this market community, Anna's rural identity merges with and against the urban identity of her neighbors who do not know this "delicate ongoing dance." Her scrapbook presents an added historical dimension when she discusses the changes that have taken place in the Farmer's Market since her childhood. Anna writes that "farm language is now translated into Spanish, as Hispanics glean fields in Alabama and north Florida and sell their produce beside Alabama farmers." The Market has expanded in size and variety, and an ongoing flea market runs alongside the produce stands. The city streets directly outside the Market have seen shootouts and knife fights and drugs, yet "it remains relatively safe and peaceful inside the fences of the Market." Despite the transformations that she has witnessed in this place, Anna continues to feel accepted as a "regular" at the Market, or as one who "relates [her] family history there."

A project such as Anna's illustrates one way in which urban students can claim their own identities inside the composition classroom, rather than simply accommodating identities that have been prepackaged for them. By validating students' recollections of people and places in the city alongside histories presented by more traditionally authoritative sources (e.g., textbooks, newspapers, brochures), students are able to construct how and with whom they wish to be identified. And leaving open the format for revealing these identities, whether through a scrapbook or a video or an essay, encourages students to bring the values of their own communities to the telling of a city's story.

Principle 3: Prepare Students to Offer
Alternative Myths and Identities

This third principle acknowledges that however well we educate our students within our classrooms, the composing skills they learn need to empower them outside the academy as well. Birmingham is a city bustling with career opportunities for college graduates, especially for those with keen communication skills. As our students leave UAB and enter this larger professional community, we hope to equip them with strategies for participating in personal and institutional negotiating practices. While many students will remain in the area, others will enter different urban and rural environments where they might also benefit from such critical knowledge.

Editing in Professional Contexts is a junior-level course recently added to the professional writing curriculum. This course is designed specifically for individuals interested in editing careers or in positions in business, industry, or education that involve producing annual reports, newsletters, or other internal and external publications. Students who enter this class are highly motivated, as Birmingham is home to more than sixty book and magazine publishing companies and city newspapers. Perhaps the best known of these organizations is Southern Progress Corporation, whose head office in Birmingham produces such periodicals as *Southern Living, Cooking Light, Coastal Living,* and *Progressive Farmer.* Southern Progress Corporation (along with many other local publishing companies) is eager to hire UAB students with astute writing, marketing, and creativity skills, offering internships and other incentives to introduce them to the organization. So students enrolled in this course often have a clear goal attached to the skills they will read about and apply in class.

Students in this course are taught to identify the uniqueness of existing corporate cultures, that is, the ways in which particular organizations present themselves to the public, set up internal channels of communication, and prioritize certain values for their employees. The environment in which an organization is located greatly influences the ways in which it establishes and reinforces its corporate culture. Students interested in joining a publishing company in Birmingham will find many tensions between the mythologized city and the idealized institution for which they will work, tensions similar to those present throughout UAB's revised recruitment materials. For example, in a recent brochure produced by Southern Progress Corporation, students are urged to apply for internships with the company. On the first page, readers are told that the company is "a subsidiary of Time Warner," that it is one of the "largest lifestyle publishers in the country with revenues of $520 million," and that it is headquartered in Birmingham, Alabama. The organization is touted as "a progressive company that looks to the future," evidenced in part by the company's growing "national, as well as regional titles." Like UAB, this Birmingham-based organization stresses a forward- and outward-looking image, strengthened by a cover photo of the central office a few miles from the center of the city, an impressively modern building beautifully landscaped in Southern greenery.

Students in this course are encouraged to consider how the unique urban space in which they live influences the corporate culture of such organizations, as well as how their own identities have been formed in relation to such institutions. One of the first assignments students pursue in the course is a personal narrative that traces their textual history. The logic behind this assignment is that before editors create texts to be read by others, they should consider the priorities and assumptions they place on written, visual, or oral language. In addition to reading brief autobiographical excerpts that address literacy and learning, students reconstruct the ways in which they were introduced to reading and writing and explore the power of discourse in their lives. Further, they are asked to consider the impact an urban or rural environment had on these experiences, particularly on what was expected of them as readers and writers and how they were taught to participate in ongoing public and private conversations in their communities. The essays that stem from this assignment illustrate the importance of listening to how and why students portray their textual abilities in particular ways.

In one recent class, two students used their individual narratives to present a short collaborative presentation to the other students. Linda, an African American fifty-five-year-old woman from Birmingham, dressed in a long, flowing, white dress; Judy, a white fifty-five-year-old woman from a small community south of Birmingham, came to class in a straight, black suit. They engaged in a dialogue of comparisons and contrasts, beginning with some amusing similarities. Both women had the same number of children, and one of each of their daughters shared the same name. Both had recently become grandmothers for the first time, and both had been happily married for many years. But then their stories began to part. While Judy spent most of the sixties engrossed in the lives of her young children, Linda was involved in the needs of her local, black community during this time. While both Judy and Linda were raised in homes where books were valued and where their parents read to them at least weekly, Judy regularly visited her local library and brought home new and interesting books as Linda stood outside the library doors wondering what wonderful stories and adventures lay within. Both women came to view reading and writing as highly politicized activities, but for quite different reasons. Judy always knew she was a "good" reader and writer—her teachers told her so—and she was rewarded frequently for her ability to create "correct" and "pretty" sentences. Linda was also (much to her teachers' surprise) a "good" writer, and she was told that this skill would help her get ahead in life. Thus, for Judy, textual skills were a perk; for Linda, they were a tool for survival. Even today, both women admitted, these associations are strong every time they put pen to paper.

Such personal histories of literacy and the identities that emerge from these histories are significant when and if students enter institutions outside the academy where myths of the city are accommodated or resisted. The critical understandings that stem from such an exploration open up a gap through which students might negotiate their positions within an organization and perhaps influence (gradually) the ways in which an institution forges a particular urban identity for itself or those with whom it communicates. Southern Progress Corporation, in other words, is not just a company with a fixed image. It is an urban space that adds to a complex and dynamic discourse about the city, its people, its goals, its myths. And students, aware of their own histories with and responses to this greater discourse, can contribute to ongoing urban conversations.

CONCLUSION

As we close this chapter, we find ourselves still disagreeing about how Birmingham should be represented and how such representations might influence writing processes and the teaching of writing. We have grown more comfortable with our varied interpretations of Birmingham, though, and in designing the writing program at UAB, we consciously accounted for the mythologized presence of the city and the diverse individuals and communities who live here. We know that those who "write a city" must feel free to imagine its possibilities and to picture themselves as active makers of these possibilities, and there is no more productive site for such writing and imagining than the composition class.

WORKS CITED

Alabama Advisory Committee to the U.S. Commission on Civil Rights. *Civil Rights Issues in Birmingham*. Birmingham: AAC, 1988.

Baker, Tracey. "EH 102 Research Questionnaire: Community, Membership, and Identity." Student Survey. Spring 2000.

Barthes, Roland. *Mythologies*. Trans. Annette Lavers. New York: Noonday, 1972.

Bell, Daniel. *The Coming of Post-Industrial Society: A Venture in Social Forecasting*. New York: Basic, 1973.

Bloom, Harold. *The Anxiety of Influence: A Theory of Poetry*. London: Oxford UP, 1973.

Calvino, Italo. *Invisible Cities*. London: Picador, 1979.

Connerly, Charles E. "Federal Urban Policy and the Birth of Democratic Planning in Birmingham, Alabama, 1949 to 1974." *Planning the Twentieth-Century American City*. Ed. Mary Corbin Sies and Christopher Silver. Baltimore: Johns Hopkins UP, 1996. 331–58.

de Certeau, Michel. *The Practice of Everyday Life*. Trans. Steven Rendall. Berkeley: U of California P, 1984.

Hemphill, Paul. *Leaving Birmingham: Notes of a Native Son*. Tuscaloosa: U of Alabama P, 1993.

Lefebvre, Henry. *Writings on Cities*. Trans. Eleonore Kofman and Elizabeth Lebas. Cambridge, MA: Blackwell, 1996.

McKiven, Henry M., Jr. *Iron and Steel: Class, Race, and Community in Birmingham, Alabama, 1875–1920*. Chapel Hill: U of North Carolina P, 1995.

Operation New Birmingham. Birmingham: ONB, 1985.

Seibels, George G., Jr. *Citizen Participation Plan*. Birmingham: City Council, 1974.

Short, Dale. "Introduction: Birmingham Explained." *Guide to Birmingham for Newcomers and Natives Alike*. Ed. Joe O'Donnell. Birmingham: Newton, 1998. 20–21.

Southern Progress Corporation. Brochure. Birmingham, AL: Southern Progress Corporation, 2000.

Transferring to UAB. Birmingham: UAB Office of Undergraduate Admissions, 1998.

University of Alabama at Birmingham. 1998. 12 September 2000. <http://www.uab.edu>.

University of Alabama at Birmingham. CD-ROM. Birmingham: UAB Office of Undergraduate Admissions, 1998.

University of Alabama at Birmingham: Information Booklet. Birmingham: UAB Office of Undergraduate Admissions, n.d. (pre-1998).

University of Alabama at Birmingham: The Future is Here. Videotape. Birmingham: UAB Office of Undergraduate Admissions, 1998.

University of Alabama at Birmingham: Viewbook. Birmingham: UAB Office of Undergraduate Admissions, n.d. (pre-1998).

Wilson, Bobby M. *Race and Place in Birmingham: The Civil Rights and Neighborhood Movements.* New York: Rowman and Littlefield, 2000.

CHAPTER TWO

WRITING AGAINST TIME

Students Composing "Legacies"
in a History Conscious City

Elizabeth Ervin and Dan Collins

In the fall of 1998, the administration of Cape Fear Community College (CFCC), in conjunction with the CFCC Foundation, determined that it needed a campus focal point—an identifying marker that simultaneously distinguished it from other schools in the area and established its affiliation with downtown Wilmington, North Carolina, where CFCC is located. Public art was unpredictable and possibly offensive, so that idea was rejected; a fountain might attract vandals and would likely require costly long-term upkeep, so that option, too, was dismissed. Upon receiving a brochure from van Bergen, a clock manufacturer, and securing a private donor willing to finance the $35,000 project, the decision was made to build the George Henry Hutaff Memorial Clock in front of the administration building, right across the street from the main entrance to the CFCC campus.

Erected in February 1999 and formally dedicated in May of that year, the Hutaff Memorial Clock is sixteen and one-half feet high and has four faces, each three feet in diameter; at its base, it is surrounded by a shallow red brick wall enclosing seasonal flowers and shrubs. The clock comes equipped with an electronic sound system capable of digitally simulating a carillon of cast bronze bells; however, this feature was disabled once the sound, which emanates not from the clock itself but from speakers attached to an adjacent building, was found to disconcert passers-by. By virtue of its prominent location, the Hutaff Memorial Clock does appear to function as the landmark and campus meeting place that the administration envisioned. Showcased in print and television ads for the college and on "thank you" cards sent to CFCC Foundation donors, it has, moreover, become a symbol of and for the school in very short order.

As CFCC was putting the finishing touches on its public clock, a student across town—Shane Fernando, president of the 2000 senior class at the University of North Carolina at Wilmington (UNCW)—was already beginning to think like a college administrator. Fernando's goal was to organize a class gift with a millennium theme, more specifically, "some sort of timepiece" (Hirsh 6A). Using a controversial $35,000 loan from the Student Government Association as seed money, Fernando launched a sophisticated marketing campaign with the slogan "A Gift of Tradition," and in less than a year, his committee raised $92,000 from about four hundred donors, including students, faculty, alumni, businesses, and local residents. The university pitched in an additional $56,000 to purchase the Millennium Clock Tower, and indeed, it is considered to be one of the most "significant" (i.e., expensive) student gifts ever presented to a North Carolina university. The fifty-foot tower was shipped from the Verdin Company in Ohio and assembled in the center of campus just in time (!) for Spring 2000 commencement ceremonies. A local newspaper article reported that "[g]raduating seniors hope the clock tower will become a new university symbol and campus rallying point" (Schreiner 5B), and Fernando himself reasoned that $150,000 is "not really a lot of money" to pay for a symbol (qtd. in Bianchi 8).

On the contrary, some might argue that $150,000 is really quite a lot of money to pay for something that is merely, or at least primarily, symbolic; or they might point out that a hodgepodge of four hundred donors does not indicate widespread support from the 1,370 students who received their degrees at the May 2000 commencement. Predictably, though, the UNCW clock tower story has been narrated by administrators and the local media not as an arrogant waste of money and good intentions, but as an inspiring tale of student entrepreneurialism and school spirit. As Steve Bilzi, a member of the county school board, remarked, "It's wonderful that these kids are becoming such a productive part of their community and they haven't even graduated yet" (qtd. in Hirsh 1A). What the clock tower contributes to the local community—or, for that matter, the campus—remains to be seen. Like the CFCC clock, however, it is already part of UNCW's "image," showcased on its "Live on Campus" Internet link as well as on the covers of various university publications and brochures.

After discovering our institutions' mutual enthusiasm for public clocks, our initial question was: Why clocks? That is, why did these two very different schools, independently but only months apart, select clocks to embody their respective identities (histories, ambitions, legacies) and engender that elusive quality known as "community"? In an age when pretty much everybody has at least one watch and needs to look no farther than the nearest bank, computer screen, microwave, stereo, or dashboard for the current time, public clocks can perhaps only serve a symbolic purpose. What, then, do they signify, and what agendas do they endorse or suppress?

We believe that the answers to these questions have much to do with the ways in which "time" and, more specifically, "history" figure into Wilmington's rhetorical ecosystem. We borrow the term *rhetorical ecosystem* from Michael Weiler and W. Barnett Pearce, who use it to describe a mutually defining relationship between place and discourse that determines what can and can not be said (and understood), and by whom. As they explain it,

> Rhetors are forced to act within the confines of the ecosystem, and their discourses must reflect the web of relationships among its species and their surroundings. But as the rhetorical ecosystem evolves, as any living thing must, so too do its discursive possibilities, and within the system there is ample room for authorial creativity and cleverness. The rhetorical options available are thus constrained but not determined by the intertextuality of our "spaces" in the array of discourses that confront rhetors. Context both fits rhetorical action and is reconstructed by it. (14–15)

It is important to emphasize that rhetorical ecosystems are as lush as they are dense: dynamic and elastic, they invite both accommodation and innovation. By attending carefully to the people, events, artifacts, shared and contested histories, spaces, and oral and literate texts that compose—and are composed by— their cities, students can learn to navigate this context, and, in the process, create and inhabit urban spaces that are more authentic than symbolic.

HISTORY, TIME CONSCIOUSNESS, AND SELF-CONSCIOUSNESS IN WILMINGTON

Wilmington has enjoyed many urban identities in its long history. Incorporated in 1739, it has played a key role in several wars and has been shaped by Jim Crowism and the Civil Rights movement, hurricanes and race riots, shipping and real estate development and textile manufacturing. Tourism remains the city's most prominent local industry; however, since the extension of I-40 connected Wilmington to the rest of the state in 1990, the city has attracted a variety of other economic interests, including film production and pharmaceutical research. These infusions of capital have been accompanied by great wealth: pricey suburbs and gated communities as well as purveyors of yachts and other luxury items have sprouted up throughout the county, and the local political winds have shifted decidedly to the right. With so many signs of affluence, it can be easy to forget that Wilmington shares the same urban problems as cities many times its size. According to the 2000 census figures, Wilmington is home to 75,838 people, and yet it supports eleven public housing communities, its per capita homicide and child abuse rates are among the highest in North Carolina, and its public services are chronically underfunded.

The city's historic district is something of an anomaly within this urban setting. With its antebellum homes, century-old buildings, and scattered brick streets—and with the Battleship *North Carolina* providing an imposing backdrop across the river—"historic downtown Wilmington" is literally saturated with remnants of an illustrious past; in the words of a local museum, it is a place "where the past has presence." The city is proud of its rich heritage and promotes it through various preservation societies, historic sites, and special events. Problems of cost, location, and relevance make this "public" history inaccessible to many local residents, however, so the city also markets a less esoteric version in the form of horse-drawn carriages, antique stores, and trendy eateries, bars, coffee shops, and specialty boutiques.

Jerry Herron refers to this sanitized, commercialized exploitation of the past as "the humiliation of history," and he claims that it occurs and is tolerated—sometimes even celebrated—because of its historical *effect* rather than its historical *content*. And it is clearly historical effect (not content) that ultimately matters most in areas, such as downtown Wilmington, which have become so divorced from their larger urban contexts that their role is no longer to provide essential goods and services for a broad range of citizens; instead, cities such as Wilmington are forced to traffic in charm and nostalgia for a primarily middle-class clientele (110). A diverse, thriving urban district for more than two centuries, downtown Wilmington fell into decline in the 1970s before rebounding to its current state of "revitalization" (i.e., gentrification) in the last decade. Currently, it has a drug store and post office, but no laundromat or grocery stores; no movie theater, but a make-your-own pottery studio, ice cream parlor, and kite store; no veterinarian, but several lawyers and nail salons. In short, although Wilmington is a large enough urban area that most necessary goods and services can be found *somewhere* (with the exception of affordable housing, which has become scarce, even for professionals such as teachers and police officers), few of them can be found *downtown*. Much of the city's wealth and political power remains concentrated around the historic district, however, and because the tourists who flock there do spend a lot of money, the identity of and prospects for the entire metropolitan area have come to rest largely upon the humiliated history we have described.

While this marketing strategy might be lucrative in the short term, urbanists such as James Howard Kunstler suggest that it actually undermines the character of a community in the long run. Kunstler argues in *The Geography of Nowhere* that people are connected to each other and to where they live not by romantic and sterile histories, but by messy and multivalent ones that develop organically, over time, without the self-conscious crafting of boosters and chambers of commerce. When we replace this evolving historical content with bogus signifiers such as horse-drawn carriages and clock towers—that is, when we attempt to fabricate a sense of place rather than "achieve" it (see Rorty)—we lose not only the history but the vital human connections as well, leaving us feeling more estranged from our communities than ever (Kunstler 126, 169).

The attitudes and identities of UNCW and CFCC are more densely intertwined with those of downtown Wilmington than with those of the larger city. UNCW was established in 1947 as a junior college for the specific purpose of training and educating veterans returning to school on the GI Bill; it originally occupied a single building near downtown, where, like CFCC today, its students and staff were a familiar presence. In 1961, Wilmington College, as it was then known, relocated to a large tract of land across town, where it quietly thrived, attracting serious local attention only when it became part of the North Carolina state university system in 1969. Before Wilmington College even left downtown, arrangements were made for another vocational school to take its place. The Wilmington Industrial Education Center (WIEC), founded in 1959 and controlled by the county school board, became the first incarnation of this objective, and its Marine Tech program continues literally to anchor the school on the Cape Fear River at the northern edge of downtown Wilmington. In 1964, WIEC was renamed Cape Fear Technical Institute and fell under the jurisdiction of the State Board of Education and the Department of Community Colleges; it assumed its current name in 1988.

In its short existence, UNCW has rapidly developed something of a split personality. On the one hand, it enjoys an enviable academic reputation for a regional university, with increasingly talented students as well as a number of prestigious programs and faculty; it is currently the fastest-growing public university in the state and the second most selective. Despite these achievements, UNCW seems also to suffer from an inferiority complex in relation to the more celebrated universities in the state, such as Duke and UNC-Chapel Hill. Sensitive to its reputation as a "surfer school" (as evidenced by the nickname "UNC by the Sea") or a purveyor of cut-rate educational opportunities ("UNC by the K-Mart"), the school has undertaken an aggressive campaign to raise its profile locally and throughout the state. In general, this translates into courting and commending media attention—for example, by adding a "Faculty and Staff in the News" feature to the *Campus Communique* (the weekly faculty and staff newsletter), identifying those who have been quoted or have otherwise appeared in the media, and by initiating its own cable talk show, *Let's Talk! UNCW and You.* Less innocuous are the university's efforts to accommodate *Dawson's Creek,* a popular teen soap opera that films on campus, by waiving impact fees, blocking or vacating sections of campus during filming, and even adding a *Dawson's Creek* link to its homepage. In response to exasperated students and staff who feel that the school is selling its academic soul for a little publicity, administrators explain that since the show's primary audience is the very population UNCW is trying to attract, it makes sense to capitalize on the connection. Not surprisingly, the Millennium Clock Tower was immediately absorbed into the university's public relations machinery—although its status in campus folklore probably is not what administrators had in mind. In one story, a library employee left work at 10:00 P.M. shortly after the clock was erected, but noticed that it did not chime, thus prompting the joke that the clock only performs for crowds. Others have reported hearing the clock play, apparently without irony, such selections as "Dixie," "Proud Mary," and the "Showboat Overture" (which includes excerpts from the songs "Make Believe" and "Old Man River").

If UNCW's institutional psychology can be characterized as "self-conscious," CFCC's might be described as "unappreciated." CFCC has always been an awkward fit with downtown Wilmington. Its campus consists of a mish-mash of nondescript concrete structures ("in the genre of public housing," as Ira Shor once put it [13]) that add little to the historical aura Wilmington tries to project and protect. Until recently, the school's own history was one of benign neglect, with little change in the student population, academic programs, or campus size. Explosive local growth and the establishment of a college articulation agreement in 1995 (by which area community college students with a minimum GPA can automatically transfer to UNCW) changed all that, however, and CFCC now struggles to keep up with higher enrollments and a shifting academic mission. Such growth has not been universally welcomed by city stewards: whatever its value as an academic institution, the CFCC campus is also prime real estate, eyed by developers for various riverfront projects designed to cash in further on Wilmington's reputation as a tourist destination. In fact, in a 1997 study commissioned by the city and county governments and the Downtown Area Revitalization Effort, two of the three prospective visions for the downtown area over the next twenty-five years virtually ignore or, in the words of one trustee, "obliterate" CFCC (Agnoff qtd. in Hoover 1A). Laboring under the pressure to seem historical in an area where history sells, CFCC administrators are eager to pacify detractors by blending in. Enter the Hutaff Memorial Clock. While the clock's vintage style might in fact lend CFCC an air of humble immutability, this manufactured history has little to do with the realities of the school, its downtown neighborhood, or its students—most of whom commute from less affluent, more racially diverse areas of the city.

But our purpose here is not simply to mock the clocks; at issue, rather, is how these symbolic artifacts manifest Wilmington's rhetorical ecosystem.

Clocks have long been implicated in complex local, ideological, and institutional agendas. Scholars such as Lewis Mumford and E. P. Thompson have characterized clocks as the defining machines of the industrial age, and others have connected clocks to rationalism, capitalism, and even "coverage" models of education (e.g., see Bomer). As Gerhard Dohrn-van Rossum suggests in *History of the Hour*, the introduction of clocks, specifically public striking clocks, effected a sweeping transformation of "time consciousness" in European cities at around the end of the fourteenth century—a *Zeitordnung*, or "ordering of time," that comprised not only chronology and historical memory, but also a particular "temporal order" informed by prevailing intellectual and religious beliefs (233). This new time consciousness was enormously influential, regulating daily behaviors such as work, education, religious worship, and social activity, as well as conventions for structuring historical change (i.e., the relationship between past, present, and future). Dohrn-van Rossum tells us, for example, that it was this period that saw the synchronization of calendars and the reckoning of time according to consecutively counted days of the month, technologies that simplified the recording of one's date of birth, which in turn made it possible for individuals to connect their lifetimes to larger historical events (3–4). In any case, although time-keeping devices had already existed for two thousand years, by the fifteenth century public striking clocks assured two things: first, that everyone would be aware of the precise hour and local expectations for that hour (e.g., praying, starting or stopping work, confining oneself to home or city), and second, that everyone would be aware that *everyone else* was aware of these things. In other words, these clocks created not only a time-consciousness, but a self-consciousness structured by time—one that, Dohrn-van Rossum argues, alienated individuals from the "natural" rhythms of the days and seasons, giving them the sense that they no longer controlled time, but that it controlled them. Collectively, these changes represent the differences between what we call time-keeping and time-serving.

Although perfunctory references to "community welfare" were often used to justify their expense, Dohrn-van Rossum reports that public clocks were never solely utilitarian, but in fact were also considered "prestige objects" within a city and, as such, occasioned highly politicized inter- as well as intra-city competition for the most beautiful or powerful timepieces. Dohrn-van Rossum puts it simply: "Competition for prestige means that a city acquired a public clock because other cities already had one" (141). Moreover, he says,

> As a prestige-enhancing project, the public clock quickly became one of the features that distinguished a city as a city and was thus part of the urban decor. From the beginning of the fifteenth century, at the latest, possession of a public clock was part of a city's self-identity. . . . The expensive design of the public clock increased a city's renown and bolstered its self-confidence. (146)

Thus the time-consciousness that developed in the wake of public clocks was accompanied by a specific kind of self-consciousness and place identity. Schools occupy a central position in this history, for teachers in urban academic institutions were among the earliest proponents of public clocks, adopting an ancient logic that associated the observance of time with wisdom, moderation, and sensible self-control—in a word, temperance. "Making economical use of one's time," Dohrn-van Rossum points out, came to carry not just pedagogical value (by prioritizing content and systematizing the sequence of instruction) but moral value as well (251–60).

By these criteria, UNCW's Millennium Clock Tower and CFCC's Hutaff Memorial Clock represent almost paradigmatic public clocks, manifesting the temporal orders within their own geo-rhetorical ecosystems in several respects. First, they suggest an indeterminate historical consciousness: both are vaguely "traditional" in appearance, with roman numerals and other stylistic features compatible with the highly regulated architectures of Wilmington's historic district and the UNCW campus. Further, the clocks have been marketed as contributions to the welfare of their communities and indeed as key components of "community" itself, the nature of which seems to be shaped largely by fundraising and promotional efforts. Finally, the clocks are objects that represent prestige. Both, after all, come with appealing pedigrees—Verdin's clocks can also be found at such institutions as Notre Dame, the Smithsonian, the Chicago Botanical Gardens, and what formerly stood as the World Trade Center; van Bergen's customers include Clemson University, Texas A & M, and Middlebury College—and have inspired some friendly competition between the two schools (an official at CFCC confided to Dan that "our clock is prettier than [UNCW's]"). Despite certain similarities, these clocks deviate from the ancient patterns chronicled by Dohrn-van Rossum in one significant way: while the original public clocks were hailed as harbingers of modernism, the Millennium Clock Tower and the Hutaff Memorial Clock were conceived as specious historical artifacts. And because both arrived at their destinations with virtual historical content preinstalled, they can betoken only a humiliated history.[1]

In Wilmington and elsewhere, public clocks have come to be regarded as almost requisite accessories of city and campus life. Does this phenomenon represent evidence of a "disciplined" urban landscape (the triumph of synchronization and conformity over the idiosyncrasies of diversity and imagination) or of community pride (different constituencies coming together for the aesthetic enhancement of local surroundings)? In other words, if we assume that the clocks mean something to the people who occupy the same spaces, then what might those meanings be? Such questions are at the heart of learning to read and write landscapes rhetorically. As we see it, this process has two components. The first involves exploring patterns of living in our most immediate environments in order to locate the gaps, fissures, and uncertainties embedded in communal texts and artifacts. The second entails challenging and reconstituting the meanings of these texts and artifacts, taking responsibility for constructing what Cathy Fleischer and David Schaafsma call a "habitable space"— "a common place, a safe place, where conversation can begin and where meanings might be negotiated to create communities in which literacy might flourish" (xx). We believe that our classrooms can help students to begin this process, thereby demystifying the ways in which public spaces are manufactured and how they can become more life-enhancing.

SERVING TIME AND KEEPING TIME

In the remainder of this chapter, we will look at what happens when students attempt to compose habitable spaces. In the first case, the students' aims are co-opted and circumscribed by a seemingly unrevisable past; in the second, the students become agents of local rhetorical practices, using a historicized sense of place to imagine "possible worlds." Both UNCW and CFCC students have specific reasons for being concerned about their place in local histories. We will consider these in turn.

Betsy's Story

The Millennium Clock Tower movement renewed two ongoing discussions at UNCW: about a perceived lack of tradition on campus and about the "need" for a campus clock tower. It is true that participation in university-sponsored events is often disappointing, and even the most active students would be hard-pressed to identify a longstanding custom or practice unique to the school. For years, a clock tower has been advanced as the "solution" to this problem. In 1986, for example, a student named T. James Stanley wrote in the school newspaper, the *Seahawk:*

> We need a classy clocktower *[sic]* that is some way customized for our particular campus. The clocktower should be built solidly for a look of permanence, combining structural elements of antique and modern design. A symbol of the past and of the future. . . . The clocktower should be positioned on a small plot of ground somewhere on the central part of campus. It should be outstanding, but not ridiculously so. (2)

Stanley's vision is eerily prophetic: not only does it describe the appearance of the eventual Millennium Clock Tower, but it also foretells the "small plot of ground" that was actually incorporated into the redesigned "central part of campus" in 1997—at the request of the chancellor over the objections of the university's Buildings and Grounds committee—even before the most recent clock tower lobbying efforts began. In 1999, Jeremy Page, staff writer for the *Seahawk*, offered a succinct explanation for this arrangement: the Student Government Association was concerned about a lack of school tradition, and "[t]he clock tower project has been an SGA effort to establish such tradition this year" (3).

This statement reveals much about UNCW's historical anxieties. On the one hand, the school's emissaries clearly hold a reverence for history and tradition that is consistent with attitudes in Wilmington generally (the fact that the chancellor is a military historian might account for this somewhat). On the other hand, there is an impatience with history, illustrated by the desire to establish traditions immediately, "this year," rather than create a variety of living monuments or practices and wait for other people to transform them into traditions (or let them fall into oblivion). These tensions are not restricted to the clock tower project. Consider, for example, the following April Fool's Day e-mail message sent out to all faculty and staff by the former Associate Dean of the College of Arts and Sciences during the school's recent fiftieth anniversary observances:

> I am now at liberty to publicly announce the surprising find that was made during excavations for the lake at Campus Commons. The digging brought to light a collection of quill pens, ink wells, two books, eyeglass frames, a couple of lead bullets, several bottles, and, most of all, a small time capsule. UNCW archeologist Dr. Thomas Loftfield has established the origin of all the artefacts *[sic]* to be early 1700's.
>
> This is particularly exciting because some documents in the time capsule mention the existence of a "College For Ye Learned Sciences and Fine Arts" in the year 1756! As you may know, the first cornerstone for UNC-Chapel Hill was not laid until October 12, 1793, so that the site of the UNCW campus may actually be the OLDEST COLLEGE IN THE STATE. This may have extremely far-reaching implications.
>
> News of the find was withheld until excavations were complete, and an official celebration is planned for later this month. However, everybody is invited to a sneak preview of the documents and artefacts . . . on the lawn, in front of the main entrance of Bear Hall (look for the picnic tables).
>
> Dr. Thomas Loftfield will be present to explain the significance of each object, and there will be free cookies and soft drinks. Also, in celebration of the occasion, the UNCW Brass Ensemble will be playing a brief selection of tunes.
>
> EVERYBODY IS WELCOME! (Kiefer)

Despite ample clues that the announcement was a hoax (the April 1 date, for instance), the longing for "historical" status was so profound that an eager crowd—including local media—showed up to celebrate the "discovery," forcing Dean Kiefer to issue a public apology for the backfired joke.

It was out of these treacherous time-conscious waters that the UNCW History Project emerged. The project was conceived by a composition student named Angela who had become fascinated with some archival documents related to our university's history. She had stumbled across these documents during a class research assignment, and she wanted to argue in her final essay that the university should not only promote its history, but also create opportunities and incentives for faculty and students to get involved in researching this largely undocumented history of our school—perhaps by creating some sort of award or prize. I mentioned to Angela the upcoming fiftieth anniversary celebrations, and together we brainstormed specific kinds of research projects in which UNCW students might engage. She recorded these ideas and forwarded them to the chancellor. Although Angela never heard from the chancellor, I seized upon her ideas and built them into my first-year writing, reading, and research courses (also viewing this as an opportunity to learn more about the university myself, as I was a relatively new faculty member at the time), and with her permission, this is what I did. Eventually, Angela moved on to other interests, so I recruited a colleague, Lu Ellen Huntley, to assist me in planning the course, and after much discussion, the two of us established some objectives and settled on an assignment sequence that included oral history, archival research, scholarly research, and public presentation of research.

Our efforts to engage students in this project soon confirmed Angela's hunch that students would embrace opportunities to understand and participate in the history of their school. One of their first assignments was to visit and write a journal response to an exhibit at our local museum that featured various photographs, newspaper clippings, and artifacts from UNCW's early days. Many students compared various aspects of the university then and now or raised questions about what was missing; some tried to imagine themselves at the school in previous years. T.J. wrote that after seeing the exhibit,

> I began to feel that I was a part of UNCW's history. I felt that in the years to come, people would go to the same museum and see the impact that my class and my generation had on the campus at UNCW. With all the increase in construction on campus, I imagined another aerial [photograph] of the year 2001 that showed buildings that we don't have presently. I imagined newspapers that would describe the culture and attitude of the students today. A reputation would surface and that reputation would be started and held by us.

Responses like this suggest that students do desire to leave a legacy and see their lives as being linked to a larger history—both a past and a future—and at the time of the project, Lu and I took them as indications that the UNCW History Project would roll spiritedly along, powered by student curiosity and the local mania for documenting times past.

Lu and I quickly realized that in order for students to produce high-quality work, we would need some money for equipment (e.g., tape recorders), postage, photocopies, and other resources such as oral history videos. At this point we turned to UNCW's Office of University Advancement, which provided vital moral and financial support as we got our project off the ground. Most serendipitously, University Advancement had received a $500 gift certificate from a local electronics superstore in celebration of the university's anniversary, and this office donated the gift to me and Lu for the purchase of eighteen hand-held tape recorders and batteries. Despite the Office of University Advancement's generosity, however, our allies in administration had an agenda that was somewhat different from ours. Lu and I were committed to fulfilling the course goals for English 103—namely, "to give students practice in a variety of written forms, with primary attention given to writing for academic purposes . . . characterized by an inquiring, balanced, informed voice and a tolerant intellectual stance"—while the folks in University Advancement saw our project largely in terms of its public relations, recruitment, and fundraising value. They were particularly interested in producing a promotional video featuring famous UNCW graduates, and they gave us a prioritized list of different departments, programs, offices, alumni, staff, and donors whose histories they wanted chronicled, as well as key contact persons who could provide us with information and the number of students they needed for each project.

It was not long before these plans spiraled out of control and increasingly came into conflict with the purposes of the course and the more specific goals that Lu and I had identified for this project. We continually had to remind our friends in University Advancement that these were first-year students, not experienced scholars; that this was an introductory writing course, not an advanced seminar in video production; and that it was crucial that students be allowed to pursue their own research agendas, not ones imposed on them by the university bureaucracy. We had to tread lightly here, for our project depended upon the goodwill of the administration, as well as their access to resources and knowledge of university history. The administration eventually backed off and remained supportive, and by the beginning of the fall semester most misunderstandings had been ironed out. Still, the experience made us more alert to how stories can be appropriated to serve multiple agendas.

It was not just administrators who were expecting a history that could be harnessed for promotional purposes; many informants were likewise reluctant to reveal anything that might be considered even remotely controversial, and in fact they went to some effort to conceal or sugarcoat such information. For example, a man who attended UNCW from 1968 to 1972 reported that the political climate at the school was "very conservative" during the Vietnam War, and in fact he and some of his friends essentially overthrew the school newspaper staff (who insisted on writing about the war "in every edition") and replaced them with fraternity and sorority members who focused on student clubs instead. And yet the man also insisted that there were no major conflicts between pro- and anti-war groups on campus, and that "anyone from any side [could] speak his mind, all were allowed to express themselves" (Baldwin). Other informants similarly whitewashed their descriptions of such important events as campus desegregation and the system-wide "speakers ban" on suspected communists. In short, with few exceptions, they seemed determined to narrate the story of UNCW as a story of benevolent authority, technological progress, and good clean fun.

I could detail the logistical struggles and ideological frustrations of this project *ad nauseam,* but the point I wish to make here is simply that the UNCW History Project can be read as a clash of historical perspectives. Few of our students were from Wilmington, after all, while most of their informants were natives or longtime residents, active alumni, and local citizens fiercely protective of the reputation of their city and school. These two groups held very different understandings of the purpose of the project—indeed, of the purposes of history generally—and in the end, the local perspectives prevailed. Lu and I did encourage our students to challenge the information offered by the people, texts, and artifacts they encountered in their research, to find ways to interact with received accounts of the school's history, and to use these strategies to compose our school as a "habitable space." However, because we proceeded without any understanding of the local rhetorical ecosystem, we found ourselves working from a generically academic model of historiography rather than a rhetorically localized one, and the result was a history that did not fit—could not be written or read, spoken or heard—in the available discourse.

It is too soon to tell whether the Millennium Clock Tower will succeed in establishing school tradition or coating the UNCW campus with that coveted patina of age. We do not yet know how the architects of the project will be remembered. Nevertheless, it is perhaps useful to ask why so many members of the campus and local communities seem satisfied with the symbolic version of history the clock tower extols. For one thing, "clock tower" was part of the local rhetorical ecosystem for more than a decade before the actual project came to fruition, a period during which it gained support from university administrators and was even surreptitiously built into the campus landscape. For another, the clock tower participated in the discourses of economic partnership, technological innovation, and community welfare in ways that were also recognized and accepted locally. But even though the clock tower has not disrupted Wilmington's rhetorical ecosystem, opportunities for it to participate in critique and revision may yet present themselves if we insist on regarding the clock not simply as a static artifact of humiliated history, but as a moment of uncertainty ripe with multiple meanings.

Dan's Story

As Betsy explains in the previous section, histories are easily co-opted by local rhetorical ecosystems and those who identify with and/or profit from them. Can this notion of rhetorical ecosystem—its origins, movements, and effects—be taught to first-year composition students? Can students enter rhetorical ecosystems, both prescriptive and capable of being resisted, to learn something new about their localities? Can contested meanings over any element of public life—including specious historical artifacts such as public clocks—be documented to provide a greater representation of what passes for living in a given community? The following is an account of my attempt to answer such questions with my students.

In *The Age of Missing Information*, Bill McKibben asks an important yet difficult question: "Where do I live?" (37). Embedded within this question lie other questions designed to isolate what passes for living in our localities. McKibben asks that we examine regional matters glossed over by national and global issues, highlighting what he calls "diverse localness," those aspects of our communities that separate and distinguish them from others (41). Over the past year, I have used McKibben's book with my first-year composition students to create a pedagogical framework that frontloads such an examination and composition of urban place in Wilmington. Such awareness of local entities helps students move beyond a prefabricated sense of place to productive connections to their localities that are based on lived realities rather than specious historical narratives.

We begin my first-year composition course by reading and discussing McKibben's book. To guide our discussion, I offer students specific journal prompts. One of the first prompts is McKibben's own question, "Where do I live?" Seemingly simple and straightforward, the question is actually difficult for students to answer, if only because they do not see its importance initially. The broad nature of the question also throws them: afraid to answer the "wrong way," they hesitate to write anything. Once something is down on paper, we share and discuss the multitude of answers. Some students provide street addresses, others offer more existential descriptions. During the discussion that ensues, we begin to see that the array of answers reflects McKibben's point—that the particularities of our most immediate environments are not well known or valued, that the places in which we live are "simplified" by a media environment designed to downplay or eradicate "local diversity" in favor of a standardized narrative.

The next journal prompt further sets up our discussion about local urban particularities. Here I ask students to define one element of living in Wilmington that distinguishes this city from every other place; this element can be a place, a practice, almost anything they can come up with as long as it is unique to Wilmington and valuable to that particular writer. Students' choices provide insights into what they value from the local environment and how they define this region as separate from other regions. An interesting thing happens here: while students offer a wide variety of answers in response to the first prompt ("where do I live?"), a more standardized set of answers is offered in response to this second prompt. Given our location in southeastern North Carolina, surrounded by water—the Atlantic Ocean, the Cape Fear River, the Intracoastal Waterway—many students immediately offer one of these land- marks as their answer. Other answers also betray a sort of standard narrative of the city: the downtown area, for example, with its shops and restaurants and old homes, is often identified as what makes Wilmington unique. Students' responses to these journal prompts are, I believe, mediated by the prescripted narrative of local commercial and promotional values; the local features deemed important to students are also the "selling" points of the city, after all, suggesting that "standardization" itself may be a key principle of Wilmington's rhetorical ecosystem.

To generate further reflections on our urban community, I have my stu- dents read two additional selections: Kim Stafford's "A Few Miles Short of Wisdom" and a selection from Gretel Ehrlich's *The Solace of Open Spaces.* Stafford's essay describes his quest to find the undocumented history of Big Hole National Battlefield, the place where Chief Joseph and the Nez Perce were attacked by American soldiers. Although Stafford is familiar with the traditional history of the battle, he wishes to move beyond this tired narrative that is reflected in tour books and brochures, instead adding a fresh perspec- tive to the existing stories. Ehrlich describes how the Wyoming landscape is more than just a place and actually informs ways of life, patterns of living, psy- chological dispositions, and personal and collective values. Combined (and in light of our exposure to McKibben), these readings by Stafford and Ehrlich provide an additional framework that allows students to question what gets left out of local narratives and why, and how—knowingly or not—our habits of being can be influenced by the places in which we find ourselves.

After reading and discussing these essays, students then choose a partic- ular place in the city of Wilmington that they wish to document in writing. This essay assignment provides students with the opportunity to say some- thing "new" about their urban community, to expand the history of Wilming- ton with previously unheard narratives and advance representations of the city beyond the standard ones that comprise the rhetorical ecosystem of Wilm- ington. This is not an easy assignment, and I take pains to warn students not to see it as such. We are not usually taught to think about where we live, and in an age of globalization we are living in communities that increasingly look and "feel" more and more alike. I hope, then, that in the process of examining local places and practices, students will see authentic particularity as valuable, not something to be plowed over with franchised restaurants and generic, pre-fabricated "landmarks," such as clock towers.

One student, Jim, took the assignment as an opportunity to pay homage to his grandfather (the person who, essentially, raised him) by writing about the Cape Fear Memorial Bridge, which spans the Cape Fear River on the southwest side of Wilmington. The Cape Fear Memorial Bridge is by no means a pretty sight. Thus, not compatible with Wilmington's "marketable tradition," the bridge is most often overlooked in the standardized narratives of the city. Yet in his essay, Jim describes this bridge as a testament to the hard work of his grandfather who was a crane operator, pouring concrete and hoisting steel assemblies during the construction of the bridge in the mid-1960s. Recalling his grandfather's final days, Jim offers an image of the old man squirming in his hospital bed, seemingly working the clutch and the brake of his crane. It is a moving piece of writing, intricately weaving the description of the bridge with information regarding his grandfather. Jim is a Wilmington native who had recently turned forty years old and had soured on his urban community because of rampant growth and a lack of clear vision on the part of local officials to handle such growth. But in writing about the bridge as a kind of legacy, Jim began to think about what the bridge—what his hometown—meant to him, and even though the future of the city is uncertain, he learned to value and respect this place.

The cultivation of this kind of attachment to place—self-reflective, speculative—is part of the assignment, as is the reworking of standardized representations and narratives. Working within a dominant discourse of time-consciousness and "instant history," Wilmington's students struggle to navigate the competing agendas implied by different representations of and hopes for the city. Measuring their representations against existing narratives, they consider what else should be included and to what ends. As they contribute to the local rhetorical ecosystem, students offer speculative visions for the future of Wilmington based on personal understandings of its history. These visions may take time to come to fruition (and in truth, some never will) but our classrooms can be places where such conversations begin and where literacy, and other life-enhancing activities, flourish. Connecting people and places, in other words, enables a kind of investment in the further development of the place itself. Legacy becomes an active process of engagement rather than an empty signifier.

LIVING IN LOCAL TIME

There is a *Simpsons* episode from some years back in which Lisa is determined to integrate an all-male military academy called Rommelwood. As her family drives her through the solemn stone gates, we are treated to a shot of the school's motto: "A Tradition of Heritage." We laugh at the absurdity of an institution that is at once exclusive and obsolete—and that serves an increasingly symbolic purpose—but because this could just as easily be the motto for Wilmington, or an inscription on either of our schools' clocks, or indeed the fundraising slogan for the Millennium Clock Tower, we also have to take seriously the idea of history folding in on itself. We know that legacy and community are not as easy to add to a campus as a clock, which is why we believe that it is vitally important to interrupt local historical consciousness by localizing time.

In this essay we have suggested that our institutions' respective clocks represent efforts to fill a void felt by administrators (CFCC) and students (UNCW), materially in the form of "enhancing" existing landscapes and metaphorically in the form of establishing a focal point for community and tradition. The irony, however, is that both schools seem to pin their aspirations for historical legitimacy on generic, mass-produced symbols that lead away from a distinctive identity toward a culture of nowhere guided by empty signification. Kunstler denounces the impulse to accept such shortcuts:

> [T]he discontinuities of our everyday surroundings are mirrored by the discontinuities of the university. Viewing a landscape of totem objects designed to convince us that we live in a thing called *community* . . . the academics declare that these objects may be minutely observed without considering their value in relation to other things—for instance, to some notion of what makes a community authentic or false, good or bad. (123)

Kunstler sees college as a Petri dish for both enacting these discontinuities and intervening in them: as a place and a time simultaneously, it already provides the framework for thinking about the when, what, where, how, and why of our lives. Kunstler thus calls on academics, particularly those within the humanities, to return to more substantive questions of value in their work, specifically, by interrogating what constitutes "a life worth living" (123).

Examined through the rubric of this question, even "totem objects" such as the Millennium Clock Tower and the Hutaff Memorial Clock can provide useful moments of analysis and reflection. Living well involves cultivating relationships with our immediate environments that provide balance, order, identity; as we stated earlier in this essay, it involves constructing habitable spaces. If by design the clocks are intended to represent prestige, tradition, and legacy without taking up the history of UNCW and CFCC, then we can take up those histories ourselves in innumerable ways. If the legacy embodied by the clocks is only a mirage and the future is largely vacant, then we can embody a more authentic historical consciousness through our actions, including writing. In short, by documenting the uncertainty of time and the fragility of place at our respective institutions, we can sustain the possibility of deliberating local temporal orders.

Literacies are local, Robert P. Yagelski reminds us (14). When we teach rhetoric as a means of actively participating in the construction of local meanings, we can also teach our students to render more affirmative, life-enhancing choices regarding ways in which to live together. The clocks, then, need not represent dead ends that siphon off debate via misguided symbolic practice; rather, they are elements in the construction of place that need to be acknowledged, reckoned with, lived.

NOTE

1. It is worth noting that the Verdin Company's website participates fully in the discourse of humiliated history. A lengthy section on "streetclocks," for example, claims that public clocks "provide a service to your community" even as it advises potential clients on how to "[m]ake the streetclock an effective promotional vehicle." Elsewhere, Verdin appeals to those seeking to create a legacy by noting that "[a] bell is a lifetime investment, a living memorial for future generations," and that "[i]t is said that a person never forgot the sound of his village bell, no matter how many years he was away from home." Finally, any college administrator who governs in the era of TQM will be attracted to Verdin's service agreement, called, appropriately, "The Verdin Guarantee of Excellence." Van Bergen's website focuses much more on clock-making technology and craftsmanship than on the commercial advantages of public clocks.

WORKS CITED

Baldwin, John. Interview with Billy Kupferman. 16 September 1997.

Bianchi, Marybeth K. "Senior Class Leaves Clock Tower as Monument." *UNCW Magazine* (Spring/Summer 2000): 8.

Bomer, Randy. *Time for Meaning: Crafting Literate Lives in Middle and High School*. Portsmouth, NH: Heinemann, 1995.

Dohrn-van Rossum, Gerhard. *History of the Hour: Clocks and Modern Temporal Orders*. Trans. Thomas Dunlap. Chicago: U of Chicago P, 1996.

Ehrlich, Gretel. *The Solace of Open Spaces*. New York: Penguin, 1985.

Fleischer, Cathy, and David Schaafsma. "Introduction: Further Conversations: Jay Robinson, His Students, and the Study of Literacy." *Literacy and Democracy: Teacher Research and Composition Studies in Pursuit of Habitable Spaces*. Ed. Cathy Fleischer and David Schaafsma. Urbana: NCTE, 1998. xiii–xxxii.

Herron, Jerry. *Afterculture: Detroit and the Humiliation of History*. Detroit: Wayne State UP, 1993.

Hirsh, Stacey. "Class of 2000 Donates Clock as Senior Gift to University." *Wilmington Morning Star* 9 February 2000: 1A+.

Hoover, Aaron. "Will City's Plan for Growth Clash With CFCC?" *Wilmington Star News* 15 May 1997: 1A.

Kiefer, Rudi. "Preview tonight!" Email message. 1 April 1997.

Kunstler, James Howard. *The Geography of Nowhere: The Rise and Decline of America's Man-Made Landscape*. New York: Touchstone, 1993.

McKibben, Bill. *The Age of Missing Information*. New York: Plume, 1992.

Mumford, Lewis. *Technics and Civilization*. New York: Harcourt, 1963.

Page, Jeremy. "SGA Grants $50,000 for Millennium Clock Tower." *Seahawk* 8 December 1999: 3.

Rorty, Richard. *Achieving Our Country: Leftist Thought in Twentieth-Century America*. Cambridge: Harvard UP, 1998.

Schreiner, Mark. "Clock Set Up Just in Time." *Wilmington Morning Star* 12 May 2000: 1B+.

Shor, Ira. *Critical Teaching and Everyday Life*. Boston: South End, 1980.

Stafford, Kim. "A Few Miles Short of Wisdom." *Having Everything Right: Essays of Place*. Seattle: Sasquatch, 1997. 23–38.

Stanley, T. James. "Time for Chime." *Seahawk* 18 September 1986: 2.

Thompson, E. P. "Time, Work-Discipline, and Industrial Capitalism." *Past and Present* 38 (1967): 56–97.

The Verdin Company. 20 July 2000. <http://www.verdin.com/>.

Weiler, Michael, and W. Barnett Pearce. "Ceremonial Discourse: The Rhetorical Ecology of the Reagan Administration." *Reagan and Public Discourse in America*. Ed. Michael Weiler and W. Barnett Pearce. Tuscaloosa: U of Alabama P, 1992. 11–42.

Yagelski, Robert P. *Literacy Matters: Writing and Reading the Social Self*. New York: Teachers College P, 2000.

CHAPTER THREE

A Paragraph Ain't Nothin' but a Sandwich
The Effects of the GED on
Four Urban Writers and Their Writing

Krista Hiser

San Francisco's billboards tout the urban identity of the new millennium, and it is a hip, hi-tech, khaki-clad capitalism so perpetually in your face that, after a while, you begin to believe that everyone drives an SUV, works in a groovy loft space, and spends free time shopping online. The dot e-conomy and the steady gentrification of urban neighborhoods such as the Mission and the Tenderloin have transformed what it means to be a San Franciscan. The situation is summed up by an ironic graffiti art poster painted underneath the freeway near the Mission district. It reads: "Welcome to the Mission: cleaner, whiter . . . with tablecloths."

The mayor's office estimates that between 11,000 and 14,000 men and women have nowhere to sleep on any given night in San Francisco. To be homeless in the city means to be invisible, and to have your identity written upon you, a one-line tragedy on a piece of cardboard: "lost my leg in Vietnam," or "3 kids, HIV +," or "why lie—I need a beer." Activists, politicians, and service providers have different ideas about what the homeless need, but one thing is certain: they need a place to remember, or discover, who they used to be before they became statistics. Michael Holzman uses the term *zero measure* to describe the self-concept of, for example, the substance abuser, whose identity is constituted by the individual's social position—she is named by mainstream voices and mirrored by the fellow addicts with whom she forms a community (29). Urban community adult education sites have been the places where people could gather, not only to learn skills, but also to develop social networks through which they could build new identities. But as the economic and political climate of the city has changed, so too has the function of education in urban locales.

Deborah Brandt illustrates the impact that "sponsorship" has always had upon the form of literacy that is made available to those who seek it. She describes through case study how "the course of an ordinary person's literacy learning—its occasions, materials, applications, potentials—follows the transformations going on within sponsoring institutions as those institutions fight for economic and ideological position" (177). In San Francisco, what used to be about finding yourself is now about quick certification and quantifiable outcomes: welfare statistics, job placement, the GED.

I started working in San Francisco's social services "industry" nine years ago, as a literacy tutor in the basement of a shelter in the Tenderloin. My job was to tutor a middle-aged man named Marco, who wanted to improve his writing. Marco—whose father had beaten him with a belt for keeping a journal because "writing was for sissies"—taught me an enduring lesson: that learning to write is a complex social and psychological process, not merely a skill. This lesson was later reinforced by my graduate work in composition. Yet, as I studied theory and learned to teach process before product, I saw an increasing emphasis on form in the community writing classes I continued to teach and observe.

Marco had been a student at the Episcopal Community Services (ECS) Skills Center, one of the only education providers serving San Francisco's homeless and low-income community. Marco blossomed in the creative writing and poetry classes available to him. Today, however, the opportunities available to homeless or low-income literacy seekers are more likely to emphasize computers, work-readiness, and the GED. Megan Christoph, the education manager at the Skills Center, agreed that "there's definitely been a shift to the quantifiable," but unlike me, she sees this as a good thing. She is pragmatic: "You want money; you want a place to live, a better job; that's why people come here. If we can give them some computer training, it helps them with that."

"We've totally transformed our program," she continues while I reminisce about the old days in the shelter basement. "We've lost the creative writing aspect, which is too bad for some people, but we're doing a much better job for people who come for literacy, reading, writing, math, and computers. We have less funding than we did even four years ago, and something has to go. I don't even know anyone who does creative writing anymore except maybe the [Coalition on Homelessness'] Street Sheet. . . . It's just not as pressing as the need to get a job." She explained the pressure the U.S. government's General Assistance Program puts on people now to illustrate how the infamous "welfare-to-work" initiatives have transformed urban education services: payments are down from $345 a month to $265 a month, with a thirty-six month limit. Welfare recipients who go to school can receive a higher payment but have a shorter time limit at twenty-seven months. "People need our program," Megan said. "They come for a reason, because they realize they will be cut off."

Such institutionalized pressures on urban literacy sponsors cause a loss of local control over literacy education, resulting in a limited emphasis on basic skills and job training, as if to say—*for you, this is enough*. And compositionists, especially at urban universities, need to pay close attention to these kinds of institutionalized pressures, since we are all part of the same literacy system whether we are based in community or university contexts. Increasingly, writing teachers are becoming more interested in, as Anne Ruggles Gere puts it, listening "to the signals that come through the walls of our classrooms from the world outside" (76). We can learn much from this listening, but we risk condescension in our eavesdropping if we continue to ignore the real factors acting upon literacy seekers outside of the university.

The GED, a test so deeply entrenched in the literacy system that we no longer even notice it, is one example of an institutionalized pressure placed on urban literacy sponsors that results in debilitating pedagogical limitations. Despite having discredited formalist pedagogies and the five-paragraph theme decades ago, the discipline of composition continues to ignore the formalist GED essay test as a crucial aspect of literacy education, thus implicitly accepting the test and its oppressive social functions. The result is an unkind stratification of the literacy experience. For in the world outside the university, the GED has incredible power, influencing writing pedagogy in urban community programs and holding a symbolic value in people's lives in the way they think of themselves as writers and as human beings.

Writing pedagogy outside of the university is full of possibilities. Carol Heller's three-year observation of San Francisco's Tenderloin Women Writer's Workshop, for example, describes a vision of classroom "synthesis" that we are capable of creating in urban community spaces. She shows us how "the words of marginalized people, transformed in writing, in stories, in cultural performance, embody more than new narratives; they are in fact the public creation of possible worlds" (228). Such writing, Heller argues, "could constitute the backbone of new conceptions of cultural forum and liberation education" (46). She echoes bell hooks, who describes a "space of radical openness" in which marginality is "a site one stays in, clings to even, because it nourishes one's capacity to resist. It offers to one the possibility of radical perspective from which to see and create, to imagine alternatives, new worlds" (150).

Unfortunately, our work and that of our students is evaluated, not according to the fulfillment of personal or social needs, but instead by external "legitimating" forces such as the GED. Too often, the writing instruction experienced in the shelters, neighborhood centers, prisons, and other urban settings where we work is an ill-fitting, worn out hand-me-down. Rather than engaging urban literacy students on their own terms and working from there, the GED essay requirement forces students to re-imagine their identities, habits, goals, and dreams in order to fit the predetermined content of a formalist essay test.

THE ROLE OF THE GED AT THE ECS SKILLS CENTER

In 1998, more than 45.5 million adults had not finished high school, and only one percent of those adults received a GED. In California, during that same year, 5,327,621 adults did not finish high school, and only 37,463 were awarded GEDs (Hone 11). Of all the people excluded from mainstream schooling, very few actually earn GEDs. And yet our opportunities and methods for teaching literacy in urban sites are increasingly constrained by the GED, which may or may not be a relevant goal for many of the people who inhabit community classroom spaces.

When I began a ten-week observational case study at the ECS Skills Center, my research questions had nothing to do with the GED. I was still looking for the space of radical openness. I was looking at how the participants related to or employed writing in their own lives and how writing instruction affected their skills and their sense of themselves as writers, what Albert Bandura calls their "perceived self-efficacy." I soon found that I could not ask questions about identity in this context without running into the GED again and again.

Bandura defines *self-efficacy* as "people's judgements of their capabilities to organize and execute a course of action required to attain designated types of performances" (qtd. in Pajares 313). Self-esteem is a related psychological mechanism, described by Nathaniel Branden as a "disposition to experience oneself as competent to cope with the basic challenges of life and as worthy of happiness" (7). While self-efficacy steadily increases with practice, self-esteem changes constantly in relation to one's situation and surroundings. These two concepts must remain distinct, as Bandura emphasizes: "There is no fixed relationship between beliefs about one's capabilities and whether one likes or dislikes oneself. Individuals may judge themselves hopelessly inefficacious in a given activity without suffering any loss of self-esteem whatsoever" (11). It is thus possible to have a highly developed sense of self-esteem without being able to write, spell, or organize a paragraph.

When placed in a situation where formalized writing, such as the writing required for the GED, is emphasized as a high-stakes enterprise, pedagogical practices have a tremendous effect on the emerging identities of urban literacy students. Students at the ECS Skills Center intuited that writing in a supportive classroom environment helped their self-esteem, while focused GED instruction actually hindered their perceived self-efficacy in writing. I interviewed four students extensively; two of them enjoyed writing and identified strongly with it as a means of self expression. Yet when confronted with the conventions of the GED essay requirement and the paragraphing strategies taught in the GED classes, they got the message that their own urban literacies were wrong, and that there was a correct, professional way to write.

In many urban settings such as San Francisco, the GED is the great legitimator, the crossing ritual, baptism, rite of passage back into mainstream employment and schooling. Its function is heavily symbolic, both externally, in the gatekeeping function that mainstream society has ascribed to it, and internally, in the symbolic function the test holds for each person who attempts it. Many individual students, particularly at the ECS Skills Center, relate to the GED as a way to achieve an *aspiring* (or hoped for) identity, which helps them revise the *ascribed* (external, forced) identity with which they have been labeled. "Working toward my GED" is a more credible identity than "being a homeless man" or "being HIV +" or "having a learning disability." This is its positive function in that it provides a goal, an opportunity for a new self-concept. Yet when we examine the situation as urban literacy teachers, we are forced to acknowledge that aspiring identities often generate goal structures that are inconsistent with formalist methods of GED instruction.

STORIES FROM A GED CLASSROOM

This essay is not meant to be an indictment of all standardized testing, but simply a reminder that we must continue to problematize the GED. The best way to do so is to examine its role in people's lives, as they go about the complex business of negotiating new identities.

Renee

Nineteen-year-old Renee is precariously poised between her urban "street life" and some new unknown life, between adolescence and adulthood, then and now. She describes herself as a "system kid," a San Francisco native raised in a series of group and foster homes, getting in trouble at a series of schools, homeless at sixteen. One day, she pointed out to me all the places she used to have piercings—ears, nose, tongue—and it was then easier to imagine her as a panhandling street kid. She loves the beach, UB40, girlfriends, and poetry, but she also has very adult concerns. With one year left in the supportive housing program for homeless youth where she currently lives, Renee needs to finish her GED, find a job, secure new housing, and successfully break from her "old homeys" in order to make it into adulthood. "When I was livin' at the [emergency shelter], that put me down a lot." She said,

I was usin' at the time—I really didn't care—I wasn't getting' a job, I wasn't really lookin', and I didn't really care. Then, I don't know what happened, I mean I just got to the point where—first I wasn't caring then something just told me "you better start caring now 'cause you're getting older" and if you don't you're going to be stuck in this life forever. Since I didn't have a job, and since I wasn't doing anything, just hanging out on the street most of the time, and not doing anything all day, I just decided why not take the opportunity now to go to GED classes, to give me an opportunity to better myself and give me something to do during the day instead of using drugs or getting myself in trouble.

Renee says that the GED is "a way to show people 'hey, look at me, I'm tryin' to do something with my life now' instead of being just a young kid who doesn't care. I do care, and a lot of people don't know that." The GED is symbolic, to Renee and to others, of the transition from street kid to responsible adult.

Renee's transition also means that she has to change her ideas about writing. Renee identifies strongly with writing, which she uses as a way to communicate her feelings and reflect upon the past. She described for me her first experience writing poetry at the ECS Skills Center:

When I started coming to class, it was like, why don't you put your words into like a poem of what you're feeling. So one day I just sat down and started writing, how I became homeless and the life that I lived, hanging out on the streets doing drugs, panhandling, whatever, and then towards the end of the poem I talked about how I changed my life, got out of drugs, and how I'm not as scared as I was when I was homeless, and so, I don't really know how to explain it, but towards the end I felt more confident.

From the positive responses she got to her poem from members of her writing class, she began forming part of her identity around this ability to express her feelings on paper. She explains,

Growing up, I didn't have a say at all. I mean, I grew up in group homes, and no one really understood me, didn't want to communicate with me, like "who cares what she says," like I didn't have an opinion or anything. I'm still trying to learn to express myself by writing. If I tell people how I'm feeling, it might be, well, who cares, but this way it will be down on paper. I'm learning how to, instead of a closed mouth, to open my mouth instead of keeping quiet.

Renee brags about the five or six notebooks she has filled since she started writing. This writing gives her a way to hold on to those feelings, to keep track of time, her own progress toward her goals, and her increased sense of self-esteem.

Writing for the GED, however, is another story. Though she began writing essays toward the end of my observation, Renee seemed paralyzed by her perception that GED writing was drastically different from the journal writing she did, that it was more "professional" and that "there's a certain way you have to do it." During class time, Renee gave consistent cues to indicate the "split" she perceived between her own writing and the GED essays she was asked to write in class. She would slam her journal shut, push it aside, and drag out the GED workbook. It did not occur to her that the ideas in her journal could be revised or developed into a workable GED essay on some of the topics she attempted: "Why I'm in school"; "What charity I would give a million dollars to"; "Whether I prefer the city or the country."

Mimi Bong, studying student identity formation in mathematics, finds that general self-efficacy depends upon perceived similarities among different tasks or problems, yet students often have difficulty discovering these similarities (698). The GED essay has a similar effect on perceived self-efficacy in writing: not only do students tend not to see similarities between the GED essay and other forms of writing, but they also begin to doubt the literacy skills they had before beginning GED studies. This general institutionalized threat to urban literacies also more specifically threatens the precarious identity that Renee was beginning to build around writing.

One GED lesson in particular stood out as a threat to Renee's urban identity. Students were given sentences on strips of paper and asked to arrange them into a paragraph.

> Running hurts my body.
> When I run my right ankle immediately gets sore.
> Running isn't good for my back.
> Every time I run my arches shout out in pain.
> I've decided that running just doesn't work with my body.

This lesson was designed loosely around Christensen's coordinate paragraph in which the sentences all communicate "equal" ideas (Benson 29). The instructor explained how three distinct ideas about jogging could be "sandwiched" between two pieces of "bread," the topic sentence and an "echo" sentence that repeats the topic sentence. Inside the sandwich, you have your "filler" or "meat," which the instructor began to explain but was interrupted by repeated requests for clarification. In this dialogue, you can see the beginning of Renee's frustration and exclusion from the lesson:

> *Rosa:* If you see a jogger, you would know what to put in there, to tell the class. It would tell us how to run.
>
> *Instructor:* But that's not the topic. The topic is that it hurts my body . . .

[She tries to continue but is interrupted again.]

Ricardo: There's an intro, body, and end!

Instructor: The paragraph is . . . What's so cool about the GED is if you can write a paragraph with an intro and an ending, that same format can be blown up to use for your essay.

Renee: [Slamming her notebook on the table.] Why is writing so hard?

Ricardo: Who, What, Where, When, Why!

While Rosa tried to engage with the purpose of the sentences, Ricardo threw out all the cliches he has ever learned about writing, which were essentially confirmed for him. But the strict rules of this exercise frustrated Renee because this standardized knowledge is what she felt she lacked. Renee explained,

> What makes me mad is that there's a certain way you have to do it. I'm not used to how she does it, like sandwiches and topic, middle, end, or conclusion, or whatever. I'm used to just like writing things down, and however it come out, it come out. I don't think about "this is the ending of a paragraph, this is the beginning of a paragraph." Other people can catch that really fast, they can write a paragraph then skip a line and go on down, but I don't even think about it, I just keep going and going. If they can't understand it, they can come to me and I'll tell 'em.

Handing out a worksheet, the instructor continued the lesson. "You gotta write between two hundred and two hundred fifty words for the essay, so let's pad it a little—in a good way—with details." The worksheet she handed out had the original sentences about running written as a list, then the same five sentences written as a paragraph, then a "padded" version with an additional (subordinate, in the Christensen framework) three sentences (one detail for each "filler" idea). The students were, for the most part, confused.

Renee: Why is it when you write, you don't think about this stuff?

Instructor: They do when they write the GED essay.

Renee: When you're writing, you just write!

Instructor: Go back to your journal and see if one of your paragraphs fits these patterns.

Ricardo: I understand it.

Instructor: We're describing subordinate paragraphs, putting in details.

Rosa: Try walking, you don't have to jog.

Instructor: And look at this [holds up worksheet]: is this a good size paragraph? Any questions about that?

Renee: It's easier said than done.

Ellie

Ellie is two decades too late to be a San Francisco Beat poet, but her community in the city revolves largely around poetry, in the open mic café scene in which she and her husband, Mike, are involved. Mike works in the mailroom at Pitney Bowes and Ellie considers herself "basically a housewife," tending to their low-income studio apartment and pet birds. She enjoys reading romantic novels, mysteries, and her favorite poet, Allen Ginsberg. She writes voraciously—a poem a day, a diary, plus the work she does in her daily classes at the ECS Skills Center. And yet the GED is probably an impossible goal for her, though she counts it, along with getting a driver's license, as her main goal to achieve by the end of the year.

The sophisticated ideas in her poems contrast with the fat, childlike letters she forms with a blunt pencil, tightly gripped. As an adult with a learning disability, Ellie's literate identity far exceeds the formal literacy skills she is able to demonstrate. When I ask her how her writing might be helping her toward her goal of getting the GED, she focuses on the literal, saying that it "helps with my penmanship," probably referring to the difficulty she has with "getting the spaces between words."

"I take practice tests, try to get higher scores to take the real test," she says, "but sooner or later I have to write a perfect essay, to work on my writing." Her challenge in writing, she says, is "coming up with ideas, organizing them, um [silence], how to put them in sequence so they make sense." The complex ideas she can communicate perfectly in the stream-of-consciousness style of the Beats become impossible to convey when she tries to fit them into conventionally structured and punctuated paragraphs.

Ellie is trapped inside the GED paradigm. In the city, among friends and family and to herself, she is a poet, yet inside the system she is not even qualified to be a foot messenger, which is the job she wants and the job for which she needs the GED. The instructor's goal is to "weed out" Ellie's writing, to help her see a clearly defined organizational structure. During the same lesson that had frustrated Renee, and after the "sandwich" idea (top bread, filler, bottom bread) had been explained, the teacher asked students to write a paragraph beginning with the topic sentence, "There are many reasons to be in school."

Ellie's Sandwich Paragraph, Draft 1. There are many good reasons to go back to school. For myself I'm in school to learn new things that will help me pass my GED Before the year 2000 I'm learning how to pass all of my subjects. Social Studies Arts and liertature also the math test and all the other subjects that I have to pass to get my GED. I know having my GED will help me get a better paying job with all of the benfits that I deserve as an adult that wants to work.

There are many good reasons to go back to school. These are the best reasons that I know of that I'm in school.

After this first attempt, I asked Ellie how she felt about her paragraph, and she smiled and clapped her hands to say she liked it quite a lot. This was the only version to include the personal insight "I know having my GED will help me get a better paying job with all of the benefits that I deserve as an adult that wants to work," a crucial aspect of Ellie's identity in relation to school. If we ignore punctuation, it is a fairly complex and well-organized paragraph (a "mixed" paragraph in the Christensen scheme).

Yet the teacher was not satisfied, and she asked Ellie to try again, this time emphasizing the "sandwich" structure.

> *Ellie's Sandwich Paragraph, Draft 2.* There are many good reasons to go back to school. To learning to read brushing up on my math skills to learn all the material and hand out that will help me to get my GED. Do I will pass it not to far in the future having home work will help me out with my goal. There are difficulties in my life but I will concur [conquer] them. School is a real learning experience for me. The other students are in school for the same reasons that I am. There are many good reasons to go back to school.

When Ellie checked with the instructor after the second draft, she was told that she needed to have three distinct "filler" sentences, and the instructor was very firm about wanting Ellie to write according to the sandwich scheme. As I watched her working on the revisions, I could see her energy and enthusiasm leaking away, replaced with a frustration that may have crept into her writing. In one second draft sentence, she writes: "there are difficulties in my life," and she then makes the off topic comparison of herself to "other students." Her writing becomes indecipherable in this second draft—"Do I will pass it not to far in the future"—and this is not usually a characteristic of her sentence structure.

Still not satisfied, Ellie's teacher encouraged one more revision.

> *Ellie's Sandwich Paragraph, Draft 3.* There are many good reasons to go back to school. I am improving my reading and math skills. Also I am working at getting my GED. This will help me get a better paying job after I graduate. These are my reasons for returning to school.

By the third draft, Ellie's ideas have become abstract and thin in content, her confidence thoroughly diminished. It is a perfect sandwich paragraph.

Moses

Moses is a tall, athletic, and intelligent African American man in his late thirties, with a thirty-day bed at one of San Francisco's main emergency shelters. His goal is to get his GED in order to join the mainstream workforce. Being a homeless man is *not* part of how he sees and presents himself. His aspiring identity is contained in his goal: to get into the plumbers' union. He knows plumbing and has worked odd jobs with friends and family members in the business, but in order to join the union he needs the GED. "I need to brush up anyway," he said, "so it's kind of good for me to be doin' reading and calculatin' and what have you." Moses saw the GED as "basically just common sense," and commented, "to me a GED isn't nothin' but a ninth grade education. As far as I'm concerned, everybody in this country should be basically knowing what they're doing, to know how to reason and figure things out, and just know what you're doin', whether it's on paper, whether it's your mind functioning, what have you." Moses had been coming to the ECS Skills Center for about two weeks when I spoke to him. Unlike the other students, he chose not to participate in the classroom community, working according to his own plan to "cruise on through for the GED: First science and English literature, then social studies, then grammar and writing, then math."

However, the day I interviewed Moses was one of the last days anyone at the ECS Skills Center saw him; a $50 check for his GED testing fee sat on the instructor's desk for months. Moses's story is interesting because it happens all the time; people fail to meet their own expectations, they drop out or slip back into an old scene, and only then do we realize how little we knew about them. It is noteworthy that Moses (who I assume did not complete the GED) did not identify himself with the classroom community, the role of student, learner, friend. In our interview, he said, "The way I see it is I'm the only one who's gonna be here for the GED. . . . I don't feel that I have to participate in a class setting to get what I want, because I'm the only one going to be taking that GED test! Class ain't going to be giving me the answers. Teacher ain't going to be giving me the answers. I'm going to be giving the answers and that's how I'm looking at it. That's it, you know."

Moses also did not identify with or enjoy writing, though he told me, with some reticence, that he used to write poetry. "I can't voice it, but I'd just write it up, put it on paper." When I asked him why he doesn't write poetry anymore, he replied in a flat, nonchalant tone: "I just stopped. I had more important things to do with my life, that's all. I wasn't that good at it, you know, I just put whatever comes to mind on paper. But it's been so long I don't even think about it, basically. I really don't like to write, that's just me. That was a long time ago."

Tom

Tom was a student who did not enjoy writing but whose fluency in writing had risen like a thermometer of his self-confidence, and he shared with me some of his insights about how writing and the GED fit into his goals, the person he was trying to become. From a distance, Tom looks like a little boy, with a bright and sometimes nervous smile. He wears stylish, almost preppy clothes: cardigan sweaters and polo shirts that, appropriately, remind me of new "back to school" clothes. Up close, or in a low mood, his thirty-odd years sometimes show in tight, dry wrinkles around his eyes. He does not talk openly about his medical disability (for which he receives SSI), but prefers instead to identify himself with brotherhood—he bakes a cake for every single student's birthday. Tom explained,

> I'm here three hours a day, and people here like me—we go out to eat, we go to field trips, and some of the students have called me a brother, consider me as a brother, and that has been very helpful to me, because I believe for a person to learn it has to start from love, caring, real true caring, true love. It doesn't have to be a boyfriend or girlfriend, it can be anyone who really cares about you, and these classmates of mine we sort of have taken a hold of each other, we sort of are a family. We are adults, and I think there's a big gap in our lives where—in my life, my childhood was terrible, and people need to bond, and I'm bonding with the people here, and that has been very helpful to me. I feel that I'm blossoming, but slowly. I feel more confident this year of getting my GED than I did last year.

Tom said it was the ECS Skills Center classroom that helped him feel more confident:

> If a person doesn't like you, you can't really do very well, and the person must be genuine, you know. I needed a sense of pride, a sense of well being, like I could do something, like I'm important to you. I needed to be important to someone as well as that person is important to me. Because the difficulty of writing has to do with your personality, with yourself. . . . It's hard, not only because I can't spell, but also because I have been left alone, I have been abused, I have a troubled heart. Writing has to do with yourself. It doesn't necessarily have to be about not spelling right, it also has to do with your personality.

Tom is the only person in this story to actually pass all five sections of the GED. (Ellie left the ECS Skills Center when she got a full-time job at McDonalds, and Renee was seventeen points short on her last attempt before she moved to another state.) It took Tom more than five years to pass the GED. He recognizes that it was not just his skills that kept him from succeeding: "I had to start from the beginning, with self-confidence, to build self-confidence. I was feeling like everything is so difficult, and I had really low esteem of doing things."

CONCLUSION

Tom's insights really made me think about the way we quantify outcomes, about what types of literate practices actually translate into tangible successes, into transformations of identities, both personal and social. The GED experience is different for everyone who attempts it, yet it all boils down to a raw score. For Moses, it was a routine "brain function" test; for Renee, a rite of passage from street kid to responsible adult; for Ellie, a refusal to be classified as learning disabled, as less capable in terms of literate practices.

If the GED functions as a gate, it is one that swings two ways, both affecting and affected by students' identities, their sense of who they are in relationship to the test. For Ellie, the GED was a terrible fit, and the instruction she received neglected her literacy strengths, ultimately making her writing, and her perceived self-efficacy in writing, worse. Renee will probably pass the GED some day, though she seemed closest to succeeding when she was most involved in the ECS Skills Center community.

If a student's self-esteem and self-efficacy in writing are not already strong, the GED can be a destructive goal. There is a "well" of self-esteem that must be filled at least part way before students can internalize GED instruction or bend themselves to the format of the test without destroying the identities they are trying to build through succeeding at the GED. Further, material factors, such as living conditions and financial security, also affect whether the GED is a positive or negative goal. For example, when I asked Tom what had finally helped him improve the fluency of his writing, he said,

> A person's place of living can really make an effect on a person. Like I was staying on Sixth Street—I hate that street—I was living at [a shelter], and I was having a troubled—I was coming here for the first time, and I was having trouble studying because of the place I lived. . . . Now I'm more secure of my finances and the place I live is not so dark, like the place on Sixth Street.

In a social service climate obsessed with outcomes, it is easy to overlook the strengths that people start with, to judge literate performance by the clarity of a topic sentence rather than by the complexity of what is communicated. It is our job, as teachers of writing (whether inside or outside the academy), to continue to challenge and redefine the standards of the total literacy system. We should ensure that the diverse literacy goals that we set for students in universities are not watered down to an unrecognizable set of functional skills by the time they reach urban community writing programs.

WORKS CITED

Bandura, Albert. *Self Efficacy: The Exercise of Control*. New York: W.H. Freeman, 1997.

Benson, Robert. "Paragraph Modelling." *Sentence and Paragraph Modelling*. Berkeley: Bay Area Writing Project, 1982. 27–48.

Bong, Mimi. "Generality of Academic Self-Efficacy Judgments: Evidence of Hierarchical Relations." *Journal of Educational Psychology* 89 (1997): 696–709.

Branden, Nathaniel. *The Six Pillars of Self-Esteem.* New York: Bantam, 1994.

Brandt, Deborah. "Sponsors of Literacy." *College Composition and Communication* 49 (1998): 175–85.

Cooper, Marilyn M., and Michael Holzman. *Writing as Social Action.* Portsmouth: Boynton/Cook, 1989.

Gere, Anne Ruggles. "Kitchen Tables and Rented Rooms: The Extracurriculum of Composition." *College Composition and Communication* 45 (1994): 75–92.

Heller, Carol. "The Multiple Functions of the Tenderloin Women Writers Workshop: Community in the Making." Diss. UC Berkeley, 1992.

Holzman, Michael. "Community-Based Organizations as Providers of Education Services." *Writing as Social Action.* Marilyn Cooper and Michael Holzman. Portsmouth, NH: Boynton/Cook, 1989. 174–85.

Hone, Lisa Richards. "Population of Adults Without High School Diplomas and GED Credentialing Rate, by Jurisdiction." *GED Items* (Mar/Apr 1998): 11.

hooks, bell. "Choosing the Margin as a Space of Radical Openness." *Yearning: Race, Gender, and Cultural Politics.* Boston: South End, 1990. 145–53.

Pajares, Frank. "Confidence and Competence in Writing: the Role of Self-Efficacy, Outcome Expectancy, and Apprehension." *Research in the Teaching of English* 28 (1994): 313–30.

CHAPTER FOUR

"NOT YOUR MAMA'S BUS TOUR"
A Case for "Radically Insufficient" Writing

Paula Mathieu

Yvette was majoring in theater and speech at Chicago's downtown Columbia College until an unpaid tuition bill of $2,000 prevented her from registering for classes or collecting a $1,000 scholarship she had earned.[1] She works everyday selling street newspapers but does not earn enough to qualify for commercial loans.[2] Yvette has exceeded her limit on student aid, and she pays rent and utilities on the apartment she shares with her husband, daughter, and four grandchildren whom she helps raise. Whenever she can, Yvette pays $100 to Columbia College in an effort to eliminate her debt bit by bit. She hopes to return to college soon. At this rate, however, it will be four years before she can enroll again for one semester's classes.

In Fall 1998, Edward earned three As and a B at St. Augustine University, a small Northside college catering to immigrants and low-income students. He was studying to become a substance abuse counselor. A tuition bill of $1,900 now stands between him and his ability to register for more classes. A defaulted student loan from 1973 makes him ineligible for government loans, and a long record of felony convictions makes finding employment difficult. He is active in his church and is looking for steady work.

Anaya is young (probably twenty-two or twenty-three, but she will not say her age), intelligent, and eager to attend college. She owes nearly $6,000 in student loans to various city colleges, while having earned zero credit hours. This is largely the result of attending college while struggling off and on with homelessness, working full-time, and receiving no family support. Her original loan was $1,600. The rest of that amount—more than $4,000—represents late fees and interest on the debt. Homelessness and hospitalization caused notices of default from the student loan organization not to reach her. Research she has done shows that under current law, one cannot eliminate student debt through any sort of bankruptcy proceeding. "The only way to get out of it," she says, "is to pay it off or die."

Yvette, Edward, and Anaya are writers with whom I worked in a community writing group in Chicago. All three were articulate, engaged learners who were locked out of credentializing institutions of higher education. They powerfully recorded their lives and the city we inhabit through their poetry, nonfiction, and news accounts. At the same time, though, powerful records such as debt histories were also writing these writers, proscribing their futures and limiting their options.

From March 1998 until September 2000, I directed a writing group and subsequently a computer learning center at a Chicago street newspaper called *StreetWise* (a weekly publication that sells roughly 22,000 copies each printing) whose mission was to "empower the homeless or those at risk of becoming so, as they work toward gainful employment and self-sufficiency." The men and women with whom I worked were all homeless or working poor, selling the weekly paper as their primary source of income. They attended writing group meetings or computer workshops at the learning center in order to write articles for the newspaper, take part in writing-group publications and activities, or gain literacy and computer skills.

Teaching writing in this Chicago community setting required that I take into account the role that official records, such as credit histories, government identification cards, and prison records, played in determining the identities and realities of the students. Defaulted student loans, lost library books, and unpaid tuition balances determine an individual's identity to colleges and universities. Prison records, detailing histories of large or small crimes, determine one's identity to prospective employers. A lost birth certificate or misplaced GED certificate determines one's non-identity status at many state agencies or job-placement programs. In addition to these official records, a less officially recorded (but no less powerful) ideology regarding the homeless and poor pervades city policies and popular beliefs. Urban-planning mandates have called for the widespread destruction of public and low-cost housing, city-wide gentrification has led to skyrocketing rental prices, and race politics continue to segregate Chicago neighborhoods, keeping alive a history of police brutality especially against African Americans and a generalized public stigma against homeless and low-income people (Daniel). Together, all of these histories and records of the city have formed a complex web that entangles these writers, creating their identities. They negotiate their subjectivities between official labels (students in debt, former criminals, or "homeless" street paper vendors) and their own beliefs about themselves. In other words, identities are both the result of the "sum total of subject positions" to which individuals have been assigned and "the ways in which those positions have unreflexively or reflexively been incorporated into forms of self-awareness" (Sosnoski).

THE WRITING TEACHER AS RADICALLY INSUFFICIENT

[V]oice is not something to be given by those in power. Voice requires struggle and the understanding of both its possibilities and limitations. The most educators can do is to create structures that would enable submerged voices to emerge. It is not a gift. Voice is a human right. It's a democratic right.
—Donaldo Macedo

While the material and ideological manifestations of our economic system limited possibilities for the writers at *StreetWise*, these same histories and scripts also powerfully affected the relationship we developed as teacher and writers. As a white woman in graduate school who had never been homeless, I occupied a very different status than the writers. I was *in* (and in some ways, *of*) the university, one of the very institutions barring them access. Donaldo Macedo angrily and powerfully reminds teachers to be aware of such class differences and to be careful about what claims one can legitimately make, especially when working with those he calls "oppressed students":

By refusing to deal with the issue of class privilege, the pseudo-critical educator dogmatically pronounces that he or she empowers students, gives them voice. These educators are even betrayed in their own language. Instead of creating pedagogical structures that would enable oppressed students to empower themselves, they paternalistically proclaim, "We need to empower students." This position often leads to the creation of what I call literacy and poverty pimps: While proclaiming to empower students, they are in fact strengthening their own privileged position. (176)

Above and beyond our individual desires and intentions, the writers and I interacted in a complex dance of race, class, and gender politics. Issues of trust were central, and a wrong word or bad decision could call into question years of work. As Pat Caponni has noted, "People who have been screwed all their life aren't willing to trust very easily." Understanding the considerable risks and time commitments that many writers would be taking to work with me (risks in the form of hope, most significantly), I tried not to over-promise or sell too hard my writing workshops or writers' group. I asked myself, "Exactly what should I be asking students to trust?" When I first began teaching in this organization, I met several men and women with substantial literacy skills but who lacked access to avenues of credentializing. Or, when students did not possess strong writing, reading, or computer skills, acquiring those skills would often do little to improve their immediate lives. Basic material needs, such as shelter, food, dental care, and eyeglasses, were often not available and were desperately needed. What could writing instruction offer them?

The writing group became a powerful weekly exchange of stories, information, and critiques. It grew into a vibrant community where the weekly meetings appeared to be personally fulfilling and beneficial for the participants. One member, for example, called the meetings "good therapy, a good stabilizer because it allows me to put thoughts on paper" (Buccola).

The challenges facing the writers went well beyond solely personal matters, however, and the limits of the "good therapy" of the writing group were evident. Since I was teaching outside the boundaries of the university, my workshops and writing-group meetings could not offer credentials or college credit. Letters of appeal to scholarship boards and student loan agencies did not free up money. Improved communication skills and letters of recommendation did not offset histories of felony convictions to prospective employers. Allowing members to audit a class at the university where I teach did not get them a degree. I regularly faced the limits of my own writing and teaching. Thus, if I had no clear sense of how learning to write better would change the lives of these students, why, then, should they have any trust in writing or attending writing classes?

My experience at *StreetWise* confirmed Elspeth Stuckey's assertion that arguments and projects that begin with literacy are insufficient for changing the realities brought about by a broader economic system (126). Stuckey describes the role that literacy plays in regulating economic access and legitimizing social disparities. Similarly, Sharon Crowley criticizes the hope of composition teachers that "inoculation with literacy will somehow solve this country's social problems" (195). And Brian Street claims that problems of literacy are more often symptoms of poverty, not causes. Thus, the general benefit of improving literacy skills by themselves is questionable.

Is it worthwhile to teach writing if it is an insufficient act, especially when it offers no other reward, such as credit hours? Rather than seeking ways to justify composition and its sufficiency, I answer this question instead by admitting its insufficiency. I often talked with the writers in my group about what writing could *not* do, interrogating its limitations, and seeking creative ways to push against them. This approach is informed by critical theories of utopia.

UTOPIA AS A RHETORIC OF RADICAL INSUFFICIENCY

[I]t is the utopian possibility that makes for a teacher. The
utopian, I know, drives me, even when tempered by the practical.
—Victor Villanueva

"Utopia" is a word bandied about as frequently in a pejorative sense as in a
positive one. So before I try to argue that utopian theory and strategies can be
useful in thinking about teaching writing, especially in non-university urban
settings, I think it is necessary to be specific about how I am using the term.
Tom Moylan describes the utopian imagination as "the power of subversive
imagining to move people beyond the present toward a more fulfilling future"
(15–16). I am interested in how writing can express utopian desires and imagine changes to material culture. What people hope for and how they imagine
their futures are key components of identity formation. Moylan argues that
the utopian impulse can have subversive effects by radically altering how and
for what people dream. Yet this impulse can also be co-opted as part of the
"affirmative culture" of postwar capitalism, serving to lull people away from
dreaming of alternative arrangements. The existing social formation threatens
to co-opt the oppositional potential of utopian longings by channeling them
into desires for commodities. Thus, the utopian impulse is situated within ideology, both constructing it and pulling it apart. Although this utopian impulse
is not, Moylan says, "an unsullied white knight" (19), nevertheless, within the
context of ideology, utopia can play a role in reinventing the current system
toward more humane and liberatory ends. This is done, most significantly, by
reworking how people desire and imagine their futures. For such a reworking
to happen, however, the impulse must be to resist closure and systematization.

I see utopia as complex and contradictory; it is not a place, a goal, a thing,
and certainly not a blueprint of future action. Instead, utopia is an expression,
an action, an articulation that causes momentary changes in how people see
or behave within an existing hegemony. Utopia points toward that which does
not yet exist, but could be experienced in the future. In a critical utopian configuration, to acknowledge the present as radically insufficient does not imply
that one must passively accept this reality, nor does it mean that one closes
one's eyes, fantasizes, and wishes for a better world. Feminist utopian literature, for example, focuses on the future as a critique of the present, even
though future visions are always flawed. Margaret Whitford explains the
dilemma: "The critical moment is in many ways easier to pursue; it does not
commit one to any affirmative statements about women's nature. Yet in order
to move to the constructive moment, it might be felt that a commitment to
some affirmative position is necessary; and it is perhaps here that feminists
will find agreement more difficult" (17). Thus, the construction of a utopia is

a critical practice that works on the world and the individual through a dialectic of critique and hope.

Henry Giroux and Peter McLaren highlight Paulo Freire's indebtedness to utopia and a politics of hope. They describe Freire's process of *conscientization* as embodying a relationship between critique and hope. Giroux and McLaren write that "[h]ope and critical consciousness are dialectically reanimating, and together they produce the 'shock' of new knowledge and new social and cultural configurations and possibilities for human transformation" (149). At the same time, however, such hope is self-critical and always aware of its limitations. "Freire's utopian vision does not speak to a categorical set of blueprints, tactics or strategies for human freedom. . . . [He] understands full well that a pedagogy of liberation has no final answers" (159).

What does it mean, then, for me to see teaching writing as "radically insufficient" for the urban community setting in which I worked? It means admitting that writing was not a sufficient problem-solving skill; it did not offer many solutions in and of itself. To call this urban community-based writing instruction "radically insufficient" is to accept a utopian challenge: a challenge not to overestimate the adequacy of teaching writing skills to meet the local needs of the participants; a challenge to seek out new projects that might imagine better ways to live, while at the same time acknowledging the material limitations of these new projects; a challenge to encourage the personal goals and identities of writers, while helping them find ways to take part in broader discussions of poverty, homelessness, and education; a challenge to demand the impossible while acknowledging the limitations on the possible. Utopian theories of radical insufficiency might serve to remind writing teachers not to overestimate the value of literacy or our teaching or to assume the role of savior or advocate for students in oppressed groups. The rhetoric of "radical insufficiency" admits that composition skills are valuable, yet it also reminds us that such skills are seldom revolutionary. To acknowledge the radical insufficiency of one's teaching and to continue working against its limitations is a critical statement of hope.

NOT YOUR MAMA'S BUS TOUR:
INSUFFICIENT CREATION ON WHEELS

For me, education is simultaneously an act of knowing, a political act, and an artistic event.

—Paulo Freire

For two and one-half years, I struggled with how best to teach writing to people who were often painfully aware of how their identities and possibilities were limited by institutions beyond their control. At the same time, however, I experienced the writing and the collaborative nature of the writing group at *StreetWise* as a powerful force, for creation as well as critique. I often sought to provide the writing group with public audiences, allowing them avenues to speak back and create counter-discourses, in efforts to change what they saw as public misconceptions about homelessness and poverty. As a writing teacher, this approach appealed to me because it placed the writers in the role of authorities. My role became one of coach or editor, helping writers communicate real and pressing concerns to actual audiences. Certainly, *StreetWise* was one such outlet, as were public readings and other publications. But those publications presented the writing as individual works and did not allow the writers immediate interaction with an audience. Public readings did provide some immediate interaction, but they were infrequent and usually took place in institutional locations, such as classrooms or the street paper offices.

After completing a drama writing course at Columbia College, Yvette suggested that the writing group work on a play together. I had never taught drama but liked the idea of a collaborative project. In 1999, we began work on "The Real Deal." The plan was to stage events in the lives of the writers, strung together by a narrative device of staged writing group discussions. This project provided much creative fuel and energy to the group for about six months. Eventually, though, the demands of a large collaboration and peoples' inability to make meetings ended the play idea. As one member described it, "the play died a natural death." While unsuccessful, that effort did set the stage for a future and more ambitious project.

In May 2000, I accepted a request from Theater Madarijn, a Dutch theater company of homeless actors, to host a visit to Chicago and to help arrange audiences for them to perform their interactive play entitled "Why is Johan Homeless?" I asked Edward, a member of my *StreetWise* writing group, to help schedule performances at schools, churches, and shelters. He was subsequently hired by the director, Berthold Gunster, to escort the Dutch theater group around the city and to their performances. During their five-day visit, the group spent three and one-half days with Edward. As they traveled around the city via buses and the El (Chicago's elevated train system), Edward told many stories about his life. Berthold and I met during the last two days of his visit to talk about the writing group and its previous theatrical aspirations. I also shared with him some of the writers' work. In the car on the way to the airport, the first time in five days he had been off of a bus or train, Berthold had an intriguing vision: a bus traveling from place to place, taking an audience to hear scenes from the lives of the writers at the actual places where they occurred. Theater on wheels. After a few weeks of e-mails, discussions with writing group members, and phone calls, plans for "Not Your Mama's Bus Tour" were born.[3]

Because of our Dutch director's limited availability and the need to stage this event when Chicago weather and daylight were cooperative, we either had to move very quickly or wait nearly a year. The group was enthusiastic, so we decided to go ahead with a pilot project. The goal was to put a story-telling bus on the road to prove to ourselves we could do it and to see if the public liked the idea. The entire creation process lasted just six weeks. During the first three weeks, the writers worked together, inventing story ideas and fragments from handouts and questions I had prepared. Then came three intensely chaotic weeks of creating, editing, planning, and directing. One reporter described it this way: "After a whirlwind three weeks of preparation, including the construction of an informational Web site (http://www.uic.edu/~pmathieu/bustour), alerting the press and—oh yea, writing and rehearsing the script—the preview evening had finally come" (Buccola). Our cast of a dozen homeless or formerly homeless writers-turned-actors kept to a rigorous rehearsal schedule, working simultaneously with me on story editing and with the director on performance guidelines. We quickly raised money and support, and the writers negotiated a group agreement with the organization for payment for their writing as well as their rehearsal and performance time.[4] The process was hectic and energizing. Days were spent editing and rehearsing scenes, while nights were spent driving through the city, planning the route, and timing distances from place to place.

On a warm night in mid-August, a yellow school bus filled with press, friends, and supporters paused momentarily before driving northbound on Michigan Avenue toward Grant Park, the scene of the 1968 Democratic Convention riots and the location of our first scene. Curly, one of the two tour guides, announced the following to the forty-four passengers on the bus:

> Ladies and gentleman, I'd like to welcome you aboard tonight and go over a few rules. According to the National Transportation and Safety Board, we are required to tell you that:
>
> This is not a Gray Line, Blue Line, or Happy Face Tour.
>
> At 7:07, we will not strain our necks at Navy Pier to look at some McFerris Wheel and pay $14.95 for a sandwich named after a city 767 miles away.
>
> At 7:18, we will not entomb ourselves in a stomach turning elevator climbing to the 104th floor of the Sears Catalogue.
>
> At 7:29, we will not pass go or City Hall, where Richard sits only because his father sat all over this city.
>
> At 7:38, we will not even discuss corporatized cows or public ping-pong.
>
> At 7:57, we will not contemplate John Hancock in any form. The name alone indicates just how obscene it is.
>
> And finally, at no time during this tour will we stop at any McDonalds, let alone some Rock-n-Roll McDonalds, for a way too boring double

cheeseburger combo super-sized, as if there isn't already enough wiener envy in this city.

This is "Not Your Mama's Bus Tour," but depending on your mama, this may be her kind of ride. Welcome aboard.

Over the next two hours, our bus made six stops at some typical tourist destinations around Chicago, such as Grant Park and Orchestra Hall, and at some not-so-touristy spots. Among these were, first, the location of the death of a *StreetWise* vendor who was shot in the head by an off-duty Chicago police officer who was leaving a bar, and then Maxwell Street, the birthplace of Chicago blues and a historical gateway for immigrants, which is now all-but-demolished due to the expansion of the University of Illinois at Chicago (or "Paula's university," as one of the tour guides called it). While the bus drove from place to place, the passengers heard stories told by two tour guides, as well as poetry, songs, and music. At each stop the passengers got off the bus and watched a scene based on a story from a writer's life.

Anaya performed her scene in front of Malcolm X College. Because she was nervous about the public exposure this event might bring, she, the director, and I worked together to create a scene in which she could feel comfortable and not too exposed. Anaya wanted to share fragments of writing about her life, yet at the same time she wanted to protect her privacy. We decided to use the format of a game, combining several topics about her life—some were areas she was willing to discuss and others were not. As the crowd exited the bus, she stood in a paved open courtyard, just at sunset, as a huge sign reading "Malcolm X College" was lit high above her head in the background. She smiled a radiant smile, sporting long braids and a bright purple jacket.

Hello everyone and welcome. You can call me Anaya. Anaya only. I am homeless. There are many stories I could tell you about my life and some things I don't want to talk about. So let's play a little game. To do so, I need two assistants. *[She then chose two audience members.]* On these cards are subjects related to my life—Family, God, Age, Childhood, Malcolm X College, Sex, Exercise, Drugs, Relationships, Recovery House, and Mental Health. If you choose a topic I am willing to talk about, this is the sound you'll hear. *[To the first volunteer, she says]* Please give us a sound! Thank you, let's give her a big hand. And if you've chosen a topic I am NOT willing to talk about, this is the sound you'll hear. *[To the second volunteer, she says]* Please give us a different sound. And two more rules: no pictures and no questions. Let's play.

When someone selected the card "Malcolm X College," the audience heard the following:

I am standing twenty steps from the door of Malcolm X College. Six thousand dollars in student debt separates me from Malcolm X or any other college. How long would it take you to pay off this debt? For some people it might be two years, a year, two months, two weeks, or even one day. For me, it's been five years, and I still haven't made a dent. I have worked homeless and gone to school homeless. How can a girl who loves education and longs to go to college make her way when the earth trembles and the ground beneath her begins to shake?

Anaya's scene was filled with poetry, singing, and personal details, such as the fact that she had never used drugs, was mentally healthy, wanted to wait until marriage for sex, and was a devout Christian. When an audience member selected the card "Dream," she said,

> I long to go to college without worrying about how to pay for it. I want to owe no man anything, except for the love that all humans deserve. And now I'd like to recite a poem: I see myself in my new house, with two bathrooms. One for myself, all decked out, and one for guests. When the Body Shop sees me coming, they roll out the red carpet. I am one of their favorite customers.

At the end of the scene, she explained the game: "I used to say yes to any request, providing any information, regardless of whether I wanted to or not. But now, I can say no. I am not my experiences, I am not my debt, and I am not my past. You can call me Anaya. I am a child of God." In the tour's program, she stated her reason for doing her scene: "Relax. Enjoy the performance. If you come away with a better understanding of how inadequate it is to simply put a band-aid on the issue of homelessness, that's great too."

Anaya's request for the audience to "relax" and "enjoy" the performance was genuine. The writers and the directors all felt that this tour should not wallow in misery or lack humor or artistic pleasure. Many scenes had nothing to do with homelessness at all, because the writers wanted the audience to see that being homeless was just one aspect of their lives. Homelessness did not explain who they were or encompass their identities. Thus, music, both recorded and live, dancing, and poetry were all elements of the tour. There was humor, too, especially playing with stereotypes. Our introduction featured Will, a legally blind member of our group, seated in the driver's seat, reading aloud an announcement thanking the organization for "reintegrating people like me into society" by giving him the job of bus driver. He then proudly announced that this was his first day on the job. With his face inches from the page, he used a magnifying glass to read. He took extreme pleasure to learn that at several performances, people really feared he was the bus driver. Later in the tour, he sang "Take the El to Hell," an original tune he wrote with his band.

As the bus wound its way through Chicago's medical district, one guide described this area as "the largest concentration of hospitals in the city. It sits ironically just east of the part of the city where the fewest residents have health insurance." He dryly added, "Well, at least they have a nice view of the hospitals." He went on to describe the Byzantine procedure for seeing a dentist at Cook County Hospital, "the only place in the world where people run to, and not away from, the dentist." The "Toothless Olympics," as he called it, was a process begun by a qualifying phone call, followed by a 7 A.M. foot race down a series of hospital hallways to try to beat out the sixty-nine other "tooth-achin" qualifiers for a number to wait several hours on a hard bench to see a dentist and have a tooth pulled. "That's right, the only dental care available at County is getting a bad tooth pulled. No fixings, no fillings, just pulled. So don't forget to brush!" At that point, the masochistic "Dentist" song from "Little Shop of Horrors" played while the hostess passed out toothbrushes to each passenger.

Our group staged six two-hour-plus tours over the course of three weeks. Press coverage was excellent, including local news coverage, print stories in seven newspapers including the *Chicago Tribune,* top coverage on a local theater website, performances recorded by two documentary filmmakers, and interviews on two radio stations, including a news piece on the local NPR affiliate. The reviews were all positive. One reporter called the project a mixture of "Chicago history, street theater and candor" (Rumpf 14). Another described it as bringing "an unconventional history lesson to life through street theater. At times, it is also a poetry slam, a jam session, and a sing along" (Vogell 2). The headline from the theater website said, "This bus'll school ya . . ." (Buccola). All the shows sold out (with a suggested donation price of $25), and the public responded warmly to the tour and to the actors. Audiences lingered after the performances, asking questions of the cast and getting autographs. People called and e-mailed words of gratitude and praise. Of the twelve cast members, none missed a performance and almost no one missed a rehearsal, an unprecedented reality in the two-and-one-half-year history of our group.

EPILOGUE: THE UTOPIAN MOMENT PASSES

It would be tempting to label this project an artistic, political, and personal success for the writers. During the three weeks of rehearsals and three weeks of performances, there was a high level of commitment and shared vision. I felt alive and engaged while submerged in the creative process, as I believe many of my co-creators also felt. None of us were sure we could pull off this event, but we pushed ourselves and each other to make it happen. This was a short-term project, however, with a beginning and ending point. After the performances, the director returned to Holland, I prepared to leave the organization to complete my graduate work, and the group members became preoccupied once again with the pressing realities of their lives. During the first scene of our last performance, police arrived and threatened to tow our bus away. As the creative demands of the project diminished, the built-up trust began to give way to more usual levels of individual anxieties and uncertainties. The *StreetWise* organization is discussing ways to keep the tour continuing, but these plans are still developing. The writers' group continues as a body that is self-run by the members.

This improbable utopian project did manage to create a new, albeit temporary, reality. It was a reality of collaboration, where sixteen people of different ages, races, and economic backgrounds worked together toward one vision of a yellow school bus. The writers negotiated their own working conditions, were paid a living wage to share their wisdom and perform life stories, taking people to the actual city spaces where they occurred. We drew a paying public; more than 150 people heard stories about living with debt, experiencing police brutality, discovering sexuality, and finding hope. Twelve homeless actors received not only pleasure and good experiences, but also a job for six weeks. They honed their writing skills in creative and engaging ways to directly and immediately address a public audience. And indirectly, the writers responded to the powerful records and institutions framing their lives. Perhaps this fleeting experience allowed us a glimpse of how life could be lived otherwise, a life where work is a meaningful act of creation. Perhaps it gave us a bit of hope, to keep struggling and keep risking.

But how far did this bus tour really take anyone? After the performances, even the most well-intentioned audience members returned to their homes. Anaya still has her debts, as do Edward and Yvette. The rest of the writers still face their challenges. Despite the press and the success, the utopian moment passed and structural realities reappeared. Words were radically insufficient to change the world in such a way.

NOTES

1. I have changed the names of the writers, since I am discussing financial and criminal records. The published work of the writing group uses real names or pseudonyms, depending on the writers' wishes.

2. Street newspapers can be found in most major cities around the world, including Chicago's *StreetWise* newspaper, where I worked. Homeless people or those at risk of homelessness can become vendors of the paper, which, in Chicago, they buy for thirty-five cents and sell to the public for one dollar. Additional services, such as refer-

rals for housing, substance abuse treatment, and educational classes are frequently offered to vendors of street papers. These unusual hybrids of newspapers and social-service-advocacy organizations are affiliated through two cooperative networks, the North American Street Newspaper Association (NASNA) and the International Network of Street Papers (INSP). NASNA has roughly fifty members across the United States and Canada, while the INSP has another thirty-eight members across Europe, Asia, Africa, and South America. Writing groups like the one I began in Chicago are common at many of these papers. A survey I conducted at the 2000 INSP conference revealed more than a dozen active writing groups at papers in Europe, Africa, South America, and Asia. In North America, writing groups and discussions of vendor writing have been part of the conference proceedings since its inaugural meeting in 1995.

3. The rights to the name "Not Your Mama's Bus Tour" are registered to Street-Wise, Inc.

4. The most significant support for this project came from Deborah Epstein at the Chicago-based Neighborhood Writing Alliance. Our writing group had been a member of the Alliance, and Deborah agreed to co-produce the project after just a phone call. She raised most of the money, found a production assistant, and worked night and day to make this project happen.

WORKS CITED

Buccola, Gina. "Not Your Mama's Bus Tour: This Bus'll School Ya." Online Review. Site of Big Shoulders. 1 September 2000. <http://www.sobs.org>.

Capponi, Pat. Keynote Address. Conference of the North American Street Newspaper Association. Edmonton, Alberta. 22 July 2000.

Crowley, Sharon. "Reimagining the Writing Scene: Curmudgeonly Remarks about *Contending with Words.*" *Contending with Words.* Ed. Patricia Harkin and John Schilb. New York: MLA, 1991. 189–97.

Daniel, Jamie Owen. "Rituals of Disqualification: Competing Publics and Public Housing in Contemporary Chicago." *Masses, Classes, and the Public Sphere.* Ed. Mike Hill and Warren Montag. London: Verso, 2000. 62–82.

Giroux, Henry, and Peter McLaren. "Paulo Freire, Postmodernism, and the Utopian Imagination: A Blochian Reading." *Not Yet: Reconsidering Ernst Bloch.* Ed. Jamie Owen Daniel and Tom Moylen. London: Verso, 1997. 138–62.

Macedo, Donaldo. *Literacies of Power: What Americans are Not Allowed to Know.* Boulder, CO: Westview, 1994.

Moylan, Tom. *Demand the Impossible: Science Fiction and the Utopian Imagination.* New York: Methuen, 1986.

Rumpf, Caesréa. "Vendors Take Their Show on the Road." *StreetWise* 21 August 2000. 14.

Sosnoski, James. "Subjectivity." Online Glossary. 28 August 2000. <http://www.crhet. com>.

Street, Brian V. *Social Literacies: Critical Approaches to Literacy in Development, Ethnography, and Education.* London: Longman, 1995.

Stuckey, J. Elspeth. *The Violence of Literacy.* Portsmouth, NH: Boynton/Cook, 1991.

Villanueva, Victor. *Bootstraps: From an American Academic of Color.* Urbana: NCTE, 1993.

Vogell, Heather. "Bus Tour Takes Ride on the Gritty Side: Program Explores Life Via Street Theater." *Chicago Tribune* 27 August 2000: 4:1+.

Whitford, Margaret. *Luce Irigaray: Philosophy in the Feminine.* New York: Routledge, 1991.

CHAPTER FIVE

FROM URBAN CLASSROOM TO URBAN COMMUNITY

Susan Swan

Founded in the eighteenth century, Pittsburgh began as a set of forts designed to ward off French and Native American populations, and it soon coalesced into a modern city with fur trading and some of America's first glass factories. Early settlers discovered that Pittsburgh was built on mountains containing an endless supply of the raw materials necessary for making steel. From the nineteenth century to the 1980s, Pittsburgh's economy was supported by steel milling and fabrication, with its three rivers providing cheap and easy access to the ports of the east coast and the rapidly expanding Midwest (Lorant). Immigrants, working-class whites, and post-slavery/pre–civil rights blacks flocked to Pittsburgh with varying degrees of success. A thriving working and middle class made Pittsburgh an excellent choice for workers—if they were the "right" gender and ethnicity. As Tony Buba's 1996 film *Lightning Over Braddock: A Rustbowl Fantasy* documents, the mills were host to racism and sexism, problems that did not begin to subside until the rise of unions in the mid-twentieth century. Working-class blacks, women, and Chinese immigrants found themselves locked out of almost all careers in the mills, even if they were highly trained machinists (see also Dickerson). The 1970s and 1980s brought stiff competition from Japanese steel mills that sold their products at extremely low prices. Pittsburgh's mills could not compete, and by the late 1980s only a few remained in operation throughout the city. Those mills that did remain in production held drastically reduced employee rolls. The three rivers were lined with abandoned steel mills, and Pittsburgh soon came to be known as the Rust Belt.

The collapse of the steel industry left Pittsburgh's working-class citizens devastated. Families used to union wages and benefits now struggled to make ends meet with minimum wage jobs or government aid. The culture of work that used to spell economic success in Pittsburgh now means little in what remains of the city's meager steel industry. The mills are gone, and manual labor has been replaced by professions in technology, medicine, education, and the service industries. A low cost of living and attractive professional wages make Pittsburgh a good choice for many middle-class families. However, the emergence of Pittsburgh's postindustrial economy has barely affected its inner city communities— especially those that are primarily African American. In Pittsburgh's new economy, black workers have been largely left behind. Ralph Bangs reports that in 1999 only one in six young black men from urban Pittsburgh who were looking for work could find it, while nine of ten young white suburban youth (male or female) were able to find work. Further, Pittsburgh's inner city unemployment rate is two to four times higher than the rate of unemployment in its suburbs.

Although much has been written about the changing culture of work in America generally, and Pittsburgh specifically, I believe that historical and critical knowledge gleaned from even more specific intra-urban communities can lead toward activities that promote "social justice"—that is, the pursuit of egalitarian political arrangements through the intersection of education, community services, and the labor movement. Scholars in policy analysis, education, and sociology have struggled to construct a large-scale representation of how our economy has changed over the past several decades (see Datcher-Loury and Loury; Holzer; Ihlandfeldt and Sjoquist; Lynch; and Tannock). While this generalized literature is helpful in understanding (and criticizing) our current economic situation, it is not always helpful for those interested in making immediate interventions in the lives of specific people in specific places. As scholars struggle to give us the big picture, the voices of actual people fail to come through. It is my belief that this failure is a loss to the practice and real possibilities of social justice.

What I have found is that speaking with community members about work issues uncovers new and vital information about Pittsburgh's urban employment problems. My own research into Pittsburgh's food service industry examines what community expertise can add to situated problem analyses. Scott Goodrich and I have conducted several critical incident interviews (see Flanagan) in which local Pittsburgh food service workers were asked to recount instances of problems and successes from their own experience. The preliminary results of these interviews confirm that situated knowledge is crucial to solving problems. For example, the food service workers who spoke with me complained about missing their buses when management asked them to stay past their shift. Buses only run on half-hour intervals in Pittsburgh, and all stops are outside and unprotected. This data points to both a job-specific problem of miscommunication and a Pittsburgh-specific problem of when and where bus pickups happen.

Because I believe that we should teach what we know, I decided to base my own freshman composition course on local employment issues, culminating in an extended project on Pittsburgh's food service industry. Although at first glance the course seems unlike a typical composition class, I believe that the content and practice of the course support a growth in the skills of argument and interpretation, as well as a commitment to critical thinking and socially just rhetorical practices.

WRITING ABOUT WORK IN PITTSBURGH

Through exploratory and critical writing, this composition course helps students understand the culture of work in specific Pittsburgh communities; it also teaches students to construct rhetorical documents that have at least the possibility of improving working conditions at a particular Pittsburgh workplace. I derive the pedagogical philosophy for the course from three related disciplines: progressive education, cultural studies, and sociocognitive theories of learning. These disciplines, and my own pedagogical methods, encourage active learning through experience-based and student-centered practices, acknowledge the importance of context to the process of cognition, and promote social change through specific methods of analysis and intervention (such as Paulo Freire's generative terms and Stuart Hall's method of articulation). In the rest of this chapter, I will discuss each major activity that students complete for the course, starting chronologically from the beginning of the semester.

Work Autobiography

On the first day of class, I ask my students to write a short essay about their own work histories. The assignment is due the next day, when each student summarizes his or her working life while I make a "map" of our class history on the board. This work autobiography centers the course curriculum in the students' own experience, validating them as writers who already have expertise. In this way, student experience becomes the curricular melting pot for the course—I cannot teach about work, or its culture and rhetoric, until I know how we as a class represent it, how we know it, what our attitudes are toward it, and how we define it.

Even though this composition class is centered on Pittsburgh's employment environment, the connection between personal experience and culture, and the changing nature of the American economy, few of these general issues are addressed at the beginning of the class. Instead, working from students' own experiences, we slowly relate their own knowledge (life experiences, connections to popular culture, class readings, and the experiences of their family and community) to these larger issues and, perhaps, unfamiliar contexts.

Eventually, these issues and contexts become their own. For example, I work Pittsburgh's urban context into the discussion when students discuss the jobs they have held. For most of them, their summer jobs were easy to attain (usually through personal connections). I contrast their experiences with those of black youths in Pittsburgh, who struggle to find and keep even low-paying fast food jobs.

The work autobiography thus offers a platform for critical reflection. I want students to understand how politics, culture, and ethics affect their daily lives and the daily lives of people outside their circle of experience. The first question I always ask after I have mapped out my students' work autobiographies is, "What types of work don't we as a group represent?" This simple question leads to a barrage of answers. Students begin to see many new things as work: religious faith, sports, art, music, parenting, feeding oneself and others, keeping safe in "bad neighborhoods," staying healthy, studying, fulfilling dreams, having fun, and being good sons and daughters (among many other things). This first critical reflection is thus an important part of the process of the course; it places students in the position of being both knowledge producers and knowledge users.

Immediately after completing their work autobiographies, I have students read Paulo Freire's *Pedagogy of the Oppressed*. This reading takes about two weeks, and students are asked to understand the difficult terms in the book through their own work experiences. For example, I want my students to see Freire's term *limit situations* as something that has happened to them. I also connect these terms and ideas to Pittsburgh's labor problems, relating limit situations to the urban youth I have spoken with who will not even look for jobs because of racist hiring practices and impossible transportation problems. My goal here is to offer my students a method for decoding the experiences of self and others in new ways.

In addition to the generative ideas found in Freire's *Pedagogy of the Oppressed*, I also introduce students to Stuart Hall's method of articulation, and we read Jennifer Daryl Slack's article "The Theory and Method of Articulation in Cultural Studies." Articulation is a method of situating reality in its cultural, ideological, historical, political, institutional, physical, gendered, economic, and affective environments. Through the process of articulation, students describe what "links" one cultural artifact to another, what cultural glue binds institutional structures to particular institutional practices; they then explore how those links might be "re-articulated" into more socially just configurations. Students analyze representations of work in television, music, movies, the Web, print advertising, and newspapers. Then students are asked a series of questions. Why does this TV show represent work in this way? What is behind it? Are there particular "links" that are oppressive? How could they be changed (re-articulated) to be more representative, more just, more educative? Again, I work Pittsburgh's specific history into our discussions and articulations about work and popular culture. For example, when we examine song lyrics about work, I bring in the recording of and lyrics for Billy Joel's "Allentown." The song, which focuses on the closing of a town's steel mills, is an opening for us to discuss Pittsburgh's own lengthy history with steel, how the industry's downfall affected Pittsburgh's residents, and how it still affects Pittsburgh's inner city African American population.

Three Generations Work History

The first long paper I assign my students is a three generations family work history. Students must interview at least one member from three different generations in their families (themselves included) about their working lives. Students ask their family to be as specific as possible regarding each major job they have held. Once the interviews are complete, students analyze them for a theme—family "work traits" (such as farming), gender roles, social class, education, sacrifice, etc. They then must tie this theme to each member of their family in a formal essay. This assignment serves several functions. Many of my middle-class students recognize (for the first time and to their great surprise) that their families were "working class" only one or two generations before. Other students discover in their interviews that their families have dealt with gender discrimination, class discrimination, and the fight for a good education. Students begin to see the struggles of the oppressed as their own, and they begin the process of seeing their parents and grandparents as subjects rather than parent-objects. I have had students whose fathers were union organizers in Pittsburgh steel mills, whose grandfathers were killed in the mills, whose families had to re-create themselves after the industrial base fell, and whose families are still struggling with the lower paying jobs that replaced their union jobs.

Workplace Observation

After the three generations work history assignment, and in preparation for their next essay assignment, students then read selections, including official policy papers, about urban unemployment in Pittsburgh. Students discuss these issues in class by performing skits about such issues as the changing culture of work, low wages, and racism. The second major assignment in the course, the "workplace observation" paper, requires students to travel outside of the university to do research. I ask students to go to an urban service industry worksite (there are many within walking distance of the university) and to observe this site until "something happens." This "something" may be positive or negative, though it is usually negative. They then correlate this observation with the readings from the class and ask themselves if these readings completely explain what they saw.

This assignment respects students as knowledge makers, asking them to think about how the course readings do or do not explain the problems they see. For example, many of my students have focused their observation papers on the behavior of customers in the restaurant industry—very few policy papers talk about the role of this "third party," instead focusing on the role of workers or managers. Students have made eloquent and convincing arguments, backed by accounts of rude customers, that the behavior of the customer is a large part of the problems inherent in the food service industry. These students argue that customers should be more sensitive to worker issues, that they should, in short, stop objectifying fast food workers as objects without feelings.

This observation paper assignment asks students to construct sensitive arguments from disparate sources of knowledge. Students may negotiate between Freire's work, class discussions, and their actual observations. The problem most students have with this assignment is where to stop—they find evidence for so many "articulation links" that they have trouble deciding which is the most vital to write about. But perhaps the most important result of this assignment is that students come to realize that real-world problems are complex, conflicting, and impossible to solve with "quick fix" solutions.

Community Problem-Solving Dialogue

Writers and readers build constructions of knowledge from a toolbox of ideas, experiences, goals, and words. Expert writers have both a diverse toolbox and a strategic arsenal for efficiently negotiating and building effective knowledge constructions, while novice writers may work from limited content and ineffective strategies (Flower). However, although expert writers may begin with a full toolbox, their composing processes often do not fully represent all possible perspectives in any given rhetorical situation, especially in urban contexts. Further, as we have seen from my discussion of the work autobiography assignment, many CMU students, in particular, construct limited representations of work, omitting from their essays the experiences of marginalized populations. Such incomplete representations may result from students: 1) living in privileged academic environments; 2) studying disciplinary discourses that define "expertise" in restricting ways; and 3) leaving their classrooms each day ill-equipped to access marginalized expertise. My goals are that students will leave my composition course with more experiences in their toolbox, better strategies for discovering knowledge on their own, and more effective processes for transforming their experiences and knowledge into coherent and convincing written arguments.

One pedagogical method that I have used to achieve these goals with my students is called "community problem-solving dialogue," developed at the

Community House on Pittsburgh's North Side. Community problem-solving dialogue is an intercultural discussion based on three powerful problem-solving strategies for building more elaborated problem analyses and hypotheses: seeking the story behind the story, gaining rival hypotheses, and testing options and outcomes. These three strategies help students acknowledge and benefit from community expertise in situations of intercultural communication and collaboration.

The first strategy in a community problem-solving dialogue is seeking the story behind the story. This strategy has the knowledge-building goal of finding the unspoken narratives behind specific community understandings of a problem. Seeking the story behind the story leads students and community members to reveal the logic, motivations, or implications that are visible from their insider perspectives. For example, one of my students found, through his interactions with workers at a local fast food restaurant, that some of these workers had to take three bus transfers to arrive at their minimum wage jobs. These bus transfers took more than an hour each way, were often delayed up to thirty minutes, and cost about twenty dollars per week. However, even though the workers had no choice in their mode of transportation (a car with insurance and parking fees was out of the question), they noted that many of their past coworkers had been fired for being late because of bus delays. This story behind the story points both to a deeper understanding of how transportation affects Pittsburgh's urban workers and how a lack of intercultural communication between workers and managers (who may never have taken the bus) may lead to unjust actions.

In gaining rival hypotheses, the second strategy in the process of community problem-solving dialogue, students and community members work and role-play together to see a shared problem from as many points of view as possible. Linda Flower, Elenore Long, and Lorraine Higgins define the rival hypotheses stance as "an attitude toward inquiry" that "addresses itself to genuinely open questions"; as a "strategy for inquiry that not only seeks out other voices, alternative interpretations, and their supporting evidence, but actively generates strong rival hypotheses that challenge and conditionalize favored claims—including one's own"; and as "a constructive process, attempting to build a 'better' conclusion in the midst of strong alternatives" (2). In this sense, rival hypotheses do not always replace an original problem-statement; rather, "rivals" flesh out a problem-context by including viewpoints from as many angles as possible (including angles that are traditionally left out or deemed non-expert). Rival hypotheses, therefore, add breadth to the experience from which students and community members are trying to solve a problem. Students and community members use rival hypotheses to construct more viable problem representations and solutions that take many arenas of expertise into consideration (even if these arenas conflict). For example, if students are studying why Pittsburgh workers keep quitting fast-food jobs, their understanding will be much more realistic and inclusive if actual fast food workers, restaurant managers, policy experts, and customers elaborate the problem-analysis from their multiple perspectives.

The final strategy in a community problem-solving dialogue is options and outcomes. With this strategy, students and community experts test possible problem-solutions by projecting their probable consequences. Because this collaborative move seeks to take many possible consequences into consideration, community expertise is essential. The options and outcomes strategy generates more solutions from a larger pool of expertise, increasing the chance that a solution will emerge that is viable from multiple community perspectives. Seen in this light, obtaining multiple perspectives is not just a step toward liberal inclusiveness; it is a sensible move toward solutions that work for as many people as possible.

Interview

In the final assignment, students interview actual food service workers about problems in the workplace. Students plan their interviews around the community problem-solving dialogue strategies, usually taking conclusions from their observation papers and asking community members to rival these ideas, asking for stories behind the story, and then collaboratively brainstorming options and outcomes. This final paper asks students to engage in a discussion about why problems exist and how best to solve them. In addition, the students engage in praxis by constructing rhetorical documents meant to solve real problems, even in small ways. The final project does not always, therefore, result in a typical academic paper. I have had students write letters to the editor about customer behavior, construct brochures on how to prepare for college while working at the same time, write guides on how to start a new job in an unfamiliar career, and publish online guides to problem-solving strategies for worker/manager disputes. In one case, a student hand-made a board game about how to succeed at work—this game took approximately three weeks to make, and included art work, instructions, and 250 small cards with "success suggestions" on them. Of course, many students also choose to prepare academic papers; these papers are geared toward the audience of my own prospective students, and I keep them as reference materials for future classes.

Students almost always find that their conclusions from the observation paper are refined by discussions with actual workers. They learn about Pittsburgh history, current employment practices (and racism) in the city, and particular problems that are unique to the university neighborhoods they live in. They find problems with Pittsburgh's minimum wage, racist and classist customers and managers, neighborhoods that are poorly connected to transportation and located far from good jobs, and education systems that are not training urban youth to work in a technological economy. Students take action against these problems by writing letters to policy makers, posting signs about customer service, recording and singing songs about work and its difficulties, and writing papers, brochures, and pamphlets geared toward helping local workers succeed in Pittsburgh's new culture of work.

CONCLUSION

In my students' final papers, I find traces of every activity we have done in class, even though using course resources is not a requirement of the assignment. Students talk about Freire, examine Pittsburgh labor history, use the articulation method, write about data from the community problem-solving dialogue, and see themselves, their families, and the people they interview as workers situated in culture and history. By the end of the course, many students are able to construct sophisticated arguments about a subject they knew little about only sixteen weeks earlier. Moreover, the lessons about social justice seem to stay with many of my students. As I stay in contact with them, I know that some work in outreach programs, take additional service learning classes, and continue to use the methods of articulation and community problem-solving dialogue well past the last day of our class together.

WORKS CITED

Bangs, Ralph. *The State of Black Youth in Pittsburgh: Perspectives on Young African-Americans in the City of Pittsburgh and Allegheny County*. Pittsburgh: Urban League of Pittsburgh, 1999.

Datcher-Loury, Linda, and Glenn Loury. "The Effects of Attitudes and Aspirations on the Labor Supply of Young Men." *The Black Youth Employment Crisis*. Ed. Richard Freeman and Harry J. Holzer. Chicago: U of Chicago P, 1986. 377–401.

Dewey, John. *Experience and Education*. New York: Colliers, 1963.

Dickerson, Dennis C. *Out of the Crucible: Black Steelworkers in Western Pennsylvania 1875–1980*. New York: SUNY Press, 1986.

Flanagan, J. C. "The Critical Incident." *Psychological Bulletin* 51 (1954): 327–58.

Flower, Linda. *The Construction of Negotiated Meaning: A Social Cognitive Theory of Writing*. Carbondale: Southern Illinois UP, 1994.

Flower, Linda, Elenore Long, and Lorraine D. Higgins. *Learning to Rival: A Literate Practice for Intercultural Inquiry*. New Jersey: Lawrence Erlbaum, 2000.

Freire, Paulo. *Pedagogy of the Oppressed.* Trans. Myra Bergman Ramos. New York: Continuum, 1989.

Holzer, Harry J. "Black Employment Problems: New Evidence, Old Questions." *Journal of Policy Analysis and Management* 13 (1994): 699–722.

Ihlanfeldt, Keith R., and David L. Sjoquist. "Job Accessibility and Racial Differences in Youth Employment Rates." *The American Economic Review* 80 (1990): 267–76.

Lightning Over Braddock: A Rustbowl Fantasy. Dir. Tony Buba. Zeitgeist Films, 1986.

Lorant, Stefan. *Pittsburgh: The Story of an American City.* New York: Doubleday, 1964.

Lynch, Lisa. "The Youth Labor Market in the Eighties: Determinants of Re-employment Probabilities for Young Men and Women." *The Review of Economics and Statistics* 71 (1989): 37–45.

Slack, Jennifer Daryl. "The Theory and Method of Articulation in Cultural Studies." *Stuart Hall: Critical Dialogues in Cultural Studies.* Ed. David Morley and Kuan-Hsing Chen. London: Routledge, 1996. 112–27.

Tannock, Stuart. "Positioning the Worker: Discursive Practice in a Workplace Literacy Program." *Discourse and Society* 8 (1997): 85–116.

PART II

COMPOSING SPACES

CHAPTER SIX

SIMULATED DESTINATIONS IN THE DESERT

The Southern Nevada Writing Project

Ed Nagelhout and Marilyn McKinney

Las Vegas is well known for its casinos, for its gambling, for The Strip. It remains one of the premier travel destinations in the world. Visitors come to experience the transitory gratification of the wager, the opportunity to "win." Gambling is the primary attraction, a reason for coming to the desert. But gambling is no longer the sole purpose for visiting Las Vegas, for the casinos now offer high-tech and richly decorated simulacra, destinations of "place" that present "genuine" substitutions for Venice, Paris, New York. Visitors experience a variety of visual stimulants that are more than real, that are other than what the senses perceive at first glance as authentic. The casinos seek to capture the essence of a "place" in ways normally associated with Disneyland, where, according to Michael Sorkin, "one is constantly poised in a condition of becoming, always someplace that is 'like' someplace else. The simulation's referent is ever elsewhere; the 'authenticity' of the substitution always depends on the knowledge, however faded, of some absent genuine" ("Disneyland" 216). Within this realm of the simulacra, visitors are constantly tempted by what might be, by dreams of the possible (the quick score, the jackpot). At the same time, Las Vegas is a city growing at the rate of 8,000 new residents per month, home to a burgeoning population who live and work in the shadow of the simulacra that dominate the city. New residents travel to the desert seeking the myriad opportunities for employment in the gaming and service industries, and current residents travel from job to job, always in search of the ever more lucrative position. Thus, Las Vegas becomes an "other" kind of "destination."

In this chapter, based on the above description of Las Vegas, we analyze writing as a core urban experience at the University of Nevada, Las Vegas (UNLV), using the Southern Nevada Writing Project (SNWP) as a primary point of reference. Grounding our analysis in travel theories inspired by Michael Sorkin's work, we examine underlying assumptions that SNWP participants make about writing instruction, as well as the environments to which they return after the Summer Institute is completed, in order to better understand local configurations of writing instruction at the K-12 level. We are particularly interested in exploring how both simulacra and travel work to sustain reductive models for teaching writing in the Las Vegas valley and the ways in which writing and writing instruction become "simulated destinations" within the larger educational system.

TRAVELING AND ARRIVING

Las Vegas is a place where travel is ubiquitous for visitors and residents alike, yet it remains only a "simulated destination" for most people. This concept of the simulated destination is not only effective for explaining Las Vegas as an urban place; it is also effective for examining the underlying features of writing programs and pedagogies. More specifically, the concept of simulated destinations helps us focus on ways that the Southern Nevada Writing Project must contend with exigencies unique to Las Vegas, and it assists us in developing strategies to address our particular needs.

An understanding of simulated destinations begins with an understanding of movement. In general, movement underscores relationships between parts and wholes, and examinations of movement can be done on macro- and micro-levels. For example, spatial theorists such as Sorkin argue that automobile-dependent cities "seek to create a consistent culture of the particle, in which ostensibly egalitarian relationships of property are matched with appropriate circulation" (*Traffic* 24). In this respect, patterns of movement within a particular context such as Las Vegas, can define how various elements interact with each other as part of a larger whole.

Of course, in order to track movement analysts must begin with certain points of reference, what might be called start points and end points. While these points are usually arbitrary, they serve the function of highlighting spaces where movement occurs: they specify a context for analysis. We concur with Nigel J. Thrift's definition of context: "By 'context' I most decidedly do not mean an impassive backdrop to situated human activity. Rather, I take context to be a necessary constitutive element of interaction, something active, differentially extensive and able to problematize and work on the bounds of subjectivity" (3). Context is not passive, for context has a definite impact on the ways in which movement can occur. We must also keep in mind, as Sorkin tells us, that "no theory of movement will make a difference if the character and variety of places between end points of circulation become impoverished" (*Traffic* 19). Examining movement as a context between beginning and end points is imperative, since how we get to a place is at least as important as where we arrive.

Critical to our work is the end point that names a "destination" for analysis. Sorkin writes, "The implication is double, enfolding the acts of traveling and of arriving. The element of arrival is especially crucial, the idea that one is not passing through some intermediate station but has come to someplace where there is a definitive 'there.' In the larger discourse of travel, these places are vested with a kind of equivalence" ("Disneyland" 215). A destination, therefore, marks a definitive place of arrival, and the process of travel is clearly connected to this end point. A destination is neither a representation nor a simulacrum; instead, it designates the culmination of travel within the context of a particular social setting and has no other referent to displace.

"Simulated destinations," however, are *apparent* (but not real) places of arrival, and in order for the simulation to be complete, these apparent destinations must dis-place their originary referents. These places on the surface seem definitive, with a sense of stability, and the travel that leads to them seems to clearly mark the beginning points of departure and the end points of arrival. Yet such certainty is merely a representational illusion. A simulated destination seems to have a clear referent—a "genuine destination"—but arrival means reaching an end point that is always someplace other than the genuine destination: "One has gone nowhere," writes Sorkin, "in spite of the equivalent ease of going somewhere. One has preferred the simulation to the reality" ("Disneyland" 216). Simulated destinations are *equivalent* to other "places," but they are not "real" because the genuine destination is ever absent. Thus, the simulated destination maintains authentic characteristics of the "real" within the minds of the participants but can never be more than a place that is like someplace else. One way to recognize a simulated destination is to look for travel that appears to lead to multiple destinations, for here the space for movement becomes impoverished as it attempts to express the character of multiple points of reference and address often competing goals. Travel within and between simulated destinations may also take the form of transience, a kind of aimless wandering between points. This transience may end up at a destination, but the means for reaching it are incoherent, limited to a single traveler who traversed a single path that was lost in the passing.

Simulated destinations are prevalent in formal educational settings because educators often associate end points—destinations—both with classroom and larger societal contexts. This is a form of latent doubling that too often loses sight of the immediate reality of a particular educational context by seeking to project a value that extends beyond the scope of that particular setting. For example, students in a technical writing class create written products to earn a grade for the course. This is the immediate context, the destination. At the same time, there is an assumption that these products, and the skills used to create them, are somehow equivalent to the products developed in "real" technical writing situations. This is the invented context, the simulated destination—the place that is assumed to be there, by virtue of imaginative role-playing, but is not really there at all. What we teach in writing classes, then, are not skills and knowledges that have a direct equivalence to those learned in nonacademic contexts; instead, we teach the inquiry skills necessary for *discovering* the most effective rhetorical strategies that are available in any given context. This view treats rhetoric as a process of inquiry, not as a universal set of rules that can transfer neatly from one context to another.

SIMULATED DESTINATIONS IN THE LAS VEGAS VALLEY

In preparation for our discussion of the Southern Nevada Writing Project (SNWP), we begin with brief analyses of composition courses at UNLV and the Nevada English Language Arts Standards and Proficiency Exam. We examine these two simulated destinations for writing instruction in order to establish some assumptions that many writing teachers bring to the SNWP Summer Institutes.

As stated earlier, the Las Vegas valley is one of the fastest growing areas in the United States, and because of this population growth, UNLV anticipates doubling in size to 40,000 students within the next ten years. But as an urban university, it remains primarily a nonresidential, commuter campus. While the university seeks to simulate a traditional, residential campus, the transitory experience of the traveler permeates this space, and the university students, especially, travel from home to school to work, from course to course, and from year to year until they have fulfilled the necessary requirements for graduation, until they have reached that particular destination.

First-year composition, a required two-course sequence in the UNLV core curriculum, offers a simulated destination for students. As the sole writing requirement at UNLV, these courses provide an underlying set of assumptions about writing and the teaching of writing at the university and beyond. UNLV's first-year writing requirement is designed to offer students a comprehensive introduction to writing, as stated in the *UNLV Undergraduate Catalog:*

ENG 101—Composition I
Develops fluency and confidence in writing by extensive practice in the narrative, descriptive, and expository modes of discourse.

ENG 102—Composition II
Continuation of ENG 101 with emphasis on critical thinking and practice
in persuasive discourse, as applied to selected literary texts. Research paper
and library orientation required. (255)

Here composition is posited as an "end," and the implication is that comple-
tion of these courses signifies a level of competency that is transferable to
every situation and for all time. But too often these classes hold little connection to reality for students, and the writing that occurs is often a mere simulation of the kinds of writing done outside of the composition classroom. Narrative, descriptive, and expository modes of discourse describe limited textual
forms, but the implication is that practicing these modes will develop the fluency necessary for successful writing in any context. Once students have completed the composition sequence, they will have reached their simulated destination as "good writers." In short, students' experiences in first-year
composition classrooms teach them that writing means generalizable skills,
which often translates into exercises in grammar, usage, and formulaic essays.
Even peer review takes on the trappings of response as correction.

Recently, the state of Nevada developed a new set of "standards" (intimately tied to state proficiency exams) that are designed to make teachers
more accountable for student learning. These standards "are intended to give
Nevada children the tools and experiences that will help them not only to
succeed in school but also to become lifelong and adept readers, writers, listeners, and speakers" ("Nevada English Language Arts Standards"). Nevada
is one of twenty states in the country that require high school students to pass
a standardized test to graduate, and the implication is that the Nevada state
standards will not only help students succeed in school, but will also show
students the value of lifelong learning, apparently as they prepare for the
many "tests" they will face throughout their lives. Thus, the dual goals of
these standards represent a "simulated destination," a goal for achievement in
writing that is both quantifiable and measurable because accountability is
converted into a standardized test score. But in this rendering, writing is
acontextual; writing is form without genre; writing is arhetorical. K-12 writing teachers face the inequities of these reductive expectations for writing on
a daily basis, with the pressures of accountability seemingly limiting the
options for writing instruction. Thus, in spite of what they may have learned
in teacher education classes about the importance of choice, extended practice time, peer response, revision workshops, discourse communities, or ownership over learning, teachers are forced into awkward assumptions and
unreasonable expectations.

These two "places" for writing instruction, English Composition at
UNLV and the Nevada English Language Arts Standards, create simulated

destinations for how and why people write. They assume that "good writing" is a discrete set of generalizable skills that can be mastered once and for all time, and the means for arriving are described by institutional documents such as the *UNLV Undergraduate Catalog* and "The Nevada English Language Arts Standards." These documents situate the thinking of teachers and students within the parameters of a simulated destination, "good writing," and create expectations of long-term value in a single learning experience. As we will discuss shortly, the Southern Nevada Writing Project works both to acknowledge and to disrupt the ways that writing is defined for students and teachers as a simulated destination.

SIMULATED DESTINATIONS AND THE SOUTHERN NEVADA WRITING PROJECT

Within the urban landscape of the Las Vegas valley, the Clark County School District was recently named the sixth largest in the nation and remains the sole school district of southern Nevada. Here, where context is characterized by travel and transience, movement between points becomes a constant way of life, one that is often accepted, taken for granted, left unexamined. With a new school building constructed about every thirty days, teachers and administrators are constantly on the move, either because they have been selected to open a new school or because they decide to transfer to a new school to find more compatible surroundings.

Students, too, are in a constant state of flux, moving from school to school for a variety of reasons: they change schools as parents move to a more "upscale" area; the family simply tries to survive by moving from one apartment with a month's "free rent" to another; they change schools to meet new school zone boundary changes; or they attempt to meet individual learning needs by transferring to one of the magnet schools. This constant motion by students, teachers, and administrators makes it difficult to maintain a sense of community within schools, and there are frequent attempts by central administrators to standardize the curricular offerings, to force test-prep curriculum, and to embrace models of school reform that offer expensive, formulaic "quick fixes."

Amidst this perpetual travel and arrival, the Southern Nevada Writing Project—one of 168 sites supported by the National Writing Project—has sought to provide professional development opportunities for K-16 teachers with the hope that the environments for student writing will be improved at all levels. Facilitators of the SNWP Summer Institute are guided by the National Writing Project's mission, which seeks in part "to improve the teaching of writing and improve learning in the nation's schools. Through its model of sustained professional development, the National Writing Project recognizes the primary importance of teacher knowledge, expertise, and leadership" ("About the NWP"). In a five-week Summer Institute, participants engage as writers and learners with other institute participants who collaborate to construct the summer curriculum. Throughout this intensive program of study, participants' confidence as writers, learners, and teachers grows. Once the institute ends, participants are expected to become teacher consultants at their school sites and throughout the Clark County School District. Consistent with the National Writing Project's mission, the SNWP seeks to build long- and short-term relationships with teachers through the outreach of previous participants.

Using the simulated destination framework, our analysis of SNWP Summer Institutes begins by defining start points, end points, and movement. Beginning with these definitions allows us to examine how both simulacra and travel influence, first, the teaching of writing in the Las Vegas valley, and second, the ways that writing and writing instruction become "simulated destinations" within the larger educational system.

As start points for our analysis, we began to examine the assumptions that teachers bring to the SNWP Summer Institute, such as those they may have developed as students in the first-year composition courses that we describe above. For example, Jodi, an elementary intermediate grade teacher, came to a recent Summer Institute with the problematic assumption that "good" academic writing is highly structured, based mostly on personal experience, and explores generally safe topics. This kind of "good" writing occupied much of Jodi's time during the early days of the institute. Yet as Jodi began research for an inquiry-based demonstration about the use of nonfiction texts, the practice of multi-genre composition began to intrigue her. Over time, Jodi began to write about her grandfather, an Auschwitz survivor. As she wrote, she found the need to do more extensive research, both within her family and through other written and visual artifacts; she became intimately involved as a learner, using writing to craft pieces of text in different genres and from multiple perspectives. This project consumed her waking and sleeping hours, and she began to plan ways to involve her students in the study of family heritage during the following school year. Jodi's energy and excitement were contagious within the institute's community, and one might surmise that her assumptions about the teaching of writing changed as a result of the experience.

While this example may appear to represent the disruption of a set of assumptions about writing and learning that many participants bring with them (e.g., writing instruction needs to focus on rules, grammar, and spelling, etc.), we believe that it also has the potential to become an "activity" that is too easily dropped into a classroom of elementary school students with no consideration of the very different exigencies of this new context. Thus, the engagement felt by Jodi while composing her family heritage project (an engagement that was also witnessed and felt by others in the Summer Institute), unless unpacked and carefully planned for each new audience, has the potential to become just one more simulated destination that may not work for others. Indeed, the very features that make Jodi's project authentic—time for reflection, personal engagement, frequent peer response, and an inquiry/learner stance—are the very features that become problematic once the assignment is transported back to the classroom.

As end points for our analysis, we examined the classroom spaces where teachers return, which include the overwhelming specter of the Nevada English Language Arts Standards and a proficiency exam that does not reward good writing developed over time. End points, however, can also provide us with departures from the norm and with opportunities to disrupt the status quo. And yet, during the institute and after the teachers return to their schools, these disruptions for a few teacher participants will most certainly feel uncomfortable. For many teachers, it is challenging to bring progressive pedagogical strategies back into their classrooms due to a host of factors, primarily school contexts that do not support process approaches to writing. For example, during a recent institute, one of the participants commented that teachers often "look the other way," that it becomes too time-consuming to care about teaching or encourage students to care about a particular issue. Sara, a high school English teacher deeply committed to issues of social justice, sparked a controversial discussion in responding to the comment. She described the writing and research she had done over the summer regarding Afghani women's absence of voice and power. She also described her long-term passionate involvement with Amnesty International, explaining how she and a team of local Amnesty members fought to disrupt student and teacher complacency during the school year.

The writing and teaching practices engaged by Jodi and Sara are nothing new to writing project participants; however, we feel it is important to highlight them as a way of documenting that even in a writing project environment, teachers/writers need time to engage in topics of their own choice, ones that are real and tangible, in order to forget old assumptions about "universal" pedagogies such as grammar drills and modal structures. But for many institute participants, a real dissonance arises from an inability to see ways to integrate progressive writing activities into their classrooms in the face of many obstacles—especially threats of accountability mandates and standardized tests. We mark these spaces as beginning and end points because a major challenge comes in sustaining innovative energy once the institute is over and teachers travel back to the isolation of their own classrooms.

Movement, in our analysis, is the professional development experience of the SNWP Summer Institute. In some ways the Summer Institute provides a sanctuary from the frenetic pace of most teachers' everyday lives. It is a safe place for exploring writing and the teaching of writing from a variety of perspectives. Thus, for most participants, the Summer Institute can be viewed as a context radically different from their school experiences. Teachers become involved with each other, providing demonstrations of successful pedagogical practice and conversing about applications in their classrooms. They come to know writing as writers because they engage in the practices of writing and responding within a variety of configurations, such as response groups, silent response, and whole group sharing. In short, they recapture their enthusiasm for writing and research, and they explore ways to transfer that enthusiasm to the students in their own classrooms.

The institute offers teachers the time to think about their research, their writing, and the ways that these activities transfer into their classrooms. As teachers become writers and learners, they see writing instruction in more complex ways and grapple with various approaches for facilitating writing activities in their classrooms. More importantly, the institute helps teachers acknowledge that learning and writing happen over time. As they examine these processes in themselves, teachers realize that good writing is not something that can be forced or standardized, but instead that writing skills grow out of reflective practices. Students will improve their writing through an understanding of the composing process, rather than the delivery of a perfect product. In discussions as well as written evaluations, the SNWP Summer Institute's participants consistently describe time—both the lack of time and the lack of acknowledgement within their educational contexts that learning and writing develop over time—as the most salient challenge they face in moving back into the classroom.

In its current configuration, then, the SNWP Summer Institute offers teachers in Las Vegas a broader, more diverse place for understanding and problematizing the teaching of writing at the K-12 level. This movement between teachers' assumptions (start points) and their classroom contexts (end points) highlights the value of research, revision, and response. Moreover, the SNWP Summer Institute helps teachers develop a writing community that validates their efforts and provides necessary support for success. And while the institute, as a contextual "place," is not impoverished, our analysis reveals that it and the SNWP site have not fully articulated how to deal effectively with the simulated destinations for writing that are prevalent in the Las Vegas valley.

Examined within our framework, we have located two primary gaps or discontinuities particularly salient to the work of the SNWP: sustaining involvement in the institute and attracting a broader range of participants. We believe that if we are able to fill these gaps, we will begin to help Summer Institute participants discover more readily the contextual (rather than standardized) nature of both writing and teaching. However, as students, teachers, and administrators move from school to school, the Nevada State Proficiency Exam—not students' writing processes—becomes the central component, the simulated destination, for what constitutes "good" writing. In other words, these gaps result from power struggles between competing stakeholders (e.g., teachers, administrators, school board members, the Nevada State Board of Education, and local and state legislators) who define writing practices and outcomes in the schools. We acknowledge that these gaps are typical of many National Writing Project sites; however, as we will show, simulated destination theory helps us problematize issues relevant to southern Nevada and provides us with a framework for developing effective strategies to manage and attend to these issues.

Sustained involvement with the SNWP is crucial to the vitality of both individual teachers and the site itself. If we situate the SNWP Summer Institute as movement between points (i.e., "real"/"ideal" destinations or simulated destinations such as the Nevada State Proficiency Exam), then each participant's school functions as the central point of reference, the "destination," for further teacher development. An implicit assumption of the National Writing Project model is that the participants who have completed the institute have the leadership abilities and the necessary resources to go back and lead faculty development workshops. However, they are often undermined in their efforts by resistant colleagues who are skeptical about process approaches to writing and by administrators who expect a standardized curriculum. Because of the opportunity the institute provides to examine practice, participants have moved through a different experience, one that is incongruous with the unexamined simulated destination to which they return and seek to infiltrate. The community support so vital to the five-week institute evaporates with the isolation that participants may feel upon returning to their schools.

In order to meet the insatiable need for classroom space, more than half of the district's elementary schools are now on year-round schedules; consequently, three-month-long summer vacations have been replaced by three-week-long track breaks at various times throughout the year, precluding attendance at a five-week intensive summer institute. Attracting a broad range of K-12 teachers to participate in SNWP Summer Institutes is also necessary to the dynamism of the site and to individual teacher development. This gap/discontinuity, primarily a result of the population boom, is important to acknowledge since the SNWP is the primary source of professional development for teachers of writing. Thus, a broad range of teachers is necessary to ensure that writing is taught in the most effective ways in the greatest number of schools.

TRAVELING AND ARRIVING IN LAS VEGAS

One particularly powerful way to sustain involvement in the Southern Nevada Writing Project is through acknowledging and articulating the role of inquiry in the development of writing project sites, as well as in the development of teachers and students. Within the SNWP, we have attempted to thread inquiry through the work of the site in multiple ways—through developing and engaging teachers in demonstrations, through inquiry or study circles, and through teacher research. Recognizing the importance of teacher research, the National Writing Project is making a concerted effort to support and systematically study six writing project sites across the country, all at various stages of incorporating teacher research. The SNWP, as one of those sites, is in the beginning stages of this journey.

By placing inquiry at the center of teacher activity, the SNWP hopes to encourage an inquiry stance, promoting reflection about how writing and research impact the ways that students develop as learners inside and outside of the classroom. Inquiry generates enthusiasm and excitement when it is invoked as a way of understanding one's practice, through an intentional and systematic collection and analysis of classroom data, through study groups and inquiry circles, and through assigned institute writing such as I-Search or multi-genre papers. Inquiry also serves to validate what teachers know implicitly about learning but often have lost touch with in classrooms and schools where simulated destinations of unexamined and disembodied practice have become the norm.

The institute provides time for teachers to engage in sustained exploration of topics of interest through ongoing inquiry circles. The goal here is to encourage participants to examine specific experiences in the classroom through face-to-face and on-line peer discussions, incorporating written reflections about current thinking in the field. With a book cart of professional resources at their fingertips, participants can probe their experience, examining both successful and unsuccessful practices. The idea here is that as time unfolds teachers will recognize that they are not the only ones dealing with a specific issue in the classroom or school community. This practice begins to lay the foundation for extending the community of writing teachers beyond the bounds of the Summer Institute. Moreover, these inquiry circles have the potential to serve as a model for teachers to use in forming study groups when they return to their schools.

Yet in its present iteration, inquiry within the SNWP Summer Institute, though powerful for those teachers who engage in it and embrace it, has not reached its potential for further transforming practice beyond the confines of the institute itself. Simulated destination and travel theory allows us to realize the need to extend inquiry in more intentional ways, to support teachers as they return to their schools and to develop ways to maintain a support network that extends beyond the institute. During the most recent Summer Institute, one of the facilitators, a teacher engaged in a study as part of a summer research fellowship, helped model this stance. Each week, in a "quick write" prompt, participants were asked to reflect on some aspect of the institute experience; in some cases, these prompts asked teachers to directly address feelings of dissonance they may have experienced and their plans for dealing with it upon their return to the classroom. A second part of this facilitator's study was to collect weekly reflections from volunteers; each teacher briefly listed writing activities for the week, rated her or his confidence in teaching writing, and explained why. Follow-up interviews with four teachers during the fall helped both to support teachers in continuing practices congruent with their belief systems (as opposed to simulated destination endpoints) and to inform our understanding of what it means to more intentionally examine travel beyond the institute.

The other current gap in the SNWP Summer Institute is the need to attract a broader range of participants to the project. One way that the SNWP has tried to address this gap is through the development of an institute offered during eight weekends in the fall. The goal here is to provide an opportunity for teachers (especially elementary teachers) who teach a year-round school schedule to attend. This institute is scheduled as eight Friday night and Saturday sessions and attempts to provide experiences similar to the Summer Institute. Although the Fall Institute is less a "sanctuary" than the five-week Summer Institute, participants are nevertheless able to become involved in similar practices but over a greater span of time. Teachers who have never attended the Summer Institute but who have continued to stay involved with the SNWP feel that the Fall Institute is viable and meets the needs of year-round teachers. One clear advantage to the Fall Institute model is that its participants can "try out" teaching ideas with their own students more immediately than Summer Institute participants, creating more opportunities to connect theory and practice and to emphasize an inquiry stance throughout the institute. For example, a teacher might design an assignment and get feedback from her peers during one weekend, offer it to her students the following week, and report the results of this practice back to her response group at the next institute meeting. Thus, the Fall Institute allows teachers to reflect in practice and models the ways in which a community of writing teachers can provide the support necessary to resist reductive models for teaching writing.

These are two examples of how we have used a theory of simulated destination to provide insights into the practices of the SNWP. After naming the components for analysis—start points, end points, and the movement in between—we determined gaps that were visible in our practices and we described ways that we are trying to address these gaps. Our goals have been to describe strategies developed locally to prevent teachers from allowing reductive methods for teaching writing to be their ultimate destinations and to offer more effective ways to meet the long-term needs of K-12 teachers in southern Nevada.

CONCLUSION

Our experience with the theory of simulated destinations shows us the potential that a more complete analysis might offer. We have certainly become more conscious of the ways that we help teachers move inside and outside of the classroom, for we have become more aware of the effects that our practices might have on teachers when they return to their schools. The theory has confirmed our need to make explicit that the institute is not the final destination for teachers and participants in the Las Vegas valley. The institute can only simulate the classroom that they will return to; however, the institute can provide a structure—a form of support—that allows teachers to more effectively implement the features of good writing instruction in the classroom despite any obstacles that may arise. The theory of simulated destinations has also given us the terminology for explaining the ways that teaching writing processes in the classroom can meet the mandates for writing proficiency. By describing the Writing Proficiency Exam as a simulated destination, we can articulate for teachers the arguments that they can make in defending their practices and understanding why strategies for long-term development are more fundamental to the successful growth of student writers. Finally, the theory of simulated destinations illustrates that the creation of a community of writing teachers is vital to the overall success of the project. If we acknowledge that the classroom is the ultimate destination, rather than the SNWP Summer Institute, then teachers need to maintain contact with the institute in fundamental ways. Only through these kinds of support can we help teachers maintain their enthusiasm for teaching writing in the most effective ways.

WORKS CITED

About the NWP. National Writing Project. 15 July 2000. <http://wwwgse.berkeley.edu/nwp/info.html>.

Nevada English Language Arts Standards. Nevada Department of Education. 27 July 2000. < http://www.nsn.k12.nv.us/nvdoe/index.html>.

Sorkin, Michael. "See You in Disneyland." *Variations on a Theme Park: The New American City and the End of Public Space.* Ed. Michael Sorkin. New York: Hill and Wang, 1992. 205–32.

———. *Traffic in Democracy*. Ann Arbor: U of Michigan College of Architecture and Urban Planning, 1997.

Thrift, Nigel J. *Spatial Formations*. London: Sage, 1996.

University of Nevada, Las Vegas Undergraduate Catalog, Fall 2000–Spring 2002. Las Vegas: UNLV Publications, 2000.

CHAPTER SEVEN

A PLACE IN THE CITY

Hull-House and the Architecture of Civility

Van E. Hillard

> In the case of ideologies of what is good and right it may be space
> rather than time that is crucial. Something may be good and just
> everywhere, somewhere, here or elsewhere.
> —Göran Therborn

Marking an endpoint to decades-long scrutiny of city life begun in the late nineteenth century, and carried out by the famed Chicago School of urban sociologists, Louis Wirth, a preeminent practitioner of the discipline, articulated in
summary form several defining characteristics of American urban sociability:

> [I]t becomes clear that one major characteristic of the urban-dweller is his
> dissimilarity from his fellows. Never before have such large masses of people
> of diverse traits as we find in our cities been thrown together into such close
> physical contact as in the great cities of America. Cities generally, and Amer-
> ican cities in particular, comprise a motley of peoples and cultures, of highly
> differentiated modes of life between which there often is only the faintest
> communication, the greatest indifference, and the broadest tolerance, occa-
> sionally bitter strife, but always the sharpest contrast. (61)

Though one might readily question whether or not American cities are, in
fact, historically unique in their dense diversity, Wirth echoes a central anxiety that has haunted inquiry into the nature of American city life through the

past century: how shall diverse urban persons cooperate to form democratic publics within the environmental constraints of the city where, essentially, too many persons, with too many differences, occupy too little space? Implicit in such a question lie several contestable assumptions: that communication is, de facto, thwarted by difference; that a bounded geography is, by nature, constraining; and that overt self-differentiation is, in and of itself, a dangerous thing. Such assumptions undergirded much of the rhetoric of late-nineteenth-century urban reform, which argued for public policies that would adjust or even correct the seemingly chaotic arrangement of persons within city spaces, especially as such disorder was thought to subvert normative values of publicity and privacy typically associated with American town or village life.

Paving the way for Wirth's concerns about the city, late-nineteenth and early-twentieth-century urban analysts often focused upon the nature of the built environment, with urban architectures and geographies targeted as the clearest evidence that city life was pathologically disordered. For many reformers and sociologists, the seemingly chaotic architecture of city streets, blocks, alleyways, and bounded enclaves created a confusing and confounding public geography thought to encourage various forms of disassociation among its residents—attitudes ranging from despair to disaffection to criminality. At the heart of this seemingly chaotic landscape stood the tenement buildings, structures that fostered living arrangements that tested and violated middle-class values of home, privacy, a bounded sexuality, and economic (property-holding) status.

To middle-class observers, familiar with a normative public geography of the village or town, such city spaces seemed both exotic and immoral. Of particular interest was the way in which the exigent construction of the tenements and the compression of persons into space were assumed to thwart one's formation as a civic person. At the root of such concern may simply be the troubling assumption that civic identity is a function of property holding. But beyond this, architectural concerns persisted. How can civic qualities (neighborliness, as well as mutual regard, interest, and respect) exist in the face of cheek-by-jowl living arrangements? How can something like a "reasoning public" be constructed in ethnically defined enclaves, where linguistic and cultural identification with other Americans is thwarted by material barriers and boundaries surrounding enclaves and neighborhoods? It is against such a background of concerns linking materiality to sociability that we might begin to position the nineteenth-century "urban classroom," and more particularly, the city writing class, especially in its emergence as a site of social reproduction and civic reformation in late-nineteenth-century American cities. Given the apparent disorder of urban space, the classroom, the community literacy center, and even the public library became extensions of the civic sphere, places of new association and identification, "reasonable" public spaces where one could practice civil behaviors without distraction. In these sites, a conception of civil society was as much a spatial construct as it was a communicative and sociologic one.

Taking as its chief historical example the literacy, writing, and rhetoric instruction that was made available in the late nineteenth and early twentieth centuries to diverse city persons at Chicago's Hull-House, my analysis envisions "city comp" as a form of composition instruction that grapples with the variants of urban sociability, population diversity, and material-spatial constraints in a manner characteristically different from writing instruction in non-urban spaces.

I suggest that the urban writing classroom (especially writing and reading instruction offered in literacy sites outside traditional schools) can be usefully understood in terms of civic education, where various models of deliberative rhetoric have traditionally been deployed in the effort to form citizens. This is not to imply that all sites of city comp—either historically or at present—are devoted to civic education as such, but rather to suggest that, given the context of urban education, writing instruction in cities tends to figure the classroom as a prototypical public sphere where students present themselves as relative strangers to one another correspondent to the social arrangements of urban life. By focusing on the place of writing instruction at Chicago's Hull-House, we can both consider the teaching of deliberative practices in city sites (as Hull-House provided city residents with multiple sites and occasions for sponsored deliberation on social, political, and aesthetic matters) and also value the supremely spatial aspect of instruction as it is located in particular urban geographies and architectures, spaces characteristically different from spaces of rural or suburban education.

Chicago's Hull-House was one of the most famous and also one of the most successful settlement houses of the late nineteenth and early twentieth centuries. Though differentiated from the interests of the state and compulsory public schooling, Hull-House's program of civic education highlights the ways in which the built environment of the city prompted deliberate but often overdetermined efforts at forming Americans as appropriate public persons in a space deemed suitable to carrying out the practices of civil society. Established by Jane Addams and her colleagues in 1889, and operational until midcentury, Hull-House stands as a model settlement house in America, one of hundreds of such institutions scattered throughout major American cities.

Following on the heels of the urban charity movement of the 1880s, American settlement houses distinguished themselves from other charitable ventures by occupying sites within economically underprivileged neighborhoods, with volunteer workers living and teaching as "neighbors" with the ambient population. The placement of the settlement house within the district where its clients lived and worked was an essential feature of the project, bolstering claims of involvement, accessibility, association, and social haven. By the 1920s, Hull-House established itself as a prominent site for social and political formation, offering classes free of charge in English, literature, art, dance, music, personal finance, household economics, public affairs, reading, writing, and rhetoric. In addition to its educational offerings, Hull-House sponsored a branch of the public library, series of speakers, multicultural events, a museum of labor history, and a variety of social affairs: theater, cultural exhibitions, and study groups typically addressing questions of political or economic relevance.

Positioned squarely in Chicago's nineteenth ward, Hull-House institutionally anchored the Halstead Street neighborhoods, occupying at one moment in its history an entire city block. Similar to the situatedness of an urban parish, Hull-House was architecturally differentiated from the proximate architectures of tenements, shops, flats, and saloons (for a time, one such establishment was immediately next door). Its participation in the cultural geography of the nineteenth ward also encouraged its workers and clientele to envision the neighborhood as a particular kind of sociologic and political "environment" (in the Progressivist vernacular), with Hull-House occupying roles both as an outpost of middle-class values in the urban "wilderness" and as a charitable "service provider" for impoverished persons (in addition to its curriculum, Hull-House provided dining halls, gymnasia, and even hot baths).

In its "traditional" offerings of English language instruction, rhetoric classes, and reading groups, Hull-House proves an interesting historical instance of urban literacy education, one more or less consonant with the trajectory of critical literacy education in American cities. In fact, Hull-House may be considered as a site of progressivist "critical literacy," given that it typically situated language instruction within overtly political contexts. Its English language classes for Italian immigrants, for instance, were paired with the Shirt-makers' Protective Union meetings so that English might be understood against a set of economic concerns particular to Italian laborers (Bryan). As early as 1902, Hull-House's writing classes provided spaces where students could reflect critically upon their ambient social and economic conditions. Consonant with the pedagogy fostered in its Labor Museum, its debating societies, and its reading clubs, its English Composition courses taught writing and rhetorical practices through the lens of political and economic issues pertinent to the lives of neighborhood residents. Drawing her inspiration from Tolstoy, Addams understood that the powers of close observation and analysis were best practiced in response to the conditions of everyday life.

Hilda Satt Polacheck, a Hull-House student who became a political activist and public writer, includes in her autobiography an essay titled "The Ghetto Market" that she had written in an English Composition class

(Appendix). Polacheck scrupulously catalogues the unsanitary food handling evident in a prominent open-air market. Her persona, "concerned citizen," is complemented by an ethos of careful inquiry and motivated observation, two writerly sensibilities sponsored in other Hull-House activities. Hull-House's Labor Museum, for instance, chronicled in displays and text the specifics of producing local goods, typically those made by recent immigrants. In its studied stroll through the city market, Polacheck's text mirrors the processural display of linen production available in the museum's exhibit. Polacheck details her experience of walking through the Labor Museum: "First, here was the plant; then the various steps of getting the plant ready for spinning it into thread. Then there was the finished piece of cloth in the natural color. Then pieces of cotton cloth that had been dyed. . . . The flax exhibit was a real surprise. I had seen fine linen such as tablecloths and napkins. I had even worn linen dresses. But I did not know that linen was made also of a plant" (64). The mechanism of the "guided tour" is also Polacheck's rhetorical strategy of exposition in her composition: "The woman I followed now turned to a stand opposite. Here were for sale prunes, raisins, nuts, beans, rice, salted herring, soda water, candles, matches, soap, and various other articles too numerous to mention. All these were uncovered except for the flies. Is it any wonder that this district has more typhoid than any other section of the city?" (79). Given the plethora of city ethnographies and sociologic investigations either sponsored by Hull-House or carried out by Chicago urban sociologists who frequented Hull-House and at times offered classes and presentations there, it is not surprising that Polacheck's text practices a form of exposé typically associated with the methods of critical description associated with progressivist reform texts. Clearly, the writing classroom at Hull-House was a space for focusing on the ways in which political and social critique may be carried out in language: "Papers were written on the collection of garbage, clean streets, single tax, trade unionism, and many others. . . . [O]ur subjects were influenced by what was going on at Hull-House" (Polacheck 94).

It is important to note that the modes of critical literacy promoted at Hull-House—learning to speak English not by using textbooks, but rather by engaging directly with the key terms and concepts offered in the Declaration of Independence, or by perusing naturalization manuals; practicing verbal and written argument by turning to difficult political disputes and social disagreements of the era—were typically unavailable in traditional state schools. Hull-House's contribution to defining an American form of city instruction in writing and deliberation may be found, then, in the many connections it invited its clients to form between language use and informed political and social behavior, a tendency still prevalent in urban literacy education. Its uniqueness, however, is found not merely in its sponsorship of what we would these days

term "critical literacy," but in the very ways in which it provided an architectural space for performing linguistically mediated civic roles, a space outside
that of home, church, or state-involved school.

Hull-House presents us with an example of how institutional structures
foster social reproduction by dint of their architectural solidity and material
form, constructions that in the case of nineteenth-century cities signaled specific modifications or corrections to the built environment of working-class
neighborhoods. An examination of Hull-House's streams of civic and writing
instruction may lead us to revalue the "place" of writing instruction in the city,
while reminding us of the "place of the city" within a broader category of lived
spatiality. Though at times undervalued or ignored altogether, the *place* of
instruction often carries weighty social and political significance. Certainly,
one might identify a particular school building's or classroom's ideologic architecture: rows of chairs, blackboards of public text, the presence of the clock, as
well as the hard architectures of cinder block and brick easily signal forms of
regimentation, obedience, and disciplined order. Recently, cultural geogra-
phers and spatial theorists have reminded us that the materiality of place not
only catalyzes certain behavioral choices, but it also deeply inscribes our
recognition of ourselves as public persons, as persons who sense themselves as
either "in" or "out" of place. As cultural historian Dolores Hayden puts it, our
recognition of "place" includes

> the resonance of homestead, location, and open space in the city as well as a
> position in a social hierarchy. . . . In the nineteenth century . . . place also car-
> ried a sense of the right of a person to own a piece of land, or to be part of
> the social world, and in this older sense place contains more political history.
> Phrases like "knowing one's place" or "a woman's place" still imply both spa-
> tial and political meanings. (15)

In other words, certain places in the nineteenth-century city (churches, syna-
gogues, theaters, public bathhouses, markets, nickelodeons) existed both as
physical and as cognitive sites, as knowable and habitable commonplaces, as it
were. This is not to suggest that the various architectural façades available to
residents on their daily rounds simply provided a kind of segmented aesthetic
experience; rather, they signaled that neighborhood residents experienced
such urban sites as places of association or disassociation, affiliation or dismissal, partly by the way in which such sites more or less "automatically"
inscribed social codes of inclusivity and exclusivity. Space was discerned prin-
cipally as social place. As cultural geographer Tim Cresswell puts it,

> [T]he word *place* clearly refers to something more than a spatial referent.
> Implied in these terms is a sense of the proper. Something or someone
> *belongs* in one place and not in another. What one's place is, is clearly

related to one's relation to others. . . . There is nothing logical about such observations: neither are they necessarily rules or laws. Rather they are *expectations* about behavior that relate a position to a social structure to actions in space. In this sense "place" combines the spatial with the social— it is "social space." (3)

Designed as a "model middle-class household: orderly, cultivated, temperate, and industrious" (Boyer 156), Hull-House impressed its values upon neighborhood residents in the most immediate ways. One typically might pass by its imposing brick edifice on everyday walks to and from work or to and from the market. Such locatedness permitted it to function as a kind of architectural *topos*, advocating in its stability and size certain institutional values, but doing so within the frame of a "house," styled to simulate a "home." Clients typically entered Hull-House through a vestibule, finding themselves greeted (often by Jane Addams herself) in one of its several parlors. Immediately, an etiquette of bourgeois deportment was impressed upon neighbors, a behavioral model supported not only by the niceties of greetings and introductions, but also by entrance through interior spaces clearly differentiating the teeming Chicago streets from the calm attitude within the house. Such an entrance was designed to reinforce one's sense of the appropriateness of private bounded space in contradistinction to the "permeable" doors, windows, and flimsy walls that blurred personal and social boundaries in the tenements. Hull-House's elaborate configuration of classrooms, meeting rooms, parlors, and playgrounds was designed to help its clients clearly differentiate one public role from another. Each interior space signaled its particular social and moral code, its own set of behavioral norms and rules. For Addams and her staff, civic formation—the transformation of city dwellers into reasoning members of civil society—was best accomplished in a deliberately prepared environment.

As an institution dependent upon voluntary association, Hull-House had to compete with other city attractions—the theater, the union hall, the street corner, the saloon—against which it vigorously differentiated itself. Ironically, its role as community "center" was dependent both upon its radical availability and upon its offer of transcendency. Such a confused status is evident in Addams's *Hull-House Maps and Papers*, an ambitious and innovative sociological project documenting in spatial form the ethnic and socioeconomic configuration of the nineteenth ward. The publication offered a series of graphic representations of disorder, a crazy quilt of color-coded ethnic enclaves inferred by Addams to signify a fractured public sphere. In its sponsorship of immigrant assimilation, Hull-House would help to blend the patchwork into a more unified and mutualistic form. Ironically, Addams's description of her publication complicates and betrays the very notion of Hull-House as "center"; for her, *Hull-House Maps and Papers* suggests what might be done by and through a neighborhood of working-class people, when they are touched by a common stimulus, and possess an intellectual and social centre about which they may group their various organizations and enterprises. This center of "settlement," to be effective, must contain an element of permanency, so that the neighborhood may feel that the interest and fortunes of the residents are identical with their own. The settlement must have an enthusiasm for the possibilities of locality, and an ability to bring into it and develop from it those lines of thought and action which make for the "higher life." (*Hull-House Maps* 207)

One might argue that the logical conclusion to Hull-House's effectiveness in fostering "the possibilities of locality" would be its disappearance from the scene altogether, that to truly honor the civic responsibilities of its citizens, it would position itself as impermanent, as "temporary" catalyst rather than as permanent institution, as a sponsor of residents' initiatives rather than as an institution "about which they may group their various organizations and enterprises."

In her public writings, however, Addams was quite sensitive to charges of intrusion. For her, the establishment of Hull-House within the neighborhood (the specificity of its placement) was far more authenticating for residents than was the practice of home visitation by charitable and social workers carried out in the previous decades by so-called "friendly visitors," who visited tenement families only to return home to the comfort of their middle-class surroundings. As Addams argues,

> When the agent or visitor appears among the poor, and they discover that under certain conditions food and rent and medical aid are dispensed from some unknown source, every man, woman, and child is quick to learn what the conditions may be, and to follow them. . . . [T]o the visitor they gravely laud temperance and cleanliness and thrift and religious observance. The deception in the first instances arises from a wondering inability to understand the ethical ideals which can require such impossible virtues, and from an innocent desire to please. (*Democracy* 27)

The establishment of an institution within a district—the neighborly claiming of place—was for Addams simply a "necessity," given that the core of Hull-House's work involved not simply the formation of persons, but also the reform of persons within an *environment*. The material stability of Hull-House had to stand within and apart from the neighborhood, throwing its features into problematic relief. In "The Objective Value of a Social Settlement," composed in 1892, Addams ascribes to Hull-House its geographic bearings:

> Hull-House stands on South Halstead Street, next door to the corner of Polk. South Halstead Street is thirty-two miles long and one of the great

thoroughfares of Chicago. Polk Street crosses Halstead midway between the stock-yards to the south and the ship-building yards on the north branch of the Chicago River. For the six miles between these two industries the street is lined with shops of butchers and grocers, with dingy and gorgeous saloons, and pretentious establishments for the sale of ready-made clothing. Polk Street, running west from Halstead Street, grows rapidly more respectable; running a mile east to State Street, it grows steadily worse, and crosses a network of gilded vice on the corners of Clark Street and Fourth Avenue. (45)

With this, Addams brings to mind how thoroughly Hull-House (like other educational and acculturative institutions) employed a kind of "positional ideology." An elaborate rhetoric of maps transforms the blunt facts of geography into coordinates on an economic and moral landscape. This presages the equally detailed efforts in contemporary film and media to plot the roles and responsibilities of the urban school against city desires, triangulated within a network of unpredictability and violation understood to be the ghetto. By its very nature, the attractions of the city are figured to stand in direct opposition to one's affiliation as a student. Writing to Chicago schoolteachers in 1904, Addams avers,

> The school has to compete with a great deal from the outside in addition to the distractions of the neighborhood. Nothing is more fascinating than that mysterious "down town," whither the boy longs to go to sell papers and black boots, to attend the theaters, and, if possible, to stay all night on the pretense of waiting for the early edition of the great dailies. If a boy is once thoroughly caught in these excitements, nothing can save him from overstimulation and consequent debility and worthlessness; he arrives at maturity with no habits of regular work and with a distaste for its dullness. ("Educational Methods" 3)

Certainly, this is a familiarly limited—if not thoroughly clichéd—lament regarding the competing attractions of students' lives, one readily available from the eighteenth century to the present. Addams, however, was less interested in the failures of traditional urban schooling than she was in offering up new forms of civic instruction available outside the family and beyond the state. The settlement would permit a "freer space" of association and affiliation, but would do so in light of especially aggressive concerns regarding the state of the American urban public.

Beyond the "objective facts" of poverty and the attractions of city culture, Addams went on to posit a "subjective necessity" for Hull-House, and it is here that the "material necessity" of Hull-House is also formulated. As pointedly as any of her writings, "The Subjective Necessity for Social Settlements" solidified the urgency of Addams's work. Here, Hull-House is projected to act as more than mere "place"; it will actually add space where too little exists:

The social organism has broken down through large districts of our great cities. Many of the people living there are very poor, the majority of them without leisure or energy for anything but the gain of subsistence. They move often from one wretched lodging to another. They live for the moment side by side, many of them without knowledge of each other, without fellowship, without local tradition of public spirit, without social organization of any kind. . . . [T]hese working-men are not organized socially; although living in crowded tenement-houses, they are living without corresponding social contact. The chaos is as great as it would be were they working in huge factories without foreman or superintendent. *Their ideas and resources are cramped.* The desire for higher social pleasure is extinct. They have no share in the traditions and social energy which make for progress. (52, italics added)

For Addams, as for others of her moment, the very notion of "cramping" runs immediately counter to the exercise of "freedom," an American conceit resting upon a root metaphor of open space. Though Hull-House could not significantly modify the material limitations of crowding, it could, in effect, create a "sphere of influence," a cognitive space "drawing into participation" persons who otherwise would be less able to enlarge their experience of themselves as "free" members of a relatively boundless public, in other words, as Americans. In language that betrays the limitations of her understanding of social groups (as well as a quite distinct paternalism), Addams claims Hull-House to be the very vortex of ever-widening circles of influence:

This, I think, is what the settlements are trying to do. They are trying to increase the public that shall be the medium for social developments that are of great moment to us all. They are trying to draw into participation in our culture the large numbers of persons who would otherwise remain outside and who, being outside, would not only remain undeveloped themselves, but would largely cripple our national life and in the end would cripple our generational development. ("Widening the Circle" 211)

It is difficult to envision just how the seemingly contrary centrifugal and centripetal influences Hull-House hoped to hold over its neighbors would function conjointly. If Hull-House "drew into participation," where, finally, would a remodeled public function beyond the limitations of self-promoting ethnic and European nationalist enclaves except within Hull-House walls?

The bounded publics formed within Hull-House were multi-ethnic and multi-cultural, to be sure. Italian Americans attended Polish American folk festivals; Jewish American students attended classes on Irish folklore. The labor museum displayed crafts and folkways of numerous European countries;

classes in European languages were regularly offered alongside classes in English. Just so, these were sanctioned as appropriate cross-cultural encounters orchestrated within the boundaries of the compound. Hull-House was one of the first institutions in America to sponsor a "public playground," yet even it was a space defined by certain etiquettes designed to promote a child's sense of civil behavior and to foster his or her right relationship to others. Stepping onto the playground meant, in effect, entering the world of politeness, manners, and normative social arrangements such as mutualism, with play understood as an activity free from rudeness, dispute, and anger.

It is not too extravagant to suggest that, as a kind of "city within a city," Hull-House was able to offer certain possibilities for social arrangements that were unavailable elsewhere in the nineteenth ward. Here, we might consider its architectural boundary marking both an artificial and also somewhat artful force, cognizant of the ways in which boundaries both delimit and define. However idealistically, Addams believed that Hull-House could sponsor democratic arrangements simply by "inviting" an array of immigrant groups to participate in her utopic vision. The invitation was sweetened by Hull-House's determination to keep ethnic customs and folkways alive, intact, and remembered. If not, immigrant neighbors—and especially children—would be disinherited, a condition of assimilation that Addams herself found both debilitating and abusive. Similarly, Addams felt that the "English Only" approach of the public schools unnecessarily and unfairly severed the linguistic relatedness of children to their parents and families. This disassociation held significant moral implications. Jolted into American language and culture, public school students might also disrespect parental authority. In an address to the National Education Association, delivered in 1908, Addams wonders,

> It would seem that in spite of enormous advantages which the public school gives to these children it in some way loosens them from the authority and control of their parents, and tends to send them, without a sufficient rudder and power of self-direction, into the perilous business of living. Can we not say, perhaps, that the schools ought to do more to connect these children with the best things of the past, to make them realize something of the beauty and charm of the language, the history, and the traditions which their parents represent? ("Public School" 100)

Built partly from her understanding of evolutionary biology (and its purported correspondence to trajectories of social change that flourished within certain environments) and partly from her understandings of Deweyan pragmatism (where education is best represented as a "continuous reconstruction of experience"), Addams believed that the necessity of Hull-House rested partly in the moral responsibility for middle-class Americans to usher immigrants into their new identities as citizens, a role neglected by the upper class and by the industrial orders. Hull-House, therefore, occupied a liminal space, poised somewhere between home and school, work life and family life, outside of religious affiliations and beyond the push and pull of neighborhood politics.

In this way, the social space available at Hull-House may have been a version of what Evans and Boyte call "free space": "settings between private lives and large-scale institutions where ordinary citizens can act with dignity, independence, and vision . . . voluntary forms of association with a relatively open and participatory character . . . where people experience a schooling in citizenship and learn a vision of the common good in the course of struggling for change" (17). Today, it has become commonplace to think of the American public sphere as necessarily fractured, even phantom in its appearance, existing as it does somewhere between persons, mediated by an array of electronic technologies—a placeless space. Such a vision of the public sphere may depend, however, on the co-presence of privatized interests, with certain excesses and luxuries available that permit material transcendence and a sense of placelessness. Hull-House's clients were, we might imagine, acutely aware of Hull-House as a kind of staging ground for trying out a variety of public personae, with its physical structure understood as location (its physicality and placement within the city), as locale (the ground of specified social actions), and as place (resonant with subjective meanings and personal significance). In this way, the many opportunities and venues Hull-House provided for critical exchange between residents regarding political, economic, and social conditions can be understood as provisional arrangements, preparation for one's future life as a citizen. Still, its institutional presence may have foregrounded the very sort of particularity and Balkanization of city space it purported to work against.

The Hull-House project remains a curious complexity of motives, none of them pure. As Addams herself proclaimed, seemingly unaware of the very contradictions her stance embraces, "This, then, will be my definition of the settlement: that it is an attempt to express the meaning of life in terms of itself. . . . A settlement brings to its aid all possible methods to reveal and make common its conception of life" ("Function" 188). Here, the very term *settlement* seems impossibly ambiguous, a combination of both colonizing and constructive, deeply ethical desires. Perhaps, as Walter Lippman reminded his public in 1919, it is best to consider Hull-House both as a partially realized social experiment and as an elaborate dream:

> Hull-House cannot remake Chicago. A few hundred lives can be changed, and for the rest it is a guide to the imagination. Like all utopias, it cannot succeed, but it may point the way to success. If Hull-House is unable to civilize Chicago, it at least shows Chicago and America what a civilization

might be like. Friendly, where cities are friendless; beautiful where they are
ugly; sociable and open, where our daily life is furtive; work a craft; art a participation—it is in miniature the goal of statesmanship. (122)

In his effort to reclaim the early-twentieth-century urban school as a "social
center," where students may assemble to speak their ways across lines of division in a way that honors the ethnic and national differences endemic to city
life, John Dewey turned to Hull-House as a model institution for catalyzing
new social arrangements by its very "manufacture" of occasions for dialogue
and critical exchange. Dewey argued that "the work of such an institution as
Hull-House has been primarily not that of conveying intellectual instruction,
but of being a social clearing-house. It is a place where ideas and beliefs may
be exchanged, not merely in the arena of formal discussion . . . but in ways
where ideas are incarnated in human form and clothed with the winning grace
of personal life" (107). With this, we may be reminded that perhaps one of the
necessary instrumentalities of civic and rhetorical education is the construction of a "space apart," where social exchange and critical reflection upon its
character and quality can be carried out in (relatively) safe and sustaining fash-
ion, with the understanding that such activity is, by nature, partial, provisional,
and, in its richest sense, practical.

     In his recent travels across the various economic and political geogra-
phies in which American education is situated, Mike Rose argues that civic
classrooms, lifted out of the stream of everyday life, have the responsibility to
reconstruct—however artificially—a sense of public place: "If we consider
these rooms to be miniature public spheres or preparatory arenas for civic life,
then it is essential to note how the formation of intellectually safe and
respectful space, the distribution of authority and responsibility, the maintenance of high expectations and the means to attain them—how all of this is
essential to the development of the intelligence of a people" (417). The example of Hull-House reminds us that such miniature publics must be thoughtfully constructed, and that we must pay careful attention to their materiality—in their maintenance of a cultural architecture suitable for fostering a
sense of what we might call "rhetorical space," where learners may safely present themselves as strangers to one another, as public persons who—if for just
a brief and delicate moment—identify themselves as deliberating citizens,
prepared to adopt civic personae in order to allow their differences to flourish productively. The very idea of "safe space" has perhaps hardened into
cliché, yet we might do well to remember the many ways in which the urban
writing classroom acts as haven, or refuge, or even sanctuary within the chaos
of urban living. Perhaps because of crowding, dense diversity, and the ten-
dencies toward overt self-differentiation, city residents are equipped—in
ways that the residents of town or village or suburb may not be—to under-

stand the "formation of space," distinguished and separated from other places of the city, as a social good. The city itself may be especially able to make its place for learning.

APPENDIX

"THE GHETTO MARKET" BY HILDA SATT POLACHECK

Sociologists who are studying and seeking to remedy conditions among the wretchedly poor have done vast good. The poor may now be clothed; they receive medical attention and surgical care which none but the very rich could afford to pay for. They need not be ignorant, for schools are free and there are many devoted women in the social settlements who are laboring night and day to make up whatever deficiency may exist in the capacity of the city institutions. But there is one injustice untouched; one wrong which is crying for immediate remedy. This is the unsanitary, filthy food which the poor in certain quarters are forced to eat. Not until the city takes the matter in hand and orders all vegetables, meat and fish to be sold only in adequate and sanitary rooms will this condition be entirely overcome; for as long as the old market of the Ghetto district exists, so long will the inhabitants of the district patronize it.

Few people whose work does not take them into the neighborhood have any idea what the Ghetto market is like. I took a trip through it the other night for the purpose of observation. I soon came to Jefferson and Twelfth Streets. The illumination for the stands and shops is furnished by curious gasoline lamps nailed to the houses in an irregular line, so that when I followed the crowd of shoppers, the lights in the distance looked a poorly organized torch-light parade. I walked along aimlessly for a moment till I saw a woman with an empty basket coming from a side street.

The first stop that she made was at a poultry shop, where a great many women were gathered. This shop was about six feet in height, length, and width. Trading was carried out in front of the shop. My "guide" carefully examined every fowl; she then counted the contents of her small purse and walked into the shop. I readily concluded that here everyone buys according to the size of her purse; for I saw the shopkeeper behind the counter take up the fowl and cut it into four pieces. One of these he wrapped in a newspaper and placed in the basket.

We were soon near the fish traders. The fish were kept on the window sills of the shop, somewhat smaller than the one we had just left, on stands and barrels arranged on the sidewalk. The sills and stands were made of tin, with strips along the edge to prevent the fish from slipping to the ground. In each stand

and sill a waste pipe was arranged through which the waste water from the ice took its course. But unfortunately this pipe reached the floor only, thus leaving the floor of the shop and sidewalk in front of it always covered with mud.

A man and his wife were the chief clerks, cashiers, and wrappers. The woman wore an apron which I thought at first sight was meant to protect her dress; but a second look showed me that it was tucked up on one side, letting all the slimy drippings from the fish fall unheeded on her skirt. Her head was covered with a shawl, which looked as if at one time it was black, but it had now turned green, yellow, gray, and various other colors.

The man wore a pair of overalls made of heavy blue cotton cloth, but from the constant wiping of his hands after handling the fish, looked like a leather of no particular color. The two seemed to handle their wares all day without washing their hands a single time. Not only that—I was amazed to see the man even re-fill his gasoline lamp and handle fish immediately after. The women who crowd around this stall are permitted to handle the wares to their heart's content. When they finally selected suitable portions of the fish, the shopkeeper weighed them on a dirty scale and wrapped them in a dilapidated newspaper, regardless of what substance may have been used in printing it or who handled it when it came off the press.

We next went to the cake stand which consisted of a long table standing on the edge of the sidewalk, over which was erected a heavy canvas. The table was covered with a miscellaneous assortment of cakes. These seemed to have a double mission in the world: not only did the buyers enjoy their delicious flavor, but the flies seemed very much at home, and from the constant buzzing I knew at first sight that they enjoyed the surroundings.

The woman I followed now turned to a stand opposite. Here were for sale prunes, raisins, nuts, beans, rice, salted herring, soda water, candles, matches, soap, and various other articles too numerous to mention. All these were uncovered except from the flies. Is it any wonder that this district has more typhoid fever than any other section of the city?

Nearby was a bench covered with old coats, vests, shoes, and trousers. Here second-hand shoes are bought without a thought as to who the previous wearer was. A woman will pay fifty cents for a pair of shoes and sixty cents for repairing them, whereas for one dollar her boy can be provided with a new pair that had never been worn and carried no possible taint of contagious disease.

Is this question not well worthy of consideration? Cannot the poultry shop, fish stall, and cake stand be kept off the street, free from the dust and the flies? Why should this class of people who work harder than any other be compelled to eat inferior food when they might be supplied with good food for the same money? Are there not plenty of men employed in building houses, ice boxes and various appliances for keeping provisions? Yet these people eat food sold on the street under the filthiest conditions. (78)

WORKS CITED

Addams, Jane. *Democracy and Social Ethics.* Cambridge: Harvard UP, 1964.

———. "Educational Methods." *Chicago Teachers' Federation Bulletin* 3 (1904): 1–6.

———. "A Function of the Social Settlement." *The Social Thought of Jane Addams.* Ed. Christopher Lasch. Indianapolis: Bobbs-Merrill, 1965. 183–98.

———. *Hull-House Maps and Papers: A Presentation of the Nationalities and Wages in a Congested District of Chicago.* New York: Thomas Y. Crowell, 1895.

———. "The Objective Value of a Social Settlement." *The Social Thought of Jane Addams.* Ed. Christopher Lasch. Indianapolis: Bobbs-Merrill, 1965. 44–61.

———. "The Public School and the Immigrant Child." *Journal of the Proceedings and Addresses of the National Education Association* 46 (1908): 99–102.

———. "The Subjective Necessity for Social Settlements." *Jane Addams on Education.* Ed. E. C. Lagemann. New York: Teachers College P, 1994. 49–63.

———. "Widening the Circle of Enlightenment: Hull-House and Adult Education." *Jane Addams on Education.* Ed. E. C. Lagemann. New York: Teachers College P, 1994. 204–11.

Boyer, Paul. *Urban Masses and Moral Order in America, 1820–1920.* Cambridge: Harvard UP, 1978.

Bryan, Mary Lynn McCree, ed. *The Jane Addams Papers.* Ann Arbor: University Microfilms International, 1985.

Cresswell, Tim. *In Place/Out of Place: Geography, Ideology, and Transgression.* Minneapolis: U Minnesota P, 1996.

Dewey, John. "The School as Social Center." *100 Years at Hull-House.* Ed. Mary Lynn McCree and Allen Davis. Bloomington: Indiana UP, 1990. 103–108.

Evans, Sarah, and Harry Boyte. *Free Spaces: The Sources of Democratic Change in America.* New York: Harper and Row, 1986.

Hayden, Dolores. *The Power of Place: Urban Landscapes as Public History.* Cambridge: MIT, 1995.

Lippmann, Walter. "Well Meaning but Unmeaning." *100 Years at Hull-House.* Ed. Mary Lynn McCree and Allen Davis. Bloomington: Indiana UP, 1990. 121–22.

Polacheck, Hilda Satt. *I Came a Stranger: The Story of a Hull-House Girl.* Ed. Dena J. Polacheck Epstein. Urbana: U of Illinois P, 1989.

Rose, Mike. *Possible Lives: The Promise of Public Education in America.* New York: Penguin, 1995.

Therborn, Göran. *The Ideology of Power and the Power of Ideology*. London: Routledge, 1980.

Wirth, Louis. "Urbanism as a Way of Life." *The American Journal of Sociology* 44 (1938): 52–70.

CHAPTER EIGHT

THE WRITTEN CITY
Urban Planning, Computer Networks,
and Civic Literacies

Jeffrey T. Grabill

The city is produced in many ways. . . . Cities are systems of communications
telling us who has power and how it is wielded. The configuration, use, size,
internal layout, and external design of the city embodies the nature, distribution, and contestation of power in society. The power struggle fundamentally revolves around the meaning of the city, what it represents, what it
could represent, and what it should represent. In a very real sense the city is
a system of communication, a set of signs indicating power and prestige, status and influence, victory and defeat.
                                    —John Rennie Short, *The Urban Order:
                         An Introduction to Cities, Culture, and Power* (p. 390)

There is no question that cities communicate. But what might be more difficult to see is that cities themselves are written; they are a direct and material function of complex institutional decision-making processes that produce, among other things, our built environment. This chapter is an
exploration of how cities are written, how they can be written by citizens,
and how the writing of a city can be the context for a writing class. In this
respect, I am entering a healthy conversation in rhetoric and composition
and professional and technical writing about the roles that writing plays
outside the academy, but I am also suggesting that community involvement
and civic engagement will not necessarily happen on our terms, as a func-

tion of a literacy program or a writing project. Rather, such engagement might happen—and happen more effectively—as part of other disciplinary and institutional efforts where rhetoric and writing play an integral role. The focus of this chapter, then, is not on a writing class alone, but on how a writing class can aid community building.

I am interested in the discipline and practice of urban planning and how planning produces a city. My method here will be to move back and forth between two discussions: first, of the rhetorical turn in urban planning theory; and second, of a current project in which I am working with city officials from The Atlanta Project's Office of Data and Policy Analysis (DAPA) and a Georgia State technical writing class to build one community's capacity to participate in planning and other civic processes.[1] DAPA, my technical writing class, and I are trying to create Web-based tools that will allow the residents of Mechanicsville, a neighborhood in Atlanta, to have a voice in how their neighborhood is constructed. This project raises important issues related to the status and value of citizens' knowledge and expertise, the power of citizens to participate in institutionalized decision-making processes, and the ability of information technologies to give citizens a sense of agency.

A MODEST PROPOSAL TO DEMOCRATIZE DATA

The United Way of Metro Atlanta recently began a new grant program to help build capacity in metro communities by providing money and technical assistance to small neighborhood and community organizations. At one United Way meeting that I attended, members of this organization asked if students enrolled in my service learning technical and business writing courses might provide technical assistance to grant writers, and they asked members of DAPA to help them provide data maps to grant writers so that they might better focus their efforts. As the meeting progressed, United Way representatives thought it would be a good idea to provide data and maps via the Web so that they would also be accessible to community organizations.

In urban planning discourse, giving local citizens direct access to powerful databases and mapping functions is known as "democratizing data." David Sawicki and William Craig write that the movement to democratize data is driven by two factors, the spread of computing power and the relative ease with which raw data can be turned into information. Currently, most efforts to move data, information technologies, and expertise closer to communities and neighborhoods involve the use of data intermediaries such as the Office of Data and Policy Analysis. For data to be truly democratized, however, Sawicki and Craig argue that the "locus of applications" must move closer to citizens (512).

As the capacity to access and use data becomes more common, urban planners theorize that community groups will be better able to participate in fundamental knowledge-creating processes integral to planning, such as the formulation of initial problem statements and research questions, participation in data gathering, and collaboration with "experts" in making sense of information. When community and neighborhood groups have meaningful access to information and information technologies, they can indeed be effective. Sawicki and Craig, for example, explain that The Atlanta Project played an important role in helping a local community acquire and analyze complicated tax records in order to preserve neighborhood parcels from being sold to an outside developer. Alison Cordero also writes of how a neighborhood group in Brooklyn used personal computers to create a healthier community by analyzing crime data and developing housing information systems (Sawicki and Craig 515). Too often, however, community organizations are not able to participate in these processes because they enter them too late to contribute meaningfully.

Therefore, while the United Way's impulse to democratize data was on target and is supported by a substantial body of urban planning literature, there were (and are) problems both with the idea of democratizing data and with the use of the Web and other advanced information technologies for doing so. Michael Barndt, for example, doubts that data intermediaries will ever see a diminished role and, in fact, believes that the elimination of data intermediaries would harm the communities that most need them (a position for which I have considerable sympathy). But connections between the ability to create usable knowledge and meaningful action based on that knowledge are too often assumed and not facilitated. Sawicki and Craig understand the problems with their proposal. They acknowledge that "data dumps" are ineffective and often counterproductive, that novices to complicated planning processes often need context and history that raw data do not provide, that access to databases is typically restricted, and that both the data and the information technologies needed to use the data pose significant usability issues. One answer is to work with communities to build research capacity—the ability to pose questions, drive data collection, and participate in analysis. But the problem of usability still remains. With respect to the United Way proposal, for example, we did not know if the people of Mechanicsville, who were the intended audience for the website, would or could use it. We had no idea what their information needs were or how they needed to use the information. And we had no concept of what communication tools they wanted (or even if they knew their options). In other words, we knew absolutely nothing about the users, and data without users is worthless.

Patrick Burke (from DAPA) and I voiced these concerns to the United Way, and the project eventually faded. But we did not abandon it. For the

next two years, we explored ways that we could adequately and ethically provide citizens and community groups with meaningful access to powerful data
sets and thereby better enable them to participate in planning and other civic
practices. This project, in its current form, constitutes the core of this chapter. But before I discuss this project in detail, I set the context for it by exploring urban planning theory, which should highlight why websites such as this
and the writing classes that can create them might be important tools for
civic participation.

THE RHETORICAL TURN IN URBAN PLANNING

Urban planning as an academic discipline and a pragmatic activity is like
many in the human sciences. It has one foot in the academy, with a rich tradition of empirical and theoretical inquiry, and it has another foot in the professions, with a rich tradition of planning work for governments, businesses,
and citizen groups. Therefore, planning is at once speculative and grounded,
theoretical and pragmatic, distant and local. Fundamentally, though, urban
planning is at the center of how we construct our built environments. According to Joseph Ferreira,

> Urban planning can be about the public investment, authorization, and sup-
> port for improved infrastructure (roads, transit, water and sewer, etc.), and
> for other public works and services (parks, buildings, public housing, garbage
> collection, job training, public safety, health care, etc.). It can also be about
> the regulatory processes that set, monitor, and enforce land-use and zoning
> regulations, environmental controls, economic development incentives,
> design guidelines, and the like. (166)

With such broad scope, urban planners rely on a number of methodologies to
collect the information necessary to write meaningful plans. They do land-use
studies, population studies, cost benefit analyses, large-scale planning (encom-
passing significant areas over time), survey and indicator-based data collection
and analysis (e.g., indicators of economic activity, such as applications for
business or building permits). And all of this work is framed for professional
urban planners by complex political activity—the influence of private interests, the pressures of citizen groups and associations, and the interests, values,
and decisions of political officials.

Peter Marris writes that there is always a tension in urban planning
between the political, economic, and civic functions of society, and he argues
that "planning, ideally, serves to articulate this tension and, as far as possible,
resolve it" (9). In a similar vein, Peter Hall writes that planning practice has
always been characterized by strains of anarchism and central authority. What

the history and practice of urban planning shows is that these tensions seem always to be in play. During its "anarchic" moments, planning tends toward the local, the civic, and an attendant progressive politics. During its "central" moments, planning tends to favor bureaucracies, institutional structures, conservative politics, and scientific decision-making processes. Historically, then, urban planners have found themselves favoring different sets of interests at different times, often to the exclusion or neglect of those not presently in vogue. When there are disputes about the meaning and practice of planning, they can often be understood in terms of the interplay of competing interests and the always-present strains of anarchic and central planning.

Leonie Sandercock describes five theories of urban planning that have developed since the 1940s: rational comprehensive planning, advocacy planning, radical political economy planning, equity planning, and communicative planning.[2] According to Sandercock, each of these approaches is a response to the theory that preceded it, and each approach attempts to improve both the ethics and the practice of planning. The first four theories of urban planning (rational comprehensive, advocacy, radical political economy, and equity) place the individual urban planner at the center of the planning process, favoring instrumental reasoning and privileging scientific knowledge. Sandercock's fifth theory, called communicative planning, represents the first substantive attempt to decenter the urban planner; communicative urban planners believe that the planning process is "an interactive, communicative activity" (175). It is this model that is most relevant to my discussion here.

For Patsy Healey, the communicative turn in urban planning is a move away from the privileging of instrumental reasoning and scientific knowledge. It is an attempt to understand "how people come to have the ways of thinking and ways of valuing that they do, and how policy development and policy implementation processes can be made more interactive" (28). Healey believes that communicative planning emphasizes the social construction of knowledge, multiple ways of knowing, diversity, and communication (29–30). The practice of communicative urban planning forces planners to be less like cloistered intellectuals and more like facilitators, community organizers, and master communicators. Communicative planning is always situated, multimodal in its research methodologies, and deeply rhetorical.

Once one acknowledges that overly "scientific" and expert-driven planning procedures are both intellectually limiting and procedurally suspect because they exclude people and alternative visions of the "good city," then one must revisit institutionalized procedures for creating knowledge and making decisions. This, to my mind, is rhetoric's real challenge to planning theory and to many types of civic decision making (e.g., risk communication). John Forester's understanding of this has led him to focus on the day-to-day communicative practices of planners in order to understand "the situated, performative qualities of their conversations and texts and realize how far broader institutional and structural questions of power, class, culture, ethnicity, and control manifest themselves in daily speech, writing, and gesture" (2). Forester's move places under the microscope the mundane institutional processes by which decisions are made. Rhetorical theory can be most helpful in this examination because when one begins to focus on the day-to-day procedures for making decisions, one understands, as Forester does, that these procedures are fundamentally rhetorical—they are written. The "rhetorical turn," therefore, is a potentially radical transformation of urban planning; it lays the intellectual groundwork necessary for a more participatory public life because it begins to alter institutional decision-making processes. It also foregrounds writing and positions writers to be more visible in civic life.

Communicative planning is certainly more democratizing than the planning theories that have preceded it; however, it also raises new problems for urban planners that may, in fact, be quite difficult to address. For example, when DAPA's Patrick Burke and I began talking about the possibilities of using computer networks to build community capacity to participate in planning and other civic activities, we kept coming back to issues of communication and institutional change. Specifically, we knew that those with less power in certain communities have difficulty participating in complex civic and institutional processes because they lack certain literacies and rhetorical skills, but we also knew that data and computer networks would not, by themselves, enable greater citizen involvement in planning. In fact, we knew that the opposite might be true. Nonetheless, our work in Mechanicsville is an attempt to use computer networks and writing to enable citizens to employ their knowledge and expertise to improve planning processes.

MECHANICSVILLE AND TECHNICAL WRITING

Mechanicsville is one of Atlanta's oldest neighborhoods, built on level land adjacent to the railroads tracks that were so central to the city's growth and identity (Giarrusso, Gilbreath, Tullos, and Keating 2).[3] Giarusso et al. write that "Mechanicsville has been described as a diverse neighborhood, in terms of race, ethnicity, income, and class, from the 1870s-1930s," but they also caution that while outwardly integrated, the neighborhood was internally segregated (3). Mechanicsville's African American residents, who were always present and now comprise most of the community, have always struggled against racism, and this struggle is visible in the history and geography of the neighborhood.

During what Giarusso et al. describe as Mechanicsville's early period (1845–1899), the neighborhood "exhibited one of the two 'racially-integrated' residential patterns common in the urban South. African Americans lived near the white residents in some parts of the neighborhood, but usually occupied much more modest housing 'in the rear' of the white housing" (8–9). Housing "in the rear" typically fronted alleyways instead of streets. By the 1880s, however, Giarusso et al. note that a different pattern had emerged: clusters of racial groups that over time became more stable.

In the twentieth century, Mechanicsville changed from a stable to a fluid community. During the period of 1900–1944, Mechanicsville was firmly established as an older Atlanta community and still retained its essentially working-class and diverse character.[4] The two most identifiable groups were the African American and Jewish communities who continued to coexist until the 1950s. The 1950s and 1960s were difficult times for Mechanicsville due to urban renewal efforts, highway construction projects, and the social upheaval of the Civil Rights movement. Urban renewal and the interstate construction projects are critical to any understanding of Mechanicsville and Atlanta. Urban renewal in Atlanta, while framed by laudable "great society" impulses, was often twisted to meet the agendas of Atlanta's business and political elite. Similarly, the placement of the Interstates through Atlanta dissected and destroyed a number of predominately African American communities, separating Mechanicsville, in particular, from the central business district. The result was that at the end of the 1960s, Mechanicsville was more homogeneous and uprooted than it had ever been.

Mechanicsville today is still a complicated place. Long neglected and pushed around, the neighborhood is marked by a number of run-down properties and vacant lots, and residents struggle with problems that are endemic to society as a whole but are often more noticeable in poorer communities (Giarrusso et al. 36). Still, Mechanicsville residents feel considerable pride about the neighborhood, and like many of Atlanta's communities, it is experiencing redevelopment and gentrification. While there are certainly more resources in the community because of redevelopment, gentrification in particular threatens to displace longtime and working-class residents. Planning, therefore, is once again a key civic process for Mechanicsville; however, past urban planning processes have hurt this community more than they have helped it. All too often, citizen participation has been absent in planning processes, and thus more powerful interests have inscribed themselves on the neighborhood with relative ease.

The Mechanicsville project that I have been working on with DAPA and my technical writing students attempts to achieve the following two goals: 1) to create with Mechanicsville residents a usable web-based tool that meets their civic and community needs, and 2) to build the capacity of community residents to use advanced information technologies and write with computers, particularly so that they can maintain and change the website. Accompanying these goals are the following research questions:

- What is the current state of computer access in the community (both individually and institutionally)?
- What are the features and functions of a usable website that meets community needs?
- Does the website facilitate civic and planning-related action and has community capacity to use technology effectively been increased through the project?

Using information technologies to better enable a community to participate in planning shows how communicative planning can be improved through more participatory processes and how information technologies can facilitate them. In addition, this project attempts to assist community-building efforts through the use of research and teaching resources. What I will describe here is how a technical writing class has a great deal to offer attempts to build civic capacity through the design and use of information technologies.

While I believe in the value of community-based work, I also do it with caution and, I hope, care. There is no inherent value in writing teachers and researchers moving "into the community." In fact, done thoughtlessly, community involvement is nothing more than exploitive colonization of a "community" to achieve the aims of the university (note how many articles on community service learning talk first—and sometimes exclusively—about the value of this work to students or to the university). Writing programs can, however, thoughtfully aid the process of community building and development, but they must do so in ways that respect the work and expertise of local people and institutions (Grabill). Community members must first engage in asset mapping and problem identification, and then invite outside assets, such as writing programs, to assist them. Once the writing teachers, researchers, and writing programs commit to aid the process of community development, then the commitment must be fulfilled in ways that meet the needs of the community first. The calculus that I have outlined here is actually quite rigorous, does not easily fit within the frameworks of our courses or semesters, and demands that writing teachers and programs understand that many of the literacy practices one sees in urban community contexts are functional, professional writing practices focused on achieving change or meeting specific goals. We can be of assistance to the extent that we help people achieve those goals, yet we are a hindrance if we bring to community involvement our own agendas and senses of what types of reading and writing people should be doing.

During the Spring 2001 semester at Georgia State University, the Mechanicsville website project became the centerpiece of my technical writing class. Throughout the previous year, I had done much of the necessary groundwork for this: human subjects review, relationship building, initial community maps of computer assets, and so on. Technical writers have a great deal to offer civic planning projects such as this. Many of the problems that Patrick Burke (DAPA) and I saw in "democratizing data" movements could be addressed, at least in part, through technical and professional writing. For example, many of the concerns we had about the Mechanicsville project related specifically to issues of usability, broadly conceived. So I thought that this project would be an effective way for students to learn how to do technical writing and meet the needs of Mechanicsville residents at the same time.

I taught the project as an exercise in user-driven design, which is the only way that a writing project such as this can be of use in community capacity building because such a design stance begins with citizen/user expertise. My claim for citizen expertise is based on insights gleaned from usability studies. Usability refers to a range of research that describes how real people in real situations interact with products such as instructional manuals, technologies, and any number of consumer goods. The assumption of usability is that humans are integral to the process of product design. In the course of numerous studies across industries and disciplines, usability researchers have discovered that users have considerable knowledge and expertise, and researchers have come to rely on that expertise in order to carry out effective design.

Users, therefore, are "productive." But so are citizens. Users of a computer interface are much like students in a classroom, or workers on a shop floor, or citizens in a democracy: they all occupy subordinate positions with respect to powerful systems that affect nearly every aspect of daily life. While perhaps subordinate, users, students, workers, and citizens do have some power with respect to how these systems operate. Although the nature of that power depends on the situation, it will always be linked to the ability to produce knowledge about a system. Robert Johnson argues that users generate knowledge about the technologies and systems they use and are a part of, so they should be an integral part of design. This knowledge can come in the form of adapting technologies to new and changing systems, or it can come in more explicit design situations. Regardless, Johnson asserts that user knowledge is unique and a function of certain identities and experiences. Johnson writes that "user-centered approaches should rethink the user as being an active participant in the social order that designs, develops, and implements technologies" because users experience systems much differently than "designers" or "experts," people who may not experience them at all (64).[5] This is why user knowledge constitutes a form of expertise. But it is an expertise that is wasted when traditional hierarchies of knowledge (e.g., expert/novice) are thoughtlessly maintained, particularly in situations where they may not apply.

Johnson's concern is that highly structured systems of power/knowledge do not allow us to consider that users might have something important to say about the effectiveness of a technology, or that residents have something important to say about their neighborhood or city. But when these power/knowledge systems do not cloud our vision, it becomes evident that the users of a system can effectively determine the parameters of the problem to be addressed, frame the questions that must be asked and answered, decide the information that needs to be gathered, interpret that information once collected, and therefore participate substantively in decision-making processes. One objection to participatory decision making such as this is that users lack the expertise that specialists possess and therefore cannot possibly participate meaningfully in complex decision-making processes. While it is true that there are considerable barriers to creating the shared language and knowledge necessary for meaningful participatory processes, they are not impossible to overcome. Reinforcing the power of a narrow "knowledge elite" by ignoring users not only runs the risk of perpetuating a system of domination (Sohng), but it also runs the risk of producing truly useless knowledge (see Deshler and Ewert). One way to avoid such risks is to take seriously the argument of Johnson and others and trust an alternative epistemological history that understands and respects the expertise of users and citizens.

For my purposes, of course, usability is at the heart of the website project. I gave my class the set of problems we were to solve with residents of Mechanicsville and the research questions we needed to answer in order to solve those problems. I also gave students the results of my work to that point: transcripts, notes, and institutional constraints and possibilities that influenced our work. From there, we set about designing the project. We used interviews and focus groups to generate ideas for the website. We attended civic association meetings to learn about the community and what issues were of concern. We surveyed citizens to get a sense of their experience with information technologies. We mapped the community in terms of existing information resources and networks of information sharing. And we did online research to look at models from other cities and generate directories of websites that matched residents' needs.

Based on this research, my students then created a first version of the Mechanicsville website, which, at the time of this writing, we are to test in Mechanicsville during the next two weeks. That testing will get at basic issues of usability, such as navigation and the relevance of the help system we created for the website, and we will also ask residents to help us "write" the site to meet their needs. We are attempting to draw on two aspects of the citizen/user expertise of Mechanicsville residents: 1) their needs as users of web-based technologies, and 2) their needs as citizens to use information technologies for civic purposes.

The Mechanicsville project has been rich and challenging for my students so far, and while I am pleased with their efforts, the class itself is not the only object of interest. The tendency in rhetoric and writing is to see "the community" or "the city" as our space, and the skills and expertise that we bring as the most important part of a project. We see, to be more specific, community literacy projects as fundamentally about literacy when they might more usefully be seen as sites of community activism, job training, or public health initiatives in which writing and rhetoric can play a critical role. Therefore, the seemingly "background" activities that are critical to the success of the website project, such as relationship and capacity building (e.g., short-term consulting, individual tutoring, web authoring classes), are just as important as any classroom activities that may come out of the project.

While I wish to emphasize that the terrain of the Mechanicsville project is city planning and community building, there is clearly a critical role for professional and technical writing researchers, teachers, and students, and this is due to the pervasiveness of information technologies and the issues of writing and design embedded in them. As Sawicki and Craig note, data increasingly is being published on CDs and computer networks, which makes it more accessible to the hyper- or cyber-literate and less accessible to everyone else. But the pervasiveness and use of information technologies goes much deeper. My interest in computer access, community computing, and civic activities such as urban planning stems from my belief that important civic and institutional interactions will be increasingly computer mediated. This may seem like an obvious statement (and I am certainly not the first to make it), but its implications are far-reaching. It piques the imagination to consider what a more computer-mediated civic life might look like, but it also should cause us to consider more mundane implications. So when planners like Alan and Michelle Shaw note the critical importance of computer networks in our daily lives, they are both intrigued by the possibilities and concerned about how they will play out. Like Anne Beamish, they note that the community computing movement might fail because users are too often passive consumers and never producers. Thus, "neighbors who live in a community often are not active in shaping the social setting that they face daily" because there are few constructive possibilities in the processes that shape that social setting (320). Computer networks, then, can only be helpful if they can be used as productive spaces in the process of "village building" (317), not just as conduits for information dumps and elaborate card catalogs.

The residents of Mechanicsville do not have a history of effective planning participation, but I daresay that few communities have. Planning's rhetorical turn, however, opens a space for new kinds of institutional decision making, and this rhetorical turn also opens a space in which writing researchers, particularly those concerned with professional and technical writing, can support citizen action in a more discursive public space. In order to participate in and change institutional planning procedures, however, citizens must bring something to the table. Computer networks can help, but to do so, those who want to develop these tools must pay attention to their design. And this is where writing researchers can help by conducting the research necessary to create dynamic writing technologies that help build villages.

NOTES

1. The Office of Data and Policy Analysis (DAPA) is one part of The Carter Center's antipoverty program in Atlanta known as The Atlanta Project. DAPA is the primary source of data and policy-related information for communities within The Atlanta Project area.

2. Sandercock's purpose is to use the taxonomy to create space for a sixth, as yet unrealized, theory of urban planning—empowerment planning. However, this sixth theory is not immediately relevant to my present purpose.

3. Atlanta was founded as "Terminus" in 1837 because of its location at the end of the Western and Atlantic railroad. Atlanta grew because of the railroads and quickly became the leading southern rail center just prior to the Civil War.

4. Mechanicsville's working-class character was driven by its link to the rail yards, but a healthy business district and community developed as well. Mechanicsville, in fact, was home to James Haverty, Amos Rhodes, and Morris Rich, names that most Southerners will immediately associate with their well-known furniture businesses and department stores.

5. My favorite example from Johnson's book is the story about traffic flow problems in Seattle. The quick version is this: given increasing traffic congestion, planners in Seattle turned to their experts to plan ways to ease congestion. Using standard methods (e.g., computer models and statistical analyses), planners implemented a solution that failed. Meanwhile, technical writing students from the University of Washington asked the users of the system—the drivers themselves—what they would need to alter their driving patterns and thus ease congestion. Their solution worked.

WORKS CITED

Barndt, Michael. "Transferring Technological Skills in Community Research: Options for GIS." Community Research Network Third Annual Conference. The Loka Institute, Morehouse College, Atlanta, GA. 16 June 2000.

Beamish, Anne. "Approaches to Community Computing: Bringing Technology to Low-Income Groups." *High Technology and Low-Income Communities: Prospects for the Positive Use of Advanced Information Technology.* Ed. Donald A. Schön, Bish Sanyal, and William J. Mitchell. Cambridge, MA: MIT, 1999. 349–69.

Deshler, David, and Merrill Ewert. "Participatory Action Research: Traditions and Major Assumptions." *PARnet.* (1995): Online. Available: <http://www.PARnet. org/parchive/docs/deshler_95/>.

140   JEFFREY T. GRABILL

Ferreira, Joseph, Jr. "Information Technologies that Change Relationships between Low-Income Communities and the Public, and Nonprofit Agencies that Serve Them." *High Technology and Low-Income Communities: Prospects for the Positive Use of Advanced Information Technology.* Ed. Donald A. Schön, Bish Sanyal, and William J. Mitchell. Cambridge, MA: MIT, 1999. 163–89.

Forester, John. *Critical Theory, Public Policy, and Planning Practice.* Albany: SUNY Press, 1993.

Giarrusso, Tony, Janeane Gilbreath, Kathy Tullos, and Larry Keating. "Mechanicsville, Atlanta: History of a Neighborhood Community." Unpublished Manuscript, 2000.

Grabill, Jeffrey T. *Community Literacy Programs and the Politics of Change.* Albany: SUNY Press, 2001.

Hall, Peter. *Cities of Tomorrow: An Intellectual History of Urban Planning and Design in the Twentieth Century.* London: Blackwell, 1996.

Healey, Patsy. *Collaborative Planning: Shaping Places in Fragmented Societies.* Vancouver: UBC, 1997.

Johnson, Robert R. *User-Centered Technology: A Rhetorical Theory of Computers and Other Mundane Artifacts.* Albany: SUNY Press, 1998.

Marris, Peter. "Planning and Civil Society in the Twenty-First Century: An Introduction." *Cities for Citizens: Planning and the Rise of Civil Society in a Global Age.* Ed. Mike Douglass and John Friedmann. Chichester, UK: John Wiley, 1998. 9–17.

Sandercock, Leonie. "The Death of Modernist Planning: Radical Praxis for a Postmodern Age." *Cities for Citizens: Planning and the Rise of Civil Society in a Global Age.* Ed. Mike Douglass and John Friedmann. Chichester, UK: John Wiley, 1998. 163–84.

Sawicki, David S., and William J. Craig. "The Democratization of Data: Bridging the Gap for Community Groups." *APA Journal* 62 (1996): 512–23.

Shaw, Allen, and Michelle Shaw. "Social Power through Community Networks." *High Technology and Low-Income Communities: Prospects for the Positive Use of Advanced Information Technology.* Ed. Donald A. Schön, Bish Sanyal, and William J. Mitchell. Cambridge, MA: MIT, 1999. 315–35.

Sohng, Sue. "Participatory Research and Community Organizing." *New Social Movement Network.* (1995): Online. Available: <http://www.interweb-tech.com/nsm-net/home.htm>.

Short, John Rennie. *The Urban Order: An Introduction to Cities, Culture, and Power.* London: Blackwell, 1996.

CHAPTER NINE

SPEAKING OF THE CITY AND LITERACIES OF PLACE MAKING IN COMPOSITION STUDIES

Richard Marback

Robert Beauregard, an urban planner and public policy theorist, asks a provocative question: "If the city could speak, what would it say to us?" ("If Only" 59). What makes this such a provocative question is the very fact that Beauregard can ask it and that we can imagine answers to it. Theoretically, postmodern discussions of representation have prepared us to listen to the language of objects and things such as cities, to acknowledge that they do somehow speak to us. Culturally, the presence of physical images and signs across the urban landscape has made us accustomed to seeing signification everywhere and to listening for messages from the city. Politically, the seeming concentration in inner cities of our social ills has caused us to listen closely to cities for warnings of further decline and decay. Unfortunately, despite the political, cultural, and theoretical provocations of his question, Beauregard denies that it has any real answer after all. As he puts it, "The city, of course, cannot tell us of its problems or its prospects, its successes or its failures. The city is not a speaking subject. Rather, it is the object of our discourse. We speak for the city; it is spoken about. We say what is good and what is bad, what should be done, when, and by whom. The city is represented; it does not represent itself" ("If Only" 60). Certainly, Beauregard is right. A city is not a speaking subject. It is we humans who are the subjects, who speak for and about cities. Still, his answer has not emptied this question of either its meaningfulness or its value. In asking whether cities can speak, and in answering that cities are objects incapable of speech, Beauregard places emphasis on we who do speak and on the consequences of our speaking for our cities. Through our representations of cities, our calls for civic action, and our laments of the urban condition, we tell ourselves what is good and bad, what should be done, when, and by whom.

As a compositionist working in an urban university (Wayne State was one of the first universities in the United States with a distinctly urban mission), I am drawn to Beauregard's question and to his emphasis on we who speak for cities that do not speak for themselves. His question highlights the power of language over urban space and suggests an important role for compositionists in the making of city life. As scholars and teachers of writing, we can have a say in what our cities become. But Beauregard's question also tempers any claims we might make for the dominant role of our language in the making of city life. Just as the city cannot speak for itself, our speaking cannot by itself make a city. In this chapter, I propose a place for compositionists in the making of city life by following the lead of Beauregard's question. How can we in composition studies speak of the city? What ways of speaking best do the work of composition studies in city spaces? What is the relationship between our ways of speaking and the material existence of cities? These questions force us to think hard about how we represent city spaces through our language and how city spaces condition our language. My claim is that compositionists have not yet balanced the force of rhetoric against the weight of material conditions, and so they also have yet to appreciate just how difficult it is to discuss either the rhetorical dimensions of cities or the urban and spatial dimensions of literacy, rhetoric, and writing.

I begin my discussion with Beauregard for two related reasons. First, since Beauregard is an urban planner, his turn toward rhetoric does not involve a turn away from urban materiality, that is, his articulation of rhetoric with space remains responsive to material issues. Second, Beauregard's seemingly dismissive answer to the question of the city speaking is informed by a much fuller discussion of the complex dynamics of speaking about cities and their realities, a discussion compositionists can use to judge the responsiveness of our talk to the material conditions of urban life. In *Voices of Decline: The Postwar Fate of US Cities,* Beauregard documents the range of discourses— from newspaper and magazine articles to academic books and journal articles to public policy statements and federal legislation—that speak about the decline of U.S. cities since 1945. He demonstrates that these discourses of decline weave a web of meanings that catches our attention, yet this web has open spaces, inconsistencies, even rips and tears. The discourses do not all agree, do not all overlap, and do not all directly, or even indirectly, support each other. By keeping his attention focused on the multiple discourses of we who speak for and about cities, Beauregard is able to discern the force that such multivocalic speaking has on the object itself. Cities may not speak for themselves, but in speaking for cities we do indeed transform them. Beauregard writes,

> This is not just talk, not just rumination on who we are, what we might be, and who is deserving. The discourse not only influences people's perceptions, it also shapes the choices they make in response. The discourse contains practical advice as to how people—households, investors, business owners, elected officials—can best cope with the consequences of the decline of the cities. Here we find another connection between representation and reality. Following this connection leads us to the discourse's ideological core. (*Voices* 300)

As Beauregard says, speaking the meaning of cities is an ideological act, so much so that many of those discourses have become, over time, inscribed into the spaces of cities themselves. We can never walk into a cityscape that has not already been inscribed by others and that is not always already inscribed on us. Recognizing that our speaking about cities has an impact on how cities are understood, manipulated, represented, and occupied, Beauregard has moved into the space of ideology, a space between subject and object where each influences, extends, and occupies the other. A space of discourse, of language, of representation, and of rhetoric, it has long been the space of composition studies. And, as I argue below, it is through the space of ideology that compositionists can best enter the city.

IDEOLOGY AND PLACE IN COMPOSITION STUDIES

Beauregard's claim for the ideological dynamic between rhetoric and reality has resonance for compositionists, and no one more than James Berlin has articulated the uses of discourse in the formation of ideologies and the influence of those discourses on perceptions of reality. In this section, I discuss briefly the work of James Berlin as representative of a general understanding among compositionists of the relationships among rhetoric, ideology, and reality. I then describe how Ellen Cushman has extended that understanding of rhetoric, ideology, and reality to encompass urban environments. I discuss Berlin and Cushman because I consider their work representative of larger trends in the discourse of composition studies that have turned our attention to speaking about cities.

For Berlin, as for Beauregard, we are subjects who speak about and for material objects, such as cities, and in that speaking we orient our attention toward each other, our actions, and our world. In "Revisionary History," for instance, Berlin writes, "On the one hand are the material and social conditions of society, on the other are the political and cultural. It is rhetoric—discourse—that mediates between the two, forming the core of a society's educational activities . . . and this is true whether we are discussing ancient Athens or modern Detroit" (52). Berlin argues throughout his books and articles that the ideological work of rhetoric lies in making the material resources and social conditions of society available for specific political ends. In *Rhetorics, Poetics, and Cultures,* Berlin identifies the rhetorical character of ideology, explaining that ideology "addresses and shapes" who we are as subjects through discourses that "offer directives about three important domains of experience: what exists, what is good, and what is possible" (78). By making explicit the ways in which rhetorical practices direct, influence, and distribute material and social resources, Berlin identifies avenues for compositionists to intervene in the political powers and cultural values that mediate material existence.

The furor over the 1996 Oakland Ebonics Resolution is a case in point. William Labov testified before a Congressional subcommittee investigating the Ebonics Resolution that the increased difference between the language of African Americans in the inner city and other dialects correlates with increasing residential segregation ("Testimony"). Thus, the difference in language use between African Americans in inner cities and others living elsewhere is directly caused by their geographic isolation from each other. We can say, then, that the rhetoric of contempt for the Ebonics Resolution expresses the experiences and attitudes of people largely isolated from inner city African Americans, and what critics have come to accept as real, good, and possible in this debate is a function of geography, of where they are and with whom they interact. In *American Apartheid,* Douglas Massey and Nancy Denton affirm Labov's point in terms of the material conditions of segregation. Massey and Denton document and explain how policies and practices of racial segregation organize poor African Americans in inner cities. Spatial isolation of poor African Americans limits their interactions with others to interactions that are hierarchically arranged, that are racially stereotyped, and that reinforce their ghettoization. As an intervention, the Oakland Ebonics Resolution proposed new possibilities in literacy education for rearticulating ideologies of power—our senses of the real, good, and possible—thus unlinking policies and practices of racial segregation from the geography of residential isolation.

Ellen Cushman's community-based research begins to imagine new possibilities for compositionists interested in such ideological work, yet at the same time, Cushman's attempt to renegotiate the spaces of literacy in an inner city neighborhood illustrates the limits of speaking about the ideological and spatial dynamics of cities. Near the beginning of *The Struggle and the Tools,* Cushman echoes Berlin in identifying the central role of ideology in structuring the material and social constraints of discursive interactions: "During face-to-face interactions with institutional agents, their [i.e., members of

Quayville's inner city community] struggle is both material and ideological. The tools are the linguistic strategies that these individuals use to navigate institutions in wider society and negotiate the struggles" (4). The material struggle for Quayville residents is a struggle for resources in an inner city environment that is geographically isolated, a space that physically prohibits the equitable distribution of resources. Confirming the cycle of segregation and discrimination described by Massey and Denton, Cushman documents how the spatial organization of unequal resource distribution is institutionally legitimized and maintained through stratifications of class and race. Yet unlike Massey and Denton, Cushman describes struggles for redistribution of material resources as struggles for the rhetorical strategies necessary to counter ideologies of segregation by gaining respect from institutional representatives. Here Cushman reduces the material and ideological to the rhetorical, rather than retaining the tensions among the material and rhetorical that manifest ideology. This is a point worth careful consideration. Talking about material inequality and racial discrimination in Quayville as problems addressable through discursive intervention is a way of talking about the city that has important consequences for what compositionists believe is good and possible for us to do in cities.

Cushman's desire for rhetorical interventions into the ideological practices and spatial organization of city life frames a central question near the end of her book, a question from which she proposes strategies for community work in composition studies: "How can gatekeepers and community members gather, select, and deploy the rhetorical tools necessary to promote the social and political equality of those seeking resources in the gatekeeping encounter?" (170). In many ways, the question is one of how people speak for and about a city—here, Quayville—and in that speaking represent the state of sociopolitical inequality and the related inequality of resource allocation, asserting the legitimacy of each other's demands, questioning practices of distribution, and negotiating possible reallocations of resources and respect.

Unfortunately, this form of the question also oversimplifies the multiple imbrications of ideologies in practices, spaces, and rhetorics. As Labov explained in his testimony on the Ebonics debate, the spatial organization of cities concentrates victims of poverty and contempt for these victims in inner cities, exerting the weight of physical segregation on both our practices and our rhetorics. As it is phrased, Cushman's question ignores the pressures of geographic isolation on rhetorics that segregate. It asks only about the possibilities for gaining respect and resources for the poor through a rearticulation of rhetoric; it does not ask about the articulations of space that structure residents' distinct, though interdependent, demands for respect and resources in the first place. Thus, Cushman's question shifts attention away from the force exerted by residential segregation and racial isolation on the unequal distribution of resources and respect so that the goal of intervention becomes the minimal goal of learning to speak differently. Relieved of the burden of materiality, the ideological struggle first identified by Cushman is lost to the claim for a fair share of rhetorical agency.

The difficulty inherent in engaging simultaneously in ideological struggle and in enabling broader access to rhetorical agency is all too familiar to compositionists and urban planners alike. As Beauregard explains, planning practitioners work primarily with urban constituencies who have very pragmatic concerns, but planners also work from within a discipline that increasingly theorizes such work in critical terms, terms that challenge planning practitioners to pay closer attention to power and privilege as these are exercised both spatially and rhetorically (*Voices*, xi). Learning to attend to space as much as to language, and to their influence on each other, compositionists can, like urban planners, bring together the goals of critical theory and the goals of community involvement by asking questions about rhetorical agency in specific urban settings in terms of the social and physical spaces of ideological struggle.

Urban planners who are interested in issues of ideology and who are working for a democratization of planning practice provide some terms useful to compositionists searching for nonreductive rhetorical strategies of city life. In his 1973 book *Social Justice and the City*, David Harvey sets an agenda for subsequent urban planning theory:

> We must relate social behaviour to the way in which the city assumes a certain geography, a certain spatial form. We must recognize that once a particular spatial form is created it tends to institutionalize and, in some respects, to determine the future development of social process. We need, above all, to formulate concepts which will allow us to harmonize and integrate strategies to deal with the intricacies of social process and the elements of spatial form. (27)

For urban planners such as Harvey, the spatial form of cities is the physically present material manifestation of social processes that are rhetorically mediated; or, as Beauregard puts it, urban life is a matter of how, when, and where we speak for and about the city. Understood in this way, the work of planning is to speak and to listen, to rhetorically re-mediate social processes and spatial forms so as to counter their hegemony and make possible more just relationships, processes, and forms without disregarding the exertions of spatial form and social process.

For compositionists, the rhetorical mediation of social processes and spatial forms is characterized most usefully through the concept of place making. As urban planners Lynda Schneekloth and Robert Shibley use the term, place making is a material act of building and maintaining spaces that is at the same time an ideological act of fashioning places where we can feel we belong, where we create meaning, and where we organize our relationships with others. Place making "embodies a vision of who we are and offers a hope of what we want to be as individuals and as groups who share a place in the world" (191). Here, we become aware that how we speak, what we say, how it is heard, and what consequences it has structure the places we occupy at the same time that the places we occupy determine how we speak, what we say, and how it is heard. Words and our uses of words assign significance to the places out of which and about which we speak. Our words also establish relationships between ourselves and others within the spaces of our cities. We justify going here and not there, so we convince ourselves of the need of a road here or a wall there. And as the Oakland Ebonics controversy demonstrates, we believe we are right in acknowledging these people over here and ignoring those people (because they are) over there. More than this, the concept of place making suggests that our justifications, convictions, and beliefs are as much a function of what we do and where we are as they are of what we say and to whom we say it. We go here and not there, we acknowledge these people and not those, in part because our environments constrain our choices. Place making constructs an understanding of places out of the actions, objects, and words we use when we occupy a space and fill it with meaning. Using the concept of place making, compositionists can engage the spatial dimensions of what Berlin calls the nondiscursive "formations designating the shape of social and political structures, the nature and role of the individual within these structures, and the distribution of power in society" (*Rhetoric* 4). Place making creates opportunities for using rhetoric to address issues of recognition and resources by asking us to imagine new possibilities for occupying places through a critical rearticulation of actions, objects, and words.

So Beauregard is still right—our cities cannot speak. We cannot put an ear to the ground to hear the voice of the city exclaim its decline or pronounce its renewal. But in the process of coming to terms with the fact that it is we who speak for our cities, urban planners such as Beauregard and Schneekloth and Shibley demonstrate that there is no clear and simple distinction between the subject who speaks and the object that is spoken about. Letting go of the subject/object binary, urban planners have moved onto the provocative ground of place making, where actions, attitudes, objects, spaces, values, and words intertwine. As Schneekloth and Shibley put it, place making "is about everything, because the making and sustaining of place is about living—about places, meanings, knowledges, and actions" (18).

I know of no more striking example of place making than the Heidelberg Project on the near east side of Detroit. An internationally renowned art installation, topic of documentary films, tourist destination for visitors to Detroit, subject of local debate, ground for legal actions, and, some say, an eyesore and health hazard, the Heidelberg Project exists across a number of discourses. It is a place that is made through multiple literacies. At the same time, the Heidelberg Project is a physical space that exerts force on those discourses, demonstrating all too clearly the voice of the object in the subjects who speak it. In the next section, I draw on the Heidelberg Project in order to illustrate some possibilities for the concept of place making in composition studies.

COMPOSITION STUDIES AND
LITERACIES OF PLACE MAKING

How can we identify and enact rhetorics that connect material and ideological struggles over spaces with representational practices? This question asks compositionists to enter cities attentive to the dynamics of place making and to the ways in which people assign meaningfulness to places. As I have argued, such attention is important if we are to do the work of rhetoric in city spaces, spaces such as the Heidelberg Project, where meaningfulness is achieved through multiple objects, actions, and discourses. The Heidelberg Project embodies a kind of urban struggle with meanings, a struggle expressed through competing claims about how best to (re)occupy inner city Detroit. But all is not language. The Heidelberg Project also takes shape through the objects that constitute it and the activities within and around it, even though people assert its significance by evaluating, describing, and responding to these objects and activities. More than physical reality, the Heidelberg Project is not simply the pavement of Heidelberg Street covered with brightly colored polka dots; nor is it the worn out, discarded shoes that line the sidewalk, stretching from one corner of the block to the other; nor is it the houses adorned with pieces of billboards, road signs, children's toys, and other discarded items. More than the sum of its material parts, the Heidelberg Project is an event as well as a debate about the meanings of inner city blight and urban renewal.

The material and ideological act of assembling refuse into art objects takes place in a cultural and historic space that overdetermines who occupies Detroit. The physical decay of the city began as early as the 1950s with the postwar suburban building boom. Detroit's decline continued in the 1960s as racial tensions escalated white flight. With the recession of the 1970s, jobs and residents continued to leave the city. From the 1980s on, racial animus isolated the city government from regional cooperation with virtually all suburban officials. Today, Detroit is a city of less than a million residents, mostly African American, surrounded by a suburban periphery of more than three million people. It is pointless to ask which came first, the residential segregation or the racial antagonism. For whites living in the suburbs of Detroit, the 1967 riots account for their life outside of and apart from the city and justify the plight of the poor African Americans they left behind. In fact, narratives of the riots are so pervasive and persuasive that area residents, both black and white, who were born after 1967, continue to use the riots to explain local segregation and to justify their experiences of it. In this way, very real events have become rhetorical tropes.

Tyree Guyton created the Heidelberg Project to challenge the efficient elision of meanings that make the place of inner city Detroit into abandoned evidence justifying white flight and suburbanization. Prior to 1986, the year he started assembling found art objects on Heidelberg Street (thereby transforming the street into a project), the abandoned buildings near his home had become criminalized spaces taken over by drug dealers. The area had become just another villainized inner city space. Guyton began to collect debris from around the city, bringing it to his street and assembling it into found art objects. One of his first creations, the Fun House, was an abandoned house that Guyton, his wife, and his grandfather decorated with pieces of discarded toys and broken dolls. By reinscribing the criminalized and villainized spaces of his street, Guyton dislodged the abandoned houses and vacant lots from the rhetorics that explain and justify the abandonment of inner city Detroit. By asserting meaning through a reclamation of refuse dumped in the city, he made it difficult for people to draw on dominant narratives of decline and decay to disregard him or his neighborhood. Eventually, he began to mark the buildings in the area with large purple, pink, yellow, and blue polka dots, symbols of "a coming together of the races" and "universal harmony." Terms such as "urban blight" and "inner city poverty" seem not to apply here. The Hoods, car hoods painted with faces and propped up against the trees and houses, and Noah's Ark, an old speedboat piled high with tossed-out stuffed animals, are just two of the works that defy easy description and so challenge our reductive generalization of this space as just another inner city neighborhood.

As an act of place making, the many objects collected on Heidelberg Street have heightened awareness of issues of life for the urban poor and have challenged the ways we talk about inner cities. The Heidelberg Project has been the subject of several films and one cable television documentary. In addition, many observers of cities have turned to the Heidelberg Project as a site for re-articulating the cultural politics of contemporary urban life. In his essay, "Making Sense of Detroit," David Sheridan explains that the Heidelberg Project "speaks through a 'corrupted' (visual) language, an idiom of refuse, junk, and dereliction; it is a text composed in a grapholect of orphaned object-words whose etymologies are saturated with violence of all kinds" (341). Sheridan goes on to characterize this violent language as a coming to terms with the city as it is, "an example of a city becoming accustomed to its sores, embracing the very things that it should be embarrassed about" (343). Similarly, Jerry Herron has accounted for the visual language of the Heidelberg Project in terms of the failure of our words to express the contradictions of inner cities. Observing that "description can only go so far in conveying the impact of Guyton's project" (199), Herron explains the partial demolition of parts of the project by city workers as an effort to eliminate a place that exposes the contingency of conventional narratives of decline and renewal. As Herron puts it, "By 'turning their neighborhood inside out,' Guyton and his wife and grandfather mock the failure of the historical city to conserve either objects or people; they humiliate the presumptive authority of representative culture. This is why their material insights have themselves been submitted to violent erasure" (201). In less esoteric terms, Detroit residents also struggle for the words to make sense out of the Heidelberg Project in light of their experiences of blight and renewal. As just one example, restaurateur Tom Schoenith asks why city officials are more concerned with demolishing Guyton's work than with tearing down a building abandoned over a decade ago near his restaurant, "I wish the city would tear down that building instead of this. . . . I wish they'd move all this stuff to my corner in place of the abandoned building. This stuff is junk, but it's pretty junk" (Hurt).

The "junk" is hard to make sense of and to talk about. But that is the point. To the extent that the Heidelberg Project has generated a search for a new language of place making, to the extent that it has fostered among Detroit-area residents a discussion about the meanings of urban renewal, Guyton has transformed rhetorics with which we speak for and about inner cities. Making his street in particular into a different place, he has reconnected the experience of inner city life with the material conditions of life under late capitalism, disorganizing the spatial relationship between objects of consumption and acts of living in and around a postindustrial city. For example, the great mass of bicycle frames that form the Bicycle Tree stand as a reminder of objects of consumption widely available elsewhere and easily discarded here. Some of the bicycle frames are bent and broken. All of them are missing wheels and tires. Many do not have handlebars or seats or pedals. They are wrapped around a large elm tree, reaching twelve to fifteen feet up the trunk, spreading in a tangle several feet out around the base. Arranging the bicycles as he has, Guyton makes them into an aesthetic object, reorganizing our attention to the discarded objects, drawing us into spaces that we otherwise disregard and that we have generally filled with what we no longer want. As he explained in an article about his art in *Newsweek*, "Putting art right here for them has made the people more conscious of themselves" (qtd. in Plagens 64).

The sheer weight and volume of the Bicycle Tree, the Hoods, Noah's Ark, the Dotty Wotty House, the OJ House, the Number House, and all the Polka Dots overwhelm anyone who walks down Heidelberg Street. People cannot help but become conscious of themselves in proportion to the scale of Guyton's work and of the enormity of the waste out of which he creates his art. As

Guyton has subsequently put it, he wanted to create art drawn from the lives of the urban poor, art that would "activate thoughts and feelings inside of people about issues and problems that have been too long ignored, written off, put on hold, discarded and given up on. . . . The art would carry them across the barriers that often isolate people from one another. The art would be the bridge" ("Heidelberg Project"). In a very real way, the art is a bridge. The Heidelberg Project brings people together who are otherwise isolated from each other. On any given day or night, the people on Heidelberg Street are busloads of students from outlying schools, foreign auto executives in Detroit on business, and visitors from the suburbs, all of them out of place in this inner city neighborhood. Being here, these people become more aware of the experiences of the urban poor. But the people sharing the space of Heidelberg Street do not necessarily engage each other in productive discussions of urban decline, nor do they by themselves transform the disabling rhetorics of city space. More often than not, what people have to say draws from expectations they have brought here from elsewhere, or from awareness of mass media discourses that tell us what a neighborhood should be. Even some of Guyton's own neighbors, who do not appreciate the traffic and the accumulated debris, hold up handwritten signs proclaiming, "If you think it's art, take it back to your own neighborhood."

The protestors have a point. As physical objects, the painted car hoods, tangled bicycle frames, and broken appliances are just so much junk. And while it is "pretty junk" that has aesthetic value and cultural significance in inner city Detroit, it is junk that would signify little more than deviance anywhere else. Questioning the privilege of visitors, angry local residents call into question the consumption of the inner city as a commodity. Again, the point is a reasonable one. As an object, the Heidelberg Project has brought people into Detroit, but it has not otherwise improved the material conditions of those people already living there. Even though the drug dealers now avoid the neighborhood and Guyton maintains the area by mowing the vacant lots and clearing the sidewalk of litter, these are insignificant gains for people interested in quality housing, uncluttered streets, safe neighborhoods, and reliable public services. In a way, Guyton's neighbors are demanding the same respect for property and the same access to privilege that is available just beyond the city limits. Heidelberg Street residents who challenge visitors to take some of the "trash" with them when they leave are less interested in a critique of privilege and more interested in access to that privilege.

This is not to say that the signs are not critical. They do ask visitors to consider why they have come here and to think about where they have come from. But the critique falls short of questioning the values of cleanliness that seem to apply everywhere except here. Further, the signs do not question how the ideological functioning of cleanliness in our culture contributes to making the Heidelberg Project the third most visited tourist attraction in the Detroit area. Still, the poignancy of neighbors' signs draws from their inherent claim for a fair share of well-kempt streets and lawns. Why can't they have clean, well-maintained streets? Why must they live with abandoned houses and vacant lots? Why does the interest of visitors in preserving the aesthetic value of the Heidelberg Project outweigh residents' interest in realizing some kind of normalcy? Why should they be forced to live with bicycles piled around trees and car hoods propped up in yards?

Guyton raises related questions. Why should he be forced to live with abandoned houses? Why is his city a dumping ground for the refuse of mass consumption? These questions ask for different answers than those raised by his neighbors. Guyton expressly describes his art as a challenge to the abandonment and blight of his inner city neighborhood, as he puts it, "a new creation out of chaos." The ideological critique inherent in Guyton's spatial reorganization of objects competes with the less critical, but no less important, claims of angry neighbors who think that resource redistribution will make the difference. But in his version of it, the question is not one of building order by bringing in material resources from elsewhere. His question asks for a transformation of the material and ideological conditions that distribute respect unevenly. For Guyton, the conditions must change before the resources can make a difference.

In conversations, Guyton consistently claims that one of the successes of his installation is that it has created an opportunity for people to talk about the issues. However, while it is true that people are talking about the issues, it is not clear that they are getting anywhere. In 1989, Guyton was presented with the Spirit of Detroit Award, in recognition of his work on the Heidelberg Project and its contributions to life in the city. In 1991, the mayor of Detroit ordered the demolition of parts of the project occupying city property. Over the last ten years, the cycle of recognition and condemnation has continued: Guyton has continued to receive local, regional, and international recognition at the same time that he continues to fight a protracted legal battle with the city of Detroit in an attempt to preserve what remains of the Heidelberg Project.

Whatever the final fate of the Dotty Wotty House, the OJ House, the Number House, or any of the other objects that make up the installation, the debate over the Heidelberg Project has escalated because we cannot speak for and about the city in ways that critically engage the spatial organization of resource distribution and respect. As Marion Jackson stated in a letter to Detroit Mayor Dennis Archer during the latest public debate about Guyton's creation, "I too am a citizen of Detroit and live within a short drive of the Heidelberg Project. I am strongly supportive of the Project and would be deeply embarrassed for our city if the Heidelberg Project were to be destroyed a second time, this time in the bright light of the national press and confirming in the eyes of our detractors that Detroit has little tolerance or imagination for innovation in the arts and insufficient ability or will to open a dialogue to address our differences" ("Heidelberg"). Jackson's insight is to recognize that the issues raised by the Heidelberg Project are issues of how we speak for and about the city. Speaking for and about the Heidelberg Project, Guyton, his supporters, his detractors, cultural critics, and Detroit City Council, all want—in their own ways—to win recognition for the plight of inner city residents and to gain access to material resources for urban renewal. Here, the limits of tolerance and imagination are the limits of our rhetorics, the limits of how we speak about such places as inner city Detroit and about such things as neighborhood revitalization and urban renewal. Our collective capacity to deliberate about the Heidelberg Project is limited by material conditions and ideological assertions that defy traditional expectations for renewal, even as those expectations are affirmed as realistic. Acts of tolerance and imagination that would resolve the contradictions of Heidelberg Street would redirect the debate by differently articulating expectations and realities.

To do this work, it is not enough to listen to the claims of those who call the Heidelberg Project junk and want it hauled away or to consider the claims of those who call it art and want it preserved. Invoking the concept of place making, compositionists can work to provide words that rhetorically rearticulate the spatially disconnected demands for resources and respect. As a strategy for rhetoric, place making draws all sides into a conversation that begins by acknowledging the legitimacy of all claims, that proceeds by sorting through the spatial processes and rhetorical practices that (de)legitimate these claims in relation to each other, and that ends by (re)legitimating claims for resources and respect as these are rhetorically rearticulated with each other. This means confirming the experiences of neighbors who do not want to live with the junk. It also means facilitating an interrogation of what it means not to want to live with the junk. It means involving everyone in a discussion about the kind of place they would like to make of Heidelberg Street, which also means finding ways to extend concern with dismantling (or preserving) Guyton's creation to encompass concern for dismantling and reconstructing ideological, material, and rhetorical constraints on the making of inner city places.

In the composition classroom, the Heidelberg Project has become the focus of my own curriculum and pedagogy, teaching writing as an act of place making that elides issues of historical narrative and residential segregation. Here, I would like to discuss a writing assignment that asks students to work through the meanings acquired by the Heidelberg Project. My brief discussion so far demonstrates the breadth and depth of the language used to make sense of Guyton's work. In this assignment, students go to Heidelberg Street and talk to Tyree Guyton and to his neighbors. Students then view documentaries and sift through newspaper and magazine articles focusing on the Heidelberg Project. After viewing and reading all of this material, the assignment asks students to explain the place that the Heidelberg Project becomes for them and for their community through its multiple representations and interpretations.

Recalling Beauregard's point that our talk about cities is incomplete, inconsistent, and contradictory, at the same time that it is consequential, the purpose of the assignment is to not rush to any summary conclusions. The dynamics of rhetoric, space, and ideology are too complex for that. Rather, the purpose is for students to use the many claims for what the Heidelberg Project means in order to explicitly locate it in debates, which involves further locating the debates in concerns, histories, interests, struggles, or even values. So the Heidelberg Project is important because it brings together and concentrates discourses about what matters most to us in our lives together. Students writing through the conflicts and contradictions of those discourses cannot help but inhabit the discourses and the Heidelberg Project with an enlarged sense of what others bring to the debate and of what our obligations to each other might be.

But the work of place making in composition studies does not lie exclusively with resolving the conflict over the Heidelberg Project or in the goal of teaching students spatial literacy practices. It lies as well in the capacity of compositionists to use theories to (re)locate and (re)define issues in rhetoric as issues of space. It lies in learning to ask, and to answer, such questions as, How can we identify and enact rhetorics that connect material and ideological struggles over spaces with the physical and representational practices of occupying particular places? There is really no one final answer to this question. There are too many different ways in which we speak for and about cities, too many different sites for us to speak about, too many different things that need to be said. We need not be daunted by this multiplicity, and we need not oversimplify the problem in our quest for a resolution. Place making provides a rhetorical framework for answering the question as we need to answer it, when we need to answer it. Beauregard is right, our cities cannot speak for themselves. He is also right that in the void left by their silence, we do a lot of speaking for and about them. And, as the Heidelberg Project illustrates, we do not say all that we can say, or need to say, to raise concerns for our lives in cities. Still, as much as problems of city life are problems of our speaking for cities, the prospects for making cities into just places lie in our continued commitment to speak for and about where we are with each other.

WORKS CITED

Beauregard, Robert A. "If Only the City Could Speak: The Politics of Representation." *Spatial Practices: Critical Explorations in Social/Spatial Theory.* Ed. Helen Liggett and David C. Perry. Thousand Oaks, CA: Sage, 1995. 59–80.

———. *Voices of Decline: The Postwar Fate of US Cities.* Cambridge, MA: Blackwell, 1993.

Berlin, James. "Revisionary History: The Dialectical Method." *Pre/Text* 8 (1987): 47–62.

———. *Rhetoric and Reality.* Carbondale: Southern Illinois UP, 1988.

———. *Rhetorics, Poetics, and Cultures.* Urbana: NCTE, 1996.

Cushman, Ellen. *The Struggle and the Tools: Oral and Literate Strategies in an Inner City Community.* Albany: SUNY Press, 1998.

Harvey, David. *Social Justice and the City.* Cambridge, MA: Blackwell, 1988.

The Heidelberg Project. 2 October 2000. <http://www.heidelberg.org>.

Herron, Jerry. *AfterCulture: Detroit and the Humiliation of History.* Detroit: Wayne State UP, 1993.

Hurt, Charles. "Heidelberg Project Comes Down Next Week." *The Detroit News* 18 September 1998: Online. Available: <http://www.detroitnews.com>.

Jackson, Marion. Letter to Mayor Dennis Archer. N.d. "What People Are Saying." 2 October 2000. <http://www.heidelberg.org>.

Labov, William. "Testimony on Ebonics." 23 January 1997. The Ebonics Controversy. <http://www.ling.upenn.edu/~labov/L102/Ebonics_test.html>.

Massey, Douglas S., and Nancy A. Denton. *American Apartheid: Segregation and the Making of the Underclass.* Cambridge: Harvard UP, 1993.

Plagen, Peter, with Frank Washington. "Come On-a My House." *Newsweek* 6 August 1990: 64.

Schneekloth, Lynda H., and Robert G. Shibley. *Placemaking: The Art and Practice of Building Communities.* New York: John Wiley, 1995.

Sheridan, David M. "Making Sense of Detroit." *Michigan Quarterly Review* 38 (1999): 321–53.

PART III

REDEFINING PRACTICES

CHAPTER TEN

COMPOSITION BY IMMERSION

Writing Your Way into a
Mission-Driven University

David A. Jolliffe

In an apocryphal story, Oscar Wilde, a graduate of Magdalen College at
Oxford, is asked what he learned at the university. Wilde describes a time
when one of his professors, the famous social activist and critic John Ruskin,
urged the university men to stop spending their energy on idle athletic pur-
suits and instead to use their muscle helping him build a road to Hinksey
Ferry, a village on the outskirts of Oxford. For several weeks in the autumn of
1875, Wilde joined in this enterprise, taking pleasure in loading dirt into "Mr.
Ruskin's especial wheelbarrow" (Ellman 49). Legend has it that Wilde
referred to building the road as "the only thing I learned at Oxford."
    In this tale, Wilde, to be sure, is simply being Wilde, displaying his out-
landishly quotable persona. Nonetheless, I have frequently longed for a way to
infuse the spirit of this story into college writing instruction. Two reasons
motivate this longing. First, the tale sees the value of higher education—its
only value, in Wilde's flippant estimation—as *purposeful action*, rather than
solely as *contemplative practice*. Second, the story embraces the idea of higher
education as *immersion*, an immediate, demanding-all-your-resources-at-once
response, rather than as *seriation*, where schooling proceeds bit by bit, skill by
skill, credit hour by credit hour. I realize, of course, that education at all levels, higher included, cannot simply be purposeful action alone; theoretically
grounded instruction and contemplation must precede, accompany, and follow
action. And I know, of course, that education at all levels, higher included,

must proceed serially. Though Ann Berthoff reminds us of the *at-once-ness* of composition, of a writer's need to know everything he or she might eventually learn about writing right from the start, I acknowledge that novice writers have to learn and develop over time. Depending on how the composition curriculum breaks the subject into component parts (and has anyone ever settled on the *best* way to do so?), students must proceed apace, learning first sentences, then paragraphs, then whole compositions, or first narrative writing, then descriptive, then expository, then argumentative, or first expressive writing, then transactional writing, or first process, then product, and so on.

These concessions notwithstanding, I find myself muttering Thoreau: "Simplify, simplify." What if college writing instruction were more of an experience and less of a class? What if we, as instructors, simply told students to "go, learn, do, and write"? If they wrote extensively and we interacted well with them and their writing, would they learn as much about writing as if they took a three-hour-a-week, semester-long composition class?

Fortunately, at DePaul University in Chicago, we are not faced with an either/or choice. All of our 1900–plus entering first-year students take a relatively traditional, two-course college composition sequence, the first course an introduction to academic writing in general and the second an introduction to researched argumentation. In these courses, students learn to compose like college students in general. In addition, all entering first-year students take one of two versions of a writing-intensive, experiential seminar designed to introduce them both to a particular issue or theme that influences the life of Chicago and also to the intellectual resources its citizens use to address this issue or theme. The two versions of the seminar are called Discover Chicago and Explore Chicago. Their principal difference is that Discover Chicago begins the autumn term with an "immersion week," a stretch of six days when the class meets all day from 9 A.M. to 6 P.M., and Explore Chicago meets during the regular class hours of the autumn term only. During the Discover Chicago immersion week, students are out in the city—visiting sites, talking to people, getting their hands into the issue or theme that their particular section of the seminar is investigating. During this week, the students read, write, discuss, contemplate, take public transportation, walk, and talk. In Discover Chicago, students not only work on and with their writing—they *compose* texts—but they also *compose themselves* as DePaul students in particular, writing themselves, ideally, into an integrated, personal understanding of the mission of the university they have chosen to attend and their own potential role in fulfilling it.

I want to argue that Discover Chicago is a kind of composition course, one that emphasizes the connection of writing to the construction of knowledge and one that immerses students in a writing-intensive environment. I want to maintain, as well, that a course such as Discover Chicago represents an ideal, and imitable, vehicle for colleges and universities to use to prepare their students to succeed as readers and writers throughout their undergraduate years and beyond, especially if the college or university has a distinctive mission that is manifest in its undergraduate curriculum.

WHAT MAKES A COURSE A
COLLEGE COMPOSITION COURSE?

What elements need to be present in a college-level course for it to qualify as a composition course? Certainly just naming a course *composition* does not suffice. Obviously, there must be extensive student writing. How much? That, of course, is a thorny question. Twenty or so pages of "processed," revised writing in a term? Clearly, neither the name of the course nor the volume of student writing amounts to a defining criterion. What else must a course have for it to "count" as college composition? Let me sketch out three potential answers.

James L. Kinneavy, in a chapter surveying the influences of Plato, Isocrates, and Aristotle on current teaching, provides the outlines of the first answer. Kinneavy represents the elements of composition pedagogy in a circular diagram. His chapter proposes, initially, that the elements are not static and fixed but are flexible and recursive, and, second, that each of the three classical rhetorical theorists influences composition pedagogies differently; that is, the works of Plato, Isocrates, and Aristotle each suggest a different way into and through the circle of activities. But let's examine Kinneavy's diagram in the abstract, without the influence of any of the classical theorists mapped onto it.

Kinneavy maintains that a composition course essentially can have five elements: it can 1) provide examples of writing, 2) offer students the opportunity to analyze these examples, 3) explain principles of various types—rhetorical, linguistic, literary, and so on—underlying writing, 4) provide students with an environment that fosters writing and stimulates response, and 5) sponsor a process, sketched out (perhaps too simply and sequentially) as "Think-Write-Edit-Rewrite" (73). Kinneavy explains that not all composition pedagogies order these elements in the same way. A pedagogy influenced by Aristotle, for example, begins by teaching students principles underlying good writing, then shows students examples and leads them through analysis, and then moves to the environment and stimulus and the think-write-edit-rewrite process activities (73).

No matter what qualms one has about the potential oversimplicity of Kinneavy's characterization of process, his diagram can serve as a kind of baseline checklist for what a college-level course must have (or ignore for theoretically justifiable reasons) in order for it to count as composition: examples, analysis, principles, environment and stimulus, and process. A course that assembles and orders these elements in a way that could be supported by, say, rhetorical, linguistic, literary, or psychological theory could be said to teach students to compose.

But compose to what end, one might ask? Implicit in the answer to this question is a second criterion for what a college-level course must do for it to count as composition. Consider this scenario: in a particular course, students read, say, *The Great Gatsby*, study an example of a thesis-driven paper about the symbolism of the light at the end of the pier, learn principles about writing themes about literature, then experience a classroom environment in which the teacher lectures about the symbolism of the eyes of Dr. T. J. Eckleburg and directs the students to write a thesis-driven paper about this symbolism. Would any teacher of college composition say that such a scenario is commonplace in his or her course? Would a course dominated by such pedagogy count as college composition? Probably not. In a course such as this, students would have scant opportunities to use their writing to *construct* knowledge; instead, most of their writing would be devoted to *reproduction* of knowledge that they gained from listening to lectures, reading, experimentation, or observation. As my colleagues and I argue, what makes writing instruction authentic is not simply its attention to text structure, form, and correctness, but its insistence that students learn to use their writing to interpret, analyze, synthesize, or evaluate information and to elaborate their constructions with examples, illustrations, and details (Sisserson, Manning, Knepler, and Jolliffe). In other words, a college-level composition course must embrace the composition of knowledge, not simply the composition of paragraphs, sentences, and words.

The first two criteria for what a college-level composition course must do describe how and what such courses teach students to compose. But another kind of composition also happens in these classes. Composition courses are always embedded in a particular institutional culture of the university or college where they are being offered, a culture infused with a discourse that both reflects and constrains the social, epistemological, and rhetorical practices of both students and faculty. As a result, students in these courses not only *compose* but are also *composed* themselves. They learn not only how to write but also how to behave—academically, intellectually, sometimes even socially—in the ways their institution wants them to behave. They learn what kind of student they must become in order to take up a literacy-rich project in that particular college or university—to choose a topic worth investigating, to read critically and write clearly and persuasively, to participate in class discussions and group work, to produce the genres that are recognized and honored in the institution, and so on. This discursive shaping of students as literate participants in the institution need not be viewed pejoratively, as some kind of manipulation or brainwashing. In the best of peda-gogical circumstances, students are not only composed as certain kinds of writers, readers, speakers, and listeners, but are also infused with a critical awareness that they are being so influenced.

Innovative faculty members who have incorporated community service into composition courses (e.g., Bacon) have noted how the students' writing projects help to compose them as responsible, effective contributors to the community. In the same vein, faculty members who have called upon their composition students to produce real genres of genuine public discourse (e.g., Ervin, Heilker) have pointed out how the students' work composes them as nascent, yet responsible, citizen orators. I maintain, however, that no element, such as community service or public discourse, needs to be added to a com-position course for it to discursively form students into the type of writers, the type of literate people, who will fit best in the particular institution. At a uni-versity in the western United States affiliated with a conservative religious denomination, for example, composition students devote part of their course to working on a major essay about an incident that taught them important moral laws. The composition course, perhaps tacitly, strives to compose them as people who consciously reflect on how their personal moral codes influence their lives. At Purdue University in the late 1980s, James Berlin developed a first-year composition program that explicitly tried to compose students as cultural critics of the material conditions that surround them. College com-position courses can never be content-free. Students must read and write about something, and the topics and methods they use to inquire into, exam-ine, probe, and construct knowledge with their writing work to compose them as certain types of literate people.

As I explain in the following sections, Discover Chicago meets all these criteria. Nearly all courses in the program pay extensive attention to writing, providing examples, principles, stimuli, and process-oriented writing environ-ments. Nearly all sections emphasize the students' active construction of knowledge. Most visibly, Discover Chicago introduces students, via reading, writing, listening, and discussing, to what it means to read, write, listen, and discuss as a DePaul student.

DISCOVER CHICAGO AND THE
MISSION OF DEPAUL UNIVERSITY

DePaul University has always been very open about the three distinguishing characteristics of its mission: DePaul is Catholic, urban, and Vincentian. DePaul is C/catholic, with both a capital C and a small c. It does serve the Church of Rome, and more than half of its undergraduates are Roman

Catholic. (It is worth noting, however, that no DePaul student or faculty member must make any profession of faith, it has an active Muslim Student Association, and it is the only private university in the Chicago area that has never had a quota for the admission of Jewish students.) It is also small-c catholic, believing it important for a university to be worldly and inclusive. Further, though it now has five suburban campuses in addition to its two in Chicago, DePaul is purposefully urban. The university works hard to serve the city, and it in turn capitalizes on the city's intellectual riches as a resource for its curriculum and the co-curriculum. Finally, DePaul consciously tries to build on the work of St. Vincent dePaul, the sixteenth-century French priest who focused the church's attention on the needs of the urban poor. The Vincentian character of DePaul calls on faculty, staff, and students to "respect . . . the God-given dignity of all persons, especially the materially, culturally, and spiritually deprived" and to manifest "a dedication to the service of others" (*Undergraduate Bulletin* 480).

When DePaul began revising its Liberal Studies (i.e., general education) program in the early 1990s, a planning committee examined the existing curriculum carefully, trying to identify places where these three distinctive characteristics of the university were inscribed. The committee found the Catholic, urban, Vincentian mission scattered throughout the course offerings, but they found no place where it purposefully coalesced. Out of the committee's desire to place these three missional characteristics at the university's "front doorstep," Discover Chicago was born. The course was taught for the first time at the beginning of autumn term 1995, with eight faculty and staff members and seventy-two students participating in a pilot project. Now, about 150 faculty members, staff professionals, and student mentors team-teach more than twenty sections of the course, serving nearly 450 students, or about one-quarter of the incoming first-year class at DePaul. The remainder of the entering students take Explore Chicago, a course with similar goals but taught during the regular autumn term without the immersion week. Discover Chicago serves just a portion of the incoming class for two reasons. First, it is a residential program, and DePaul's campus residences simply cannot accommodate a larger number during the week before regular autumn classes begin. Second, given the working-class profile of DePaul undergraduates (about 70 percent of our students have jobs while they are in school), not all incoming students are able to give up the last week of their summer to participate in the program.

Each section of Discover Chicago focuses on a particular theme, issue, or motif evident in the life of the city, and each course works in some way to inscribe DePaul's Catholic, urban, and Vincentian mission. Among the twenty-four sections offered in autumn term 2000 were such courses as "Walking the Streets with Chicago's Writers," "Chicago's Music Scene: What

Is There for You?" "Nature in the City: Urban Gardens and Greens," "Asian Americans in Chicago," and "Chicago's Architecture." The Discover Chicago immersion week begins on a Sunday afternoon, when the students, on their very first day at the university, meet their section's teaching team: a faculty member, a member of the university's professional staff—usually from a Student Life department, but occasionally from such sites as the library, the admissions office, or residence life—and an upper-division undergraduate student mentor. The teaching team is vital to Discover Chicago, since the course aims not only to introduce students to an issue in the city but also to acclimate them to the university—its resources, its procedures, its intellectual and social culture. The Sunday meeting is essentially an icebreaker and an informational session about the coming week.

The class begins in earnest the next day. Sections gather in their university classrooms for just a brief class session. In some classes, students have received introductory readings in the mail over the summer; in others, they have been given a brief reading at the Sunday session; in still others, they come into the first session "cold" in relation to their topic. But in most sections, students begin Monday morning by writing. The teaching team gives the students a prompt, a question or probe that focuses their attention on the places they are going to visit that day, the people they hope to encounter, the phenomena they propose to observe. Once students have had the opportunity to use writing to focus their attention on the day's work and talk briefly about their ideas, the class gets onto public transportation—the "el" or the bus in Chicago—and heads for the first of their sites. "Walking the Streets with Chicago's Writers" may head to the near west side to check out the neighborhood Nelson Algren captured in *Man With the Golden Arm;* "Chicago's Music Scene" may go backstage at the Lyric Opera House or the House of Blues; "Nature in the City" may travel to the workshop of the head horticulturist for the Chicago Park District; "Asian Americans in Chicago" may go to the corner of Cermak and Wentworth, the main intersection in the larger of Chicago's two Chinatowns; "Chicago's Architecture" may head for the loop to see the Monadnock Building, Chicago's first skyscraper, or the Rookery, the loveliest of buildings designed by James Root and later renovated by Frank Lloyd Wright.

On each of these journeys, the teaching team uses "the walk-and-talk" pedagogy: they tell students about the neighborhoods they are passing through and visiting and the issues that make the neighborhoods tick; they get to know the students personally (it is amazing what extensive conversations one can have, even on noisy trains and buses); and the students get to know the faculty member, staff professional, and student mentor as "real people"— people who eat meals, who get sweaty and tired occasionally, but above all as people who are intellectually engaged by the city in which they work. On some site visits, students hear a talk or see a demonstration given by a representative of a governmental agency, not-for-profit organization, or museum; on others, they may simply explore on their own or in groups, nearly always seeking out specific features that the teaching team has directed them to look for and that they have written about earlier in the day.

On nearly all site visits, the students write. They take notes in their journals and logbooks about what they see, hear, and experience. They jot down ideas about issues they might like to investigate further. They read their entries aloud to one another. A typical day in the immersion week contains two, occasionally three, of these site visits, and a day almost always concludes with the students and teaching team returning to the university's main campus and collecting their thoughts by writing again in their journals and logbooks.

Immersion week ends with all Discover Chicago students and teaching team members participating in New Student Service Day, when about one thousand DePaulians break into fifty or so teams and head out to sites in the city where they paint schools, clean parks, serve meals to hospice patients, and so on. Immersion week also ends, for most sections of Discover Chicago, with students writing some kind of document, generally a reflective essay, that draws together all their thoughts and experiences from the week. When the regular autumn term begins, Discover Chicago converts into a regular first-year seminar that meets for two-and-one-half hours a week and continues the inquiry students have begun during immersion week. Readings, examinations, and papers during the autumn term flesh out the issues students have encountered during the immersion week.

"INTERRELIGIOUS DIALOGUE AND COOPERATION IN CHICAGO": COMPOSING TEXTS AND STUDENTS

A specific example can illustrate how a typical Discover Chicago section pays full, careful attention to writing, leads students to use writing to construct knowledge, and composes its participants as literate students at DePaul. Jeffrey Carlson, associate professor of religious studies, regularly teaches a section of Discover Chicago entitled "Interreligious Dialogue and Cooperation in Chicago." Carlson explains his personal connection to the course:

> The sprawling, cosmopolitan, increasingly multi-ethnic-racial-religious character of metropolitan Chicago makes our urban setting an ideal context for the study of religion and its impact on the critical issues facing contemporary society. Chicago has more Buddhists than Episcopalians, more Muslims than Jews. Among the Christian community, there are distinctions between Protestant, Catholic, and Orthodox, further differentiated by race

and ethnicity, city and suburb. In the metropolitan area there are also over a dozen Hindu temples and one Zoroastrian center, alive and practicing communities among the Baha'is, Sikhs, Jains, Buddhists, and many others, as well as a host of ecumenical, interfaith, and interreligious organizations. My own involvement with the Chicago-based Council for a Parliament of the World's Religions has afforded many opportunities to develop relationships with a variety of religious communities in the city, and thereby to bring my students into contact with them. (131)

During immersion week, Carlson's students become immersed in the interreligious landscape of the city. They hear a talk from a director of a major interreligious initiative and a response to his talk from a Buddhist monk, in whose temple they sit. They meet with an interfaith organization that initiates grassroots efforts for worker justice. They hear a panel discussion on "The Inner Life" led by a Hindu, a Sufi Muslim, and a Greek Orthodox priest. Every night before a visit they read material to focus their observations. Every morning before they begin a site visit, they write and discuss.

One particular Wednesday in a recent immersion week shows clearly how the class is acting to teach students to compose and is also acting to compose the students. The class ended that day at dinner time with the students viewing the documentary *Blacks and Jews*. Then, after the film, they read an article by Cornel West, "On Black-Jewish Relations." The next morning, the students began their day by considering a quotation from the reading about media portrayals of Black-Jewish relations and by writing an entry in their logbooks, relating this quotation to an incident portrayed in the documentary, where Oakland, California, high school students were thrown out of a screening of *Schindler's List* for what was perceived to be antisemitic behavior, only to be visited by Steven Spielberg and the governor of California, Pete Wilson, a few weeks later. The students read their logbook entries aloud, and Carlson summarized them and moved the class toward drafting some theoretical statements about the issues underlying this incident. Equipped with these preliminary theoretical formulations, Carlson and the students discussed some of their possible applications and implications for action. Carlson's own words convey most forcefully what happened next.

> Then we got on the CTA. We took the Brown Line to Adams and then the Green Line to 47th Street. We walked one block to Mount Pisgah Baptist Church at 4622 S. Martin Luther King Drive. We met with Rev. Joseph Jackson, pastor at Mount Pisgah, and Ms. Jane Ramsey, executive director of the Jewish Council on Urban Affairs, who had been featured in one of the segments of the film. They gave their perspectives on the history and present status of Black/Jewish relations in this country. The students tested their theories and were generally appalled by Rev. Jackson's political conservatism

and by what they judged to be his astounding divergence from Cornel West. The distinction between personal and structural racism (with a strong emphasis on the latter) which they/we had developed in the classroom was swept away in Rev. Jackson's relentless call for personal, individual responsibility and his virtual dismissal of the existence of structural barriers to personal achievement. In this experience, the circuit from experience (of film and text) to observation/reflection, to formation of concepts, theories, and generalization, to testing the implications of these concepts, was very much a live wire. The circuit was electrified and the theory was challenged by this new experience. So back to the CTA, back to the classroom. That afternoon before dinner, we wrote in the logbooks, responding to another prompt. The process continued. (133–34)

Consider what is happening there. During the immersion week that Carlson orchestrates, students are surrounded by examples of the genre of the logbook entry; they consistently analyze one another's entries and learn principles from the daily readings and discussions about what makes a good logbook entry. Every day they are placed in environments that lead them to write in order to interpret, analyze, synthesize, and evaluate what they are seeing, hearing, and experiencing. They are learning about a certain, specific feature of living in a city where their Catholic, urban, Vincentian university embeds itself.

When the course moves into the autumn term, the students continue their inquiry into, and writing about, interreligious dialogue so that they can, in Carlson's words, "critically revisit the issues raised by the immersion week, probing more deeply and letting the initial impressions take on more mature reflective forms" (134). As an outgrowth of their mid-term examinations, students are required to propose a research project on a particular theme that they encountered in the immersion week and developed over the first half of the term. This project, which students can chose to do alone or in groups, must involve additional readings and at least two more site visits. Project topics have included "intermarriage, the relation of the Nation of Islam to global Islam, the Baha'i faith and its view of other religions, the status of minority religions in the United States in relation to Christianity, and artistic expression in several religious traditions" (135). One group of students recently undertook a particularly impressive research project. They developed a grant proposal, to be submitted to the Illinois Humanities Council, to support a project they call "Chicago's Sacred Places":

> They propose[d] a series of newspaper articles that ask Chicagoans to consider what constitutes a sacred place in the life of this city, and ask for nominations and descriptions of such sites. Then, an exhibit of sacred places nominated and selected by communities would be created, to include photographs and community narratives. (135)

The students also proposed to develop an annotated map of the sites, write an illustrated resource book for studying them, and organize a series of public liturgies to introduce the project to the city. The students' project included a sample entry for their proposed resource book, an entry on the Midwest Buddhist temple, written in collaboration with the monk who presides at the temple (135). As in the immersion week, students in "Interreligious Dialogue and Cooperation in Chicago" were spending the autumn term learning to write in both academic and public discourse genres, to use their writing to construct new knowledge, and to internalize the ways their literate behaviors and the DePaul mission are intertwined.

COLLEGE COMPOSITION, LIBERAL EDUCATION, AND INSTITUTIONAL MISSION

In the perennial debates over what Robert Connors labeled the "new abolitionism"—the issue concerning whether colleges and universities should abolish the universal requirement of first-year composition—scholars and teachers in the field, no matter what their stance on the issue, concede that it is difficult to get students to take required composition courses seriously. Proponents of abolishing the universal requirement (note: no one is proposing that the course be abolished, simply its requirement) maintain that students do not take the course seriously *because* it is required. Though I am sympathetic to many of the new abolitionists' ideas, I think they are wrong here. Students do not take required composition courses seriously, I maintain, because they do not perceive they are learning *about* anything in them. In their worst, most reductive, but unfortunately ubiquitous manifestations, required composition courses are decontextualized skill-builders, "service" courses designed to tidy up students' organizational skills, grammar, and mechanics so they can write well in their "other" courses and in the "real world" beyond academia. Given this image, it is small wonder that students try to get this course "out of the way" so they can go on to take "content" courses, both in their majors and in general education programs, the latter so they can be "well-rounded" in their education.

This dismal, yet widely accepted, image of required, first-year composition stands in stark contrast to a premise that undergirds the best college writing courses in general and sections of Discover Chicago in particular. Required, writing-intensive first-year courses are the bedrock of a college's or university's general education program. If they are designed and taught well— if they inscribe some theoretically solid version of the pedagogy Kinneavy sketches out, and if they teach students to use their writing to construct new knowledge—these courses can teach "content" to students that is every bit as vital as the substance they acquire in, say, World Civilization, Introduction to Psychology, or Physics I.

What should this content be? Why not the mission of the college or the university? Why not use required, first-year writing courses to help students understand that they have made an important choice in deciding to attend a particular institution? Why not work against the notion, so commonly held but, I believe, so misguided, that college composition is the same course, whether students take it as an advanced, dual-enrollment course in high school, at a two-year college, via the Internet, or at some other institution with a radically different mission from the one where they have matriculated? At DePaul, we use Discover Chicago to say to students, "Welcome—now read, write, listen, and discuss your way into the university." I would challenge other colleges and universities to do the same.

WORKS CITED

Bacon, Nora. "Community Service Writing: Problems, Challenges, Questions." *Writing the Community: Concepts and Models for Service-Learning in Composition.* Ed. Linda Adler-Kassner, Robert Crooks, and Ann Watters. Washington, DC: American Association for Higher Education, 1997. 39–55.

Berlin, James. "Composition Studies and Cultural Studies: Collapsing Boundaries." *Into the Field: Sites of Composition Studies.* Ed. Anne Ruggles Gere. New York: MLA, 1993. 99–116.

Berthoff, Ann. *Forming, Thinking, Writing: The Composing Imagination.* Upper Montclair, NJ: Boynton/Cook, 1982.

Carlson, Jeffrey. "From Site Unseen to Experiential Learning: Religious Studies in the 'Discover Chicago' Model." *Teaching Theology and Religion* 1 (1998): 130–37.

Connors, Robert J. "The New Abolitionism: Toward a Historical Background." *Reconceiving Writing, Rethinking Writing Instruction.* Ed. Joseph Petraglia. Mahwah, NJ: Erlbaum Associates, 1995. 3–26.

Ellman, Richard. *Oscar Wilde.* New York: Knopf, 1987.

Ervin, Elizabeth. "Encouraging Civic Participation Among First-Year Writing Students; Or, Why Composition Class Should Be More Like a Bowling Team." *Rhetoric Review* 15 (1997): 382–99.

Heilker, Paul. "Rhetoric Made Real: Civic Discourse and Writing Beyond the Curriculum." *Writing the Community: Concepts and Models for Service-Learning in Composition.* Ed. Linda Adler-Kassner, Robert Crooks, and Ann Watters. Washington, DC: American Association for Higher Education, 1997. 71–87.

Kinneavy, James L. "Translating Theory into Practice in Teaching Composition: A Historical View and a Contemporary View." *Essays on Classical Rhetoric and Modern Discourse.* Ed. Robert J. Connors, Lisa S. Ede, and Andrea A. Lunsford. Carbondale: Southern Illinois UP, 1984. 69–81.

Sisserson, Kendra, Carmen Manning, Annie Knepler, and David A. Jolliffe. "Criteria for Assessing Authentic Intellectual Achievement in Writing." *Best Practices in Composition.* Ed. Peggy O'Neill. Urbana: NCTE, forthcoming.

Undergraduate Bulletin. Chicago: DePaul University, 1999.

CHAPTER ELEVEN

WRITING PROGRAM ADMINISTRATION IN A "METROPOLITAN UNIVERSITY"

Lynee Lewis Gaillet

Compositionists have long recognized that the act of writing is a localized practice, linked in a multitude of ways to specific moments in time and writing contexts. Only recently, however, have urban studies scholars adopted a similar stance, acknowledging that although urban institutions may share certain similarities, in actuality each city offers unique educational opportunities and challenges. In this move away from essentialist constructs of urban colleges and universities, terminology becomes critical. Blaine Brownell explains that "the term 'urban university' no longer describes, as it once did, an open admission institution with mostly undergraduate and applied academic programs staffed by mostly part-time faculty." He prefers the term *metropolitan* over *urban*, emphasizing a larger, rather than smaller, area of concern (21). A growing number of administrators and teachers at urban universities who now view their institutions in these broader terms have united to develop the philosophical concept of the "metropolitan university," a construction often quite distinctive from the traditional urban university in terms of mission, community leadership and partnerships, and evaluation of traditional faculty responsibilities. In this chapter, I will define the term *metropolitan university*, discuss my own urban institution, Georgia State University, in relation to the metropolitan university philosophy of education, and, finally, describe an evolving writing course that both implements this general philosophy and takes advantage of unique writing opportunities available in my city, Atlanta, GA.

THE METROPOLITAN UNIVERSITY

The metropolitan university idea has quickly moved beyond the status of an emerging model. Its commitment to outreach and public service, within a context of focused research and a time-honored commitment to learning, is now being recognized as of critical importance for all universities in the next century.
—Al Hurley, President, University of North Texas

Charles E. Hathaway, Paige E. Mulholland, and Karen A. White define the metropolitan university as an institution that embraces an "interactive philosophy" leading to the establishment of a "symbiotic relationship" with its metropolitan area (9). Universities adopting this "interactive philosophy" have joined to form the Coalition of Urban and Metropolitan Universities (see the Declaration of Metropolitan Universities in the Appendix), which provides a network of annual conferences, publications, and grants for its members in an effort to unite "universities that share the mission of striving for national excellence while contributing to the economic development, social health, and cultural vitality" of urban and metropolitan areas *(Information on the Coalition)*. The Coalition publishes a quarterly journal, *Metropolitan Universities,* targeted primarily to departments of sociology, higher education, and policy development. However, as the Writing Program Administrator at an urban university—one that is a member of the Coalition of Urban and Metropolitan Universities—I find these articles invaluable in helping me understand both my university's broader commitment to and symbiotic relationship with the metropolitan Atlanta area, and the role the first-year composition program might play in this interactive philosophy.

Brownell's description of the role of the "true" metropolitan university (as opposed to a university simply located in an urban environment) summarizes various definitions of the "metropolitan university" found in the scholarship:

The opportunity and burden of the metropolitan university—if it is to be a metropolitan university—is to serve the entire urban region and all its diverse populations, interests, and elements. It cannot deal only with the inner-city underprepared or the suburban professionals; it must be concerned with the needs of both. It cannot identify its interests solely with the largest city in its region or with its suburbs, but rather help them to recognize mutual interests and work together. The most important role of the metropolitan university is to be a facilitator, communicator, convener, and bridge. What other institution, except perhaps the government itself, has the capacity to interpret one group to another, serve as a neutral site and forum where problems can be discussed and resolved, bring the latest knowledge and technologies to bear on the dispossessed, join the vigor and capacity of business with the compelling needs of the public at large, and, perhaps most importantly, help restore a sense of *civitas* [civic responsibility], of belonging to one polity and community? (23)

This description of the metropolitan mission leads to a broader conception of the traditional "responsibilities" of university faculty: teaching, research, and professional service. In the metropolitan university model, faculty (while meeting the highest scholarly standards of the academic community) are encouraged to reconsider and more fully integrate these duties, which are never mutually exclusive, with the university's greater city context. For example, metropolitan university faculty must seek research opportunities that link academic investigations with practical applications in real urban communities. Faculty must accept responsibility for educating students to be informed and effective citizens, as well as preparing them for their chosen professions and occupations. Additionally, faculty must contribute to the metropolitan area's "quality of life" while developing close partnerships with area enterprises in mutually beneficial ways, thus serving as more than just experts disseminating information.

Many urban studies scholars compare and contrast the modern metropolitan university's mission to that of nineteenth-century land-grant colleges created in the wake of the Morrill Act of 1862. John C. Hitt, president of the University of Central Florida, believes that "metropolitan universities are a logical extension of the land-grant mission in the new millennium" *(Information on the Coalition)*. Land-grant institutions were specifically charged to address the nation's economic problems through an emphasis on agricultural and engineering teaching and research. However, the mission of the metropolitan university has a much broader scope than the aims of earlier land-grant institutions, which successfully modernized agricultural production but addressed only in limited ways rural America's social problems (Schuh 123). According to Hathaway, Mulholland, and White, "we must think creatively of how we might utilize the entire body of the university as an urban-based experiment station." In other words, we must transform the metropolitan university "by empowering the entire campus to utilize the metropolitan area as a living laboratory" (11).

Realistically, the dual missions of research and outreach are not always compatible in university settings. In particular, faculty and administrators who embrace the "ivory tower" notion of university education often summarily dismiss aims of the "metropolitan university" and scoff at the suggestion of viewing the "university as an urban-based experiment station." The perceived incompatibility between research and outreach is heightened when traditional research universities and departments are asked to move toward adopting a metropolitan university philosophy of education, as is the case at my institution.

GEORGIA STATE UNIVERSITY'S METROPOLITAN MISSION

[T]he university community makes the most of its urban home by
drawing from the unlimited opportunities found only in a booming international city.

— Carl Patton, President, Georgia State University

I am the Writing Program Administrator at Georgia State University (GSU),
a large PhD-granting institution located in the heart of downtown Atlanta.
Like other universities in major cities, GSU, founded in 1913 to provide after-
hours education for city inhabitants, addresses a broad spectrum of instructional needs for the regional population. We offer undergraduate as well as
graduate programs not only at traditional times and places, but also at alternative times and sites to make higher education accessible to nontraditional
students and working professionals. The demographic profile of our student
body reflects the broad diversity of Atlanta and its many suburban areas. GSU
students include many racial and ethnic groups, residential students and commuters, full-time and part-time matriculants, and students spanning a broad
age range. Historically, many of our students attend more than one institution
as they work toward a baccalaureate degree and take more than four years to
graduate. Typical of many urban institutions, student profile statistics reveal
that GSU students are older than the national averages: the average age of our
undergraduates is twenty-five, the average age of graduate students is thirty-
two, and the average age of all students is twenty-seven. Graduate students
comprise 31 percent of the student body. We have 8,936 undergraduate transfers from other institutions, and students come from forty-six states and 127
countries. Last academic year, more than $93.7 million was awarded in stu-
dent financial aid *(Georgia State University)*. This statistical description of
GSU's identity situates it within expected, established parameters of urban
higher education. Far more interesting, however, is the unfolding story of how
GSU is rapidly reinventing itself in the wake of changes enacted by recent
educational reform, state legislation, the vision of the school's new president,
and the city itself.

Since my arrival in 1992 as an assistant professor in the English department, I have witnessed GSU undergo an unprecedented transformation: the
Georgia Board of Regents grandfathered in tougher admission standards
beginning in 1992; Georgia Governor Zell Miller instituted HOPE scholar-
ships, making a college education affordable for thousands of qualifying
Georgia residents; the state mandated the abolishment of learning support
courses and departments; all Georgia colleges and universities converted from
the quarter to semester system, a difficult adaptation for working students;
and the 1996 Summer Olympics held in Atlanta provided the means for con-
verting GSU from a commuter school to a residential college virtually

overnight when the Olympic Village became the GSU Village—a complex featuring four residence halls (where students live in fully furnished apartments with their own private bedrooms and full kitchens shared by either four or six students), a post office, gym, and ample parking, a rare commodity in downtown Atlanta. These combined changes, unique to our institution, have yielded a new demographic profile for the GSU student body and have redefined what GSU has to offer. Our students are now often younger, more traditional, drawn to GSU and downtown Atlanta by the promise of a free education and affordable, safe housing; and they are often better prepared academically for college than their predecessors. This list of crucial events affecting GSU is monumental for such a brief time frame; however, significantly greater change is on the horizon for our institution.

The current president, Carl Patton, also hired in 1992, is committed to expanding the university into the community both physically and philosophically. Patton has a clearly defined, "bricks and mortar" plan for integrating the campus within the downtown community, scrapping "the campus' gritty, urban feel in favor of something that more resembles a college campus—complete with its own version of Main Street" (qtd. in Suggs, "Main Street" B1). As Ernie Suggs, of the city's leading newspaper, *The Atlanta Constitution*, puts it, Patton "wants to get off what he considers the island known as Georgia State University" and further integrate the university within the fabric of downtown Atlanta ("Patton" C3). New buildings have been erected and existing buildings acquired and renovated at GSU since Patton's arrival, but his greatest plans for the changing GSU landscape are still in the works—and often quite controversial—as he moves GSU into historic Atlanta districts. Patton's passion and enthusiasm for transforming GSU are not subtle and are often met with mixed reactions. After arriving in Atlanta, Patton devised a plan to sell the GSU president's mansion in upscale Buckhead and move to a top-floor loft in the downtown Muse's building with a panoramic view of the inner city and several of GSU's buildings. His new accommodations proved profitable in his fundraising efforts. As he says, "It doesn't hurt to point to a building and mention [to potential donors] that for $10 million you could have your name on that building" (Cheakalos G5). Raising state and private funds to support his ten-year "main street" blueprint for converting GSU into a more traditional-looking university and fighting historic preservationist groups are not the only facets of Patton's vision for GSU: Patton ultimately seeks to transform GSU into "the nation's leading urban research university" (Suggs, "GSU" C1).

Tom Lewis, Vice President for External Affairs, claims that "there has never been a man more suited to being the president of GSU than Carl Patton." Lewis explains that "up until Carl, Georgia State had not accepted the fact that we are an urban institution, we had not embraced the word 'urban.' . . . The perception was it was a nice little night school for the employees of the downtown business community. Then came Carl on the scene with a vision and ready to lead this urban institution, whether or not it was ready to be led" (Cheakalos G5). Lewis raises a critical question: Is GSU ready to be led, and if so, in what direction? Faculty members in "traditional" university departments (arts and sciences, for example) do not object to Patton's initiative to elevate GSU in the Carnegie ranking of research institutions—urban or otherwise. However, problems do arise when faculty members are asked to view their teaching, research, and service as distinctively "urban."

An internal debate taking place at the moment at GSU, as we are formulating our "strategic plan" for the university, concerns a fundamental issue of self-perception. Are we to view ourselves primarily as a research institution located in an urban area *or* are we going to consider ourselves first and foremost an urban university with a "metropolitan" outreach philosophy? The university's mission statement found in the *Undergraduate Catalog, 2000–2001,* while alluding to educating a diverse student population and preparing students for civic responsibility, primarily describes GSU as a research university located in an urban environment—a description that raises little controversy among faculty:

> As the only urban research university in Georgia, Georgia State University offers educational opportunities for traditional and nontraditional students at both the graduate and undergraduate levels by blending the best of theoretical and applied inquiry, scholarly and professional pursuits, and scientific and artistic expression. As an urban research university with strong disciplinary-based departments and a wide array of problem-oriented interdisciplinary programs, the goal of the university is to develop, transmit, and utilize knowledge in order to provide access to quality education for diverse groups of students, to educate leaders for the State of Georgia and the nation, and to prepare citizens for lifelong learning in a global society. (7)

However, information found on the GSU website provides strong evidence that GSU is not only seeking to become a leading research university located in an urban setting, but a "metropolitan university" as well. The website information (without actually using the term *metropolitan university*) indicates the school's "public" adoption of the tenets of the "Declaration of Metropolitan Universities" (Appendix). For example, the following descriptions of GSU from the website echo the Coalition of Urban and Metropolitan Universities' (re)conception of faculty teaching, research, and service responsibilities: "Because of its real-world education, problem-solving research and strong community outreach, Georgia State is rapidly becoming a first-choice university." And "Georgia State University breaks the ivory tower mold of higher education and makes the most of its urban home by bringing teaching, research and service to life" *(Georgia State University).*

The following quotes from GSU's website restate the Coalition of Urban and Metropolitan Universities' mission of "linking basic investigation with practical application through interdisciplinary partnerships that attack complex urban and metropolitan problems" *(Information on the Coalition)*. According to the GSU website,

> Georgia State combines traditional university education with the unique opportunities found in a growing international city. The university's location in the heart of downtown Atlanta allows students to learn not only in the classroom but also in the busy surrounding city, where high profile companies provide hands-on experience. . . . Students enhance their education through outside work, and they bring the lessons they learn back into the classroom to share with others.

And, "New strengths emerge, but Georgia State's vision remains: to be the leading urban research university educating tomorrow's leaders, performing hands-on service in our urban regions, and conducting research that finds solutions to real problems" *(Georgia State University)*.

The following excerpts from GSU's website echo the Coalition of Urban and Metropolitan Universities' goal to "develop creative partnerships with public and private enterprises to ensure that the intellectual resources of our institutions are fully engaged in mutually beneficial ways" *(Information on the Coalition)*. The GSU website states that "[a] Georgia State student may be a physical therapy intern at a hospital, a web designer at a high-tech firm, or the owner of a business." And,

> The city is more than a place to get work experience. It is also a work site for solutions to complex urban problems. For example: Georgia State law students represent the working poor in confusing tax battles with the IRS. The School of Policy Studies has created a monitoring system to help the metro area get a handle on deteriorating air quality. Nursing students provide medical attention to grandparents who raise their grandchildren. The university's Economic Forecasting Center provides reliable, accurate advice about the state and regional economies that helps businesses prepare for the future. *(Georgia State University)*

Website information offers particularly compelling evidence that GSU wants to be recognized as a premier research university *and* an urban institution committed to a symbiotic relationship with the metropolitan Atlanta area. Are both missions with their distinct goals attainable? Can GSU resolve the inherent contradictions evident in each mission? Interestingly, the revised Carnegie Classification 2000 rankings recently "moved up" GSU's classification from the category of Doctoral I to Doctoral Extensive, the highest-ranking category, including only 3.8 percent of classified institutions. The Carnegie Foundation defines the Doctoral/Research Universities-Extensive category as follows: "These institutions offer a wide range of baccalaureate programs and are committed to graduate education through the doctorate. They award 50 or more doctoral degrees per year across at least 15 disciplines" (Basinger A34). Alexander C. McCormick, a senior scholar at the Carnegie Foundation who supervised the new classification system, explains that the categories were revised because foundation leaders were concerned that "the categories had come to weigh institutions' research activities too heavily, at the expense of other aspects of their missions, such as teaching and service" (Basinger A31). This reconfiguration of the Carnegie Classification categories is certainly beneficial for GSU (in a multitude of obvious ways) but also perhaps makes more palatable for some faculty the overt promotion of GSU as a member of the Coalition of Urban and Metropolitan Universities. Until very recently, urban universities were defined in either of two ways: as research universities in urban settings *or* as urban outreach universities committed primarily to teaching and service. The metropolitan university philosophy, which includes a strong commitment to traditional academic research, and the restructured Carnegie Classification 2000 provide other options for defining urban institutions and their missions.

When given only two choices for characterizing the university (research or urban outreach), understandably the GSU English department, along with most other departments in the College of Arts and Sciences, generally favors the "research university located in an urban setting" view of GSU over what is often defined as the "urban university" model, for perhaps obvious reasons. Historically, the English department's research and teaching interests have not meshed with the aims of institutional urban outreach. Since becoming chair in 1993, Robert Sattelmeyer has strengthened the English department in response to its Action Plan (a product of program review), recent statewide educational reform, and shifting sociocultural factors throughout Atlanta. More specifically, three critical departmental changes enacted during Sattelmeyer's tenure as chair undeniably reflect metropolitan university principles and indicate ways in which the department can create public and private partnerships, establish working relationships with area schools, and provide increased community leadership—key elements in the Coalition of Urban and Metropolitan Universities' mission statement.

First, the department has organized a secondary education committee to actively investigate and strengthen our involvement in local language arts education. We hired two tenure-line faculty members to revise curriculum and provide advice and programs for our secondary education majors. The secondary education division of the department (composed of English faculty clearly committed to, and in some cases having experience in, secondary education) has created dynamic workshops, colloquia, and seminars with metropolitan area teachers to facilitate two-way conversations about teaching. We have created an advisory board of secondary English educators to strengthen our partnerships with local schools, and on the horizon are plans for joint-enrollment classes between area high schools and GSU.

Second, the department has expanded the rhetoric and composition division by hiring two tenure-line faculty members in professional and technical writing. Sattelmeyer's willingness to spend departmental funds and his own political capital in support of this developing program is notable: the department has provided supplies, financial support for a fully developed mentoring program, software, and faculty release time; and Sattelmeyer is leading the fight for new research and classroom space (a scarce commodity in downtown Atlanta) necessary for program development. The courses in professional and technical writing (which include service learning components, internships, and writing and editing projects blending students' workplace and classroom assignments) now being offered by the English department present new opportunities for liaisons with corporate and nonprofit area organizations.

Third, with the backing of the dean of the College of Arts and Sciences, Sattelmeyer spearheaded the formation of a fully-funded Writing Across the Curriculum (WAC) program, housed in the English department. The newly hired, tenure-line WAC director is also a member of the expanding rhetoric and composition division of the department. These five new faculty lines and three new programs represent the department's greatest potential for fostering relationships between the university and metro Atlanta. However, most members of the "traditional" English faculty are involved in these initiatives in limited ways.

THE COURSE DESCRIPTION

> The uneasy compromise that exists between the English profession and the culture at large has kept Freshman English alive, but unloved for a century.
> —Sharon Crowley, "The Perilous Life and Times of Freshman English"

Upon assuming the job of Writing Program Administrator at GSU, I felt an initial conflict between disciplinary and institutional concerns on many levels. Our first-year writing program is large (offering well over one hundred sections of first-year composition, 1101 and 1102, each semester), staffed by teaching assistants and visiting instructors with varying levels of experience. Historically, these classes have been current-traditional all the way. In fact, until two years ago, we had an 1101 exit exam (a timed, prompt-driven essay, graded by external readers), which determined each student's final grade for the course, and, in large part, dictated the formalistic curriculum and pedagogy characterizing these courses. Recently, however, this exit exam was abolished.

The abolishment of the exit exam led immediately to fear from some English department faculty who believed that 1101 would now degenerate into a study of "rhetoric" devoid of basic grammar and usage instruction. For me, however, this change actually ushered in the first real opportunity to teach GSU's initial first-year writing course from a fully developed rhetorical approach; it was a prime opportunity to incorporate theoretical and pedagogical practices from the field of composition studies into our courses and launch a fully developed mentoring program for teaching assistants. Unfortunately, these efforts were met with resistance from vocal instructors who wanted to replace the former exit exam-driven curriculum of 1101 with the study of literature. These issues, in conjunction with departmental discussions concerning the portrayal of GSU's metropolitan strategic plan, prompted me to consider radical reconfigurations of the beginning writing courses. Could we offer a composition course that would satisfy my disciplinary concerns, not fuel the lit/comp debate, meet departmental expectations, *and* provide a way for the English department to engage in GSU's broader, "metropolitan university" goals?

I am currently piloting a first-year writing course that resolves many of the existing conflicts embedded in our first-year writing program and also promotes a metropolitan mission. This course borrows from ethnographic research and requires students to actively enter the communities they choose to study. We have adapted an ethnographic approach to take advantage of our urban locale and to encourage students to take advantage of the unique research opportunities available in Atlanta and its surrounding communities. Students not only read about local communities, but they also enter those communities as both observers and participants.

Higher education task forces advocating a metropolitan university philosophy of education indicate that the quality of student learning is directly related to the quality of students' involvement in their education. Charles Ruch and Eugene Trani tell us that

> boundaries between the classroom and the community can be made permeable, and the extent to which the flow of ideas and people is accelerated is the mutual benefit of both. However, the full impact on the curriculum will not be met by including only community activities. Inductive pedagogy, case methodology, and cooperative learning strategies will need to be introduced into the classroom. Only by restructuring the instructional process so classroom content is tied with community experience will the full potential of these boundary-spanning strategies be achieved. (233–34)

Not only does this pilot ethnographic writing course fulfill my own personal and professional needs and the needs of my department, but it also limits the relevance of literature to the course, circumventing the debilitating lit/comp debate. The ethnographic writing class that we have designed answers the call for incorporating community experience in the academic classroom, creating real-world research scenarios and writing assignments tied to community experiences.

The first thing our students do in this course is pick a site to investigate, and most of the course assignments concern or occur at the students' sites. Projects include mapping exercises, field observations, personal interviews, oral histories, artifact collections, urban legend recordings, as well as "traditional" research and documentation exercises. The students submit a portfolio of writing during the final week of the course, including all of the assignments, a complete narrative research paper with traditional bibliography, and a reflection essay. Each component of the final portfolio is peer-edited or presented to the class, in some cases graded, and then revised over the course of the term. To date, seven instructors have participated in this approach to first-year writing instruction with positive results. Both teachers and students are engaged and interested in the research and writing, as well as the contents of students' portfolios. We are also learning, from multiple perspectives, about the communities in which we live. Students share their work with the class throughout the semester, culminating in a "portfolio fair" during the last week of class, which provides students with an opportunity to view the final work of their classmates. We discuss the issues raised by our work and look for emerging patterns, causal relationships, and interesting trends occurring in the metro area. Students' projects cover a range of local topics and communities, some personal interest groups and others public institutions and organizations. Consider the variety in this list of my students' researched sites: snowboarding communities, nursing homes, shelters for abused women and children, pawn shops, dance studios, NASCAR racing, skydiving, punk culture, elementary schools, state funded childcare facilities, and local TV stations, to name just a few.

Although the ethnographic fieldwork model could be applicable to almost any writing class, this methodological approach is ideally suited to first-year writing courses at GSU, self-identified as the "only urban research university in Georgia" (*Undergraduate Catalog* 7). Our students are often non-traditional and work full-time; they are predominately residents of the metropolitan area—commuters rather than residential students. The (not so simple) act of just getting to campus—which is located downtown, across from the state capital building, next to the Atlanta police station, and at the intersection of three major interstates—forces students to confront social, environmental, and political issues particular to Atlanta. As a result, our students come to GSU already engaged in the community, interested in area politics and local affairs, and directly affected by localized social and environmental issues. A writing course that focuses on ethnographic research methods provides students real contexts and audiences for expressing their concerns in writing and improving the quality of life in metro Atlanta. Students choose their research sites based on their own interests and experiences within the community. They go outside of their own cultures and subcultures *or* become observers and analysts within their own cultural groups. From the first day of class, students have a concrete context for the research and writing they will produce over the course of the semester.

A REFLECTION ON CRITICAL PEDAGOGY

> To be true to their theory, critical pedagogues—in many ways—must be blunderers, teachers who wind up in the middle of difficult, politically charged teaching situations.
>
> —William Thelin and John Tassoni

Naturally, our first attempts at teaching this ethnographic writing course, although successful in the eyes of both teachers and students, reveal opportunities for improvement. Specifically, I would like to move the course more clearly in the direction of studying and practicing "civic rhetoric," eliminating sites that do not lead students from the role of observer to participant in community affairs while still allowing students to pick their own sites—one of the course's greatest strengths. Thelin and Tassoni, editors of *Blundering for a Change: Errors and Expectations in Critical Pedagogy*, explain that "blunders" in critical pedagogy "occur due to many factors, including institutional expectations, political hegemony, the malaise of our educational system, cultural assumptions about teaching/learning, and of course, instructor decisions/indecisions during any segment of the educational experience" (3). Certainly, these factors account for some of the early "blunders" in our own attempt at critical pedagogy. As a result, I am considering the following adaptations as I continue to "negotiate" this course.

Fieldworking, a composition textbook written by Elizabeth Chiseri-Strater and Bonnie Stone Sunstein, offers a comprehensive course of study in ethnographic writing, including excellent assignments and sample portfolios, and it was the ideal text for our first attempt at ethnography in GSU's first-year writing course. However, I will depart a bit from the *Fieldworking* approach in the reconfigured course, directing students to both historical and contemporary readings that address civic rhetoric. I want students to fully grasp Quintilian's concept of "a good [person] speaking well" and the phrase's historical implications (and mutations). In addition to the required handbook for first-year writing courses, I will adopt Elizabeth Ervin's *Public Literacy*, a slim text packed with clear explanations of public literacy and the public sphere, insightful examples, case studies, and challenging heuristics. Ervin encourages students to "think rhetorically" in every facet of her curriculum, grounded in the pedagogical cornerstones of peer review and the writer's notebook. *Public Literacy* is ideally suited for this reconfigured first-year writing course; it bridges the chasm between my disciplinary concerns and the desire to engage in a metropolitan university philosophy of writing instruction.

I will adopt another 2000 publication, Bruce McComiskey's *Teaching Composition as a Social Process*, as an accompanying TA manual for this course. McComiskey's work, described by James Zebroski as "one of the first books on cultural studies in composition that gets beyond postmodern theory to issues of scholarship and teaching," dovetails nicely with the Ervin text. In addition to offering teachers lucid analyses of social-process rhetorical inquiry and the post-process movement in composition, McComiskey provides detailed assignments that teachers might use to move students beyond observations of sites and artifacts toward rhetorical intervention. For example, an assignment asking students to critically examine the culture of work (a typical assignment in our fieldworking course) culminates in a heuristic asking students to identify a worksite problem and then write a letter to a member of the company in a position to improve working conditions. This particular heuristic includes detailed guidelines for analyzing the letter's audience, the audience's stance toward the problem, and the rhetorical purpose of the student's intervention (63–67).

The Ervin and McComiskey texts are instrumental in helping me solidify ways to improve upon the fieldworking approach by moving students from observation and analysis to direct civic participation and, ultimately, public writing. Atlanta affords our students a wealth of important political, cultural, and historical sites unique to our city, as well as a rich storehouse of philanthropic and social organizations where students might foster observational habits and skills leading to public discourse. When viewed against the public image of "Hotlanta," both a booming international city and "Capital of the New South," stereotypical urban social issues of homelessness, social inequity, poverty, race relations, and violence represent exigencies unique to our Southern city's history, environment, and geography, and become "crucial differences" defining the city. These localized social issues, along with environmental concerns over water pollution and treatment, urban sprawl, and air quality, provide regional examples from the bounty of resources and occasions available to our students for entering Metropolitan Atlanta's public sphere as concerned citizens and writers. For example, consider this Atlanta exigency viewed in terms of writing instruction: the metropolitan area is growing at such a fast pace that Atlanta and its suburbs are faced with escalating traffic and resulting air quality issues that at times seem insurmountable. MARTA, Atlanta's public transportation system, does not extend into two northern counties where the majority of downtown commuters (and many of our students) live; Gwinnett and Cobb counties have repeatedly rejected the public transportation system for a multitude of economic, political, and social reasons. Investigating why these counties reject MARTA and researching organizations exploring alternative solutions to perhaps the most critical, long-term problem facing the metropolitan area (and students trying to commute to our downtown campus) provide fertile opportunities for students to engage in public discourse that is both meaningful and rhetorical.

Ideally, a hybrid ethnographic writing course, which includes the study of civic rhetoric, elements of service learning, and practice in writing for diverse publics, can afford urban and suburban students unique and authentic writing opportunities, expand first-year writing students' often narrow conceptions of academic research, foster an interaction with community, realistically incorporate writing across the discipline concepts, model public intellectualism, and encourage students to view themselves as agents in "real world" rhetorical situations.

This reconfiguration of our class in ethnographic writing adopts tenets of the metropolitan university that forward GSU's urban outreach mission and addresses what Ervin has labeled composition teachers' "increasing dissatisfaction with teaching writing in ways that objectify 'society' rather than foster students' direct interaction with it" ("Course Design" 43). By encouraging our students to enter the public sphere and engage in public writing, we are helping to restore in students "a sense of *civitas*, of belonging to one polity and community" (Brownell 23). We should reconstruct first-year writing curriculum and pedagogy so that the courses are meaningful for our particular students and forward our own disciplinary and institutional concerns. The metropolitan university philosophy offers those of us teaching at urban schools a compelling model for (re)viewing the courses we teach through an institutional lens.

APPENDIX

DECLARATION OF METROPOLITAN UNIVERSITIES

A number of presidents of metropolitan universities have signed the following declaration.

We, the leaders of metropolitan universities and colleges, embracing the historical values and principles which define all universities and colleges, and which make our institutions major intellectual resources for their metropolitan regions,

- reaffirm that the creation, interpretation, dissemination, and application of knowledge are the fundamental functions of our universities;

- assert and accept a broadened responsibility to bring these functions to bear on the needs of our metropolitan regions;

- commit our institutions to be responsive to the needs of our metropolitan areas by seeking new ways of using our human and physical resources to provide leadership in addressing metropolitan problems, through teaching, research and professional service.

Our teaching must:

- educate individuals to be informed and effective citizens, as well as capable practitioners of professions and occupations;

- be adapted to the particular needs of metropolitan students, including minorities and other underserved groups, adults of all ages, and the place-bound;

- combine research-based knowledge with practical application and experience, using the best current technology and pedagogical techniques.

Our research must:

- seek and exploit opportunities for linking basic investigation with practical application, and for creating synergistic interdisciplinary and multidisciplinary scholarly partnerships for attacking complex metropolitan problems while meeting the highest scholarly standards of the academic community.

Our professional service must include:

- development of creative partnerships with public and private enterprises that ensure that the intellectual resources of our institutions are fully engaged with such enterprises in mutually beneficial ways;

- close working relationships with the elementary and secondary schools of our metropolitan regions, aimed at maximizing the effectiveness of the entire metropolitan education system, from preschool through post-doctoral levels;

- the fullest possible contributions to the cultural life and general quality of life of our metropolitan regions.

WORKS CITED

Basinger, Julianne. "A New Way of Classifying Colleges Elates Some and Perturbs Others." *The Chronicle of Higher Education* 11 August 2000: A31+.

Brownell, Blaine A. "Metropolitan Universities: Past, Present, and Future." *Metropolitan Universities: An Emerging Model in American Higher Education.* Ed. Daniel M. Johnson and David A. Bell. Denton: U of North Texas P, 1995. 17–26.

Cheakolos, Christina. "Building a Better GSU in Six Years." *The Atlanta Journal and Constitution* 7 September 1997: G5.

Chiseri-Strater, Elizabeth, and Bonnie Stone Sunstein. *Fieldworking: Reading and Writing Research.* Boston: Bedford St. Martins, 1997.

Crowley, Sharon. "The Perilous Life and Times of Freshman English." *Freshman English News* 14 (1986): 11–16.

Ervin, Elizabeth. "Course Design, English 496: Senior Seminar in Writing." *Composition Studies* 26 (1998): 37–57.

———. *Public Literacy.* New York: Longman, 2000.

Georgia State University. 24 August 2000. <http://www.gsu.edu>.

Hathaway, Charles E., Paige E. Mulhollan, and Karen A. White. "Metropolitan Universities: Models for the Twenty-First Century." *Metropolitan Universities: An Emerging Model in American Higher Education.* Ed. Daniel M. Johnson and David A. Bell. Denton: U of North Texas P, 1995. 5–16.

Information on the Coalition of Urban and Metropolitan Universities. 24 August 2000. <http://www.ucf.edu/metroplitan/ coalition.html>.

McComiskey, Bruce. *Teaching Composition as a Social Process.* Logan: Utah State UP, 2000.

Ruch, Charles P., and Eugene P. Trani. "Scope and Limitations of Community Interactions." *Metropolitan Universities: An Emerging Model in American Higher Education.* Ed. Daniel M. Johnson and David A. Bell. Denton: U of North Texas P, 1995. 231–43.

Schuh, Edward G. "The Preparation of Future Faculty for Metropolitan Universities." *Metropolitan Universities: An Emerging Model in American Higher Education.* Ed. Daniel M. Johnson and David A. Bell. Denton: U of North Texas P, 1995. 123–34.

Suggs, Ernie. "GSU and Urban Powerhouse." *The Atlanta Constitution* 28 September 1998: C1.

———. "Main Street GSU: Georgia State President Carl Patton Pitches His Vision for the University." *The Atlanta Constitution* 13 January 1999: B1.

———. "Patton to Unveil Blueprint for GSU Regents." *The Atlanta Constitution* 12 January 1999: C3.

Thelin, William H., and John Paul Tassoni, eds. *Blundering for a Change: Errors and Expectations in Critical Pedagogy.* Portsmouth, NJ: Boynton/Cook, 2000.

Undergraduate Catalog, 2000–2001. Atlanta: GSU, 2000.

CHAPTER TWELVE

URBAN LITERACIES AND THE
ETHNOGRAPHIC PROCESS
Composing Communities at the
Center for Worker Education

Barbara Gleason

As it is with any city, there are many "New Yorks." There is the New York of well-known tourist attractions, the New York of fiction and creative nonfiction, the New York of news media coverage, and the New York of film and television. Popular media images call to mind Manhattan skylines, Wall Street, bird's eye views of densely populated islands strung together by bridges, and noisy Manhattan streets lined with subway entrances, yellow cabs, pedestrians, and uniformed police. These images suggest romance, fast-paced lifestyles, professional opportunity, upward mobility, and wealth, but also risk-taking, greed, corruption, and danger. Woody Allen's *Manhattan, Annie Hall,* and *Manhattan Murder Mystery* portray comfortably established white urban professionals living in upscale Manhattan neighborhoods. Other films, such as *Wall Street* and *Serpico,* depict the greed and corruption associated with two well-known New York institutions—the stock market and the New York City Police Department. And Alfred Hitchcock's *Saboteur* and *Rear Window* foreground risk taking, intrigue, and danger in New York City. These are a few of the images and themes that come to mind if you know New York mainly through media images, but they do not represent the everyday lives of most New Yorkers.

The setting of Hitchcock's *Rear Window* does, however, suggest an important dimension of New Yorkers' lives: everyday neighborhood life depicted by a configuration of apartment buildings, as seen through the eyes of photographer L. B. Jeffries (played by Jimmy Stewart). Confined to a wheelchair with a broken leg, Jeffries stares compulsively down at a courtyard and out into the windows of his neighbors' apartments, sometimes using binoculars for close-up looks. Jeffries's voyeurism evokes a sense of local community that many New Yorkers experience, a feeling of being connected to frequently nameless neighbors by the shared common space of an apartment building or a city block or a named district within one of the five boroughs— for instance, Manhattan's Greenwich Village, Murray Hill, or Harlem; Queens' Flushing, Forest Hills, or Astoria; or Brooklyn's Bedford Stuyvesant, Park Slope, or Bay Ridge.

New York neighborhoods are home to thousands of commuter students in college. Yet we who teach in urban colleges often know little about our own students' off-campus lives and communities. Consequently, we are uninformed about who our students are and the environments in which they converse, study, read, and write. By inviting students to write about their own communities and places of special interest, we can learn about their lives and literacies away from school while better helping them develop academic literacies. Meanwhile, our students are composing college assignments in familiar linguistic and social environments, forging their own paths within "the rich interplay of purpose, genre, register, textual convention, and institutional expectation" (Rose, "Narrowing" 295).

CITY COLLEGE OF NEW YORK'S CENTER FOR WORKER EDUCATION

In New York's lower Manhattan neighborhood of Tribeca, on the sixth and seventh floors of a century-old building at 99 Hudson St., there is a bachelor's degree program for returning adults called the Center for Worker Education. This program is part of the City College of New York, an institution that began in 1847 as a tuition-free combination secondary school and college for New York City boys. Although founded far more recently (in 1981), the Center for Worker Education furthers City College's original mission: "Make [the new college] the property of the people—open the doors to all—let the children of the rich and the poor take their seats together, and know of no distinction save that of industry, good conduct, and intellect" (Traub 24).

City College has been written about extensively, some might say excessively, but there are good reasons for its popularity among authors: it has educated a long list of highly talented scientists, artists, politicians, and writers, including Ira Gershwin, Jonas Salk, Colin Powell, and Daniel Patrick Moynihan; and it has always offered educational opportunities to poor and working-class people who might not have attended college at all. But there is one more reason, perhaps the most compelling of all—City College has often been associated with controversy. In the 1930s and 1940s, the college offered a strongly intellectual climate where students of diverse political leanings (with many leaning Left) could enter into lively discussions and debates. Joseph Dorman describes a familiar scene in the City College of this era:

> In the college's cafeteria alcoves, radicals gathered in constant uninterrupted discussion from morning to night—the anti-Stalinist opponents of the Soviet Union in alcove one, their Stalinist foes in alcove two. . . . Highly competitive, intellectually agile, and loudly vocal, the young radicals were attempting to grasp the nature of their crumbling world through the lens of Marxism. (2–3)

Dorman's account focuses specifically on "New York intellectuals" Irving Kristol, Nathan Glazer, Irving Howe, and Daniel Bell, who all attended City College in the 1930s, yet it also captures the general intellectual climate of the college during these formative years.

Radical intellectuals were not the only population to find a haven in the alcoves of City College. In his fictional account of Julius and Ethel Rosenberg (who were also in attendance during the heyday of the New York intellectuals), E. L. Doctorow captures another aspect of the spirit of City College in the 1930s:

> A hill, a long hill rises from the valley of 125th Street. . . . And the trolleys pull themselves up the tracks of that hill, magnetized to the rails, jerking and gliding up the tracks of the hill of rails on spurts of current sucked by the pantography from the overhead wires; and these trolleys, in parade, carry students from their jobs through the darkness to their nighttime classes. Fences of planted spears and buildings of grey and black stone, it's not Yale but it's free and its academic standards are high . . . [a] grubby municipal accommodation for the sons and daughters of immigrants, poor people, largely Jewish. (193)

At City College, where there were no "secret quotas for Jewish students" (Dorman 2), evening classes became the avenue of access for students who had to work or who did not meet City College's increasingly stringent entrance requirements.[1] By the 1950s, a strong evening program was well in place, establishing the rationale for a separate off-campus program that would later become the Center for Worker Education.

Throughout most of its existence, City College was open to students of any social and economic background, yet it maintained high standards for admission and retention. In 1970, however, City College and all of the City

University of New York's (CUNY's) sixteen other colleges were transformed dramatically by an open admissions policy, another cause for controversy both in the national media and on the campuses themselves (Lavin and Hyllegard; Lu; Traub). With the advent of open admissions and its attending abolition of stringent entrance requirements, the students of City College became far more culturally and linguistically diverse: moreover, many of the "open admissions students" were not adequately prepared for the rigors of academic life. It was in this climate of shifting requirements and standards that Mina Shaughnessy began to administer City College's newly created basic writing program (Maher; Shaughnessy). However, soon after 1970, CUNY's senior colleges retreated from their newly instated open admissions policies, restricting their promise of unconditional access for all New York City high school graduates to community colleges only (yet another source of controversy).

But when the Center for Worker Education opened its doors in 1981, a true open admissions policy reemerged within City College, one of CUNY's senior colleges that had formerly abandoned policies providing unrestricted access.[2] Working adult students who would otherwise be admitted only to community colleges could now enter a senior college bachelor's degree program. Nearly all students at the Center for Worker Education are employed full-time during the day while attending evening and weekend classes. This off-campus branch of City College, which has its own line-item budget in the New York State Legislature, grew out of an alliance among the New York Federal Executive Board, Teamsters Union Local 237, and City College (Quinn). From 1979 to 1981, City College (based in Harlem) offered lower division college courses for federal employees at 26 Federal Plaza in lower Manhattan, and Teamsters Union Local 237 simultaneously initiated a bachelor's degree in labor studies at Empire State College of the State University of New York. In 1981, these two programs joined to create the Center for Worker Education, an entirely new City College BA program in interdisciplinary liberal arts, and in 1986 an Early Childhood Education BS with elementary education certification was added to the existing program. Today, the Center for Worker Education serves a population of approximately one thousand part- and full-time students; it has a dean, a faculty of five full-time professors, several visiting professors who are full-time faculty at City College's main campus or elsewhere, and many adjunct instructors. Academic and financial aid advisors counsel students, participate in curriculum development, and offer many other services, including student admissions workshops. Additionally, students at the Center for Worker Education benefit from a strong support staff of receptionists, writing tutors, and a technology assistant.

The ages of students at the Center for Worker Education range from eighteen to sixty-five, but most are in their thirties and forties. They are primarily women and people of color: African Americans, immigrants from the

Caribbean, Central America, or South America, and, less frequently, immigrants from countries in Europe, Asia, and Africa. A small percentage of the Center's students are working-class whites, usually from New York City, who typically have self-acknowledged ethnic identities, such as Irish, Italian, or Puerto Rican. Not surprisingly, many adult students attending classes at the Center for Worker Education retain strong roots in their neighborhoods, where they may have lived since childhood or moved to as adults for cultural and economic reasons.

WRITING ETHNOGRAPHIES OF COMMUNITY

The sociocultural identities of students at the Center for Worker Education are very often inscribed in a four-phase ethnographic writing assignment that I use in my introductory writing courses. In the first phase of this assignment, students select a local community to study and write a proposal for an ethnographic research project. In the second phase, they observe the community they have chosen and write descriptive field notes, which are turned in as part of the project. In the third phase, students interview community members and transcribe their audio recordings. In the final phase, these student ethnographers analyze their field notes, primary source documents collected from the community, and sometimes secondary sources in order to write a finished ethnographic report (see Chiseri-Strater and Sunstein; Gleason, "Returning Adults").

What do ethnographic research and writing processes offer to developing urban writers that other composing tasks frequently do not? First, ethnographic writing encourages students to use their existing oral and literate language competencies (e.g., in oral interviews and written field notes) as scaffolds for acquiring standardized language forms and academic discourse conventions that are crucial to successful communication in college and beyond (Kutz, Groden, and Zamel; Gleason, "Connected Literacies"). Second, ethnographic writing allows students a developmental space between their own need to find an "authentic voice" (e.g., by writing about issues of concern to them) and their institution's obligation to provide instruction in academic reading and writing (Bartholomae; Elbow). And finally, ethnographic research writing enables students to connect their lived experiences and literacies in home, work, and neighborhood communities with their learning in college classrooms (Cooper; Lytle; Chiseri-Strater).

Many students' ethnographic research projects portray their involvement in communities away from school. And because these ethnographies record the social streams of students' lives, they also reveal the class, race, and gender dimensions of student writers' identities. At the Center for Worker Education, my adult students' ethnographic writing often talks back to myths of writers as inspired artists. Instead, each student's writing offers evidence of what James Gee calls a *discourse:* "a sort of 'identity kit' which comes complete with the appropriate costume and instructions on how to act, talk, and often write, so as to take on a particular role that others will recognize" (526). In Gee's analysis, we all have primary discourses that we learn at home "by being [members] of a primary socializing group (family, clan, peer group)" (527). We also acquire secondary discourses in "various non-home based social institutions," such as churches, schools, and businesses, when we are allowed access to and "apprenticeships" in them (527). Gee further analyzes discourses as dominant and non-dominant: dominant discourses allow access to "wider status and social goods in the society at large" and non-dominant discourses allow "solidarity with a particular social network" (528). What Gee's discussion of discourses offers that other strictly language-based theories do not is a notion of context in which language is continually entwined with identity, agency, culture, and concrete life situations.

Gee's conceptual framework (language+culture+language acquisition) has a direct bearing on the literacy experiences of the adult students whom I teach at the Center for Worker Education. These students acquire academic literacy and mainstream culture as secondary discourses, a phenomenon that Terry Dean discusses in "Multicultural Classrooms." For such urban students in particular, thinking and writing ethnographically is especially beneficial because, as Shirley Brice Heath has shown us, ethnography helps learners acquire new ways of interpreting written and oral discourses. By practicing ethnographic research and writing strategies, students come to "see their daily actions in new terms: as the recording of events, discovering of patterns, and figuring out of options in making decisions" (Heath 339). For students whose existing literacies differ significantly from academic literacies, ethnography offers a powerful critical tool for recognizing and learning about these differences.

To illustrate the uses of ethnography as a way to teach writing in urban contexts, I will describe my experience with Audrey, a forty-one-year-old African American woman who was enrolled in my ethnographic writing course at the Center for Worker Education. During this course, Audrey experienced significant improvements in her academic writing while completing her four-phase ethnographic research project on one of her own Brooklyn neighborhood communities.

"Tired of Receiving Low Grades Due to Poor Grammar"

Audrey grew up in the Bedford Stuyvesant area of Brooklyn, the seventh of fourteen children. In her literacy autobiography (the first assignment I give in my ethnographic writing classes), she recalls a family that included an absent father, a maternal grandmother, and a strong mother. Although Audrey's mother did not complete high school herself, she supported Audrey's early childhood literacy learning at home and expressed a strong desire for Audrey to receive a good education. Toward this end, her mother arranged for Audrey to leave public schools that were close to her Bedford Stuyvesant home, where Audrey felt comfortable, in order to attend a high school in a white neighborhood. But the 1970s social environment of Audrey's new school was so hostile to black students that Audrey quit attending her freshman classes, while mentioning nothing to her mother of the problems she was encountering in school. With good academic advising, her own hard work, and summer school attendance, however, Audrey made up her lost classes and graduated within the expected four-year time frame, an accomplishment Audrey remains proud of today. After a year and a half in community college, Audrey left school and started a family. Today, Audrey is married and a mother of five children. She continues to live in Bedford Stuyvesant, where she also works as an assistant teacher in an early childhood education program.

Audrey enrolled in my writing course at the Center for Worker Education with serious concerns about language, which she communicated in a letter that I asked all students to write in the first week of classes. Here are some excerpts from Audrey's letter:[3]

> Dear Prof. Gleason,
>
> I am in your class because I need this class as a required course. I need to get help with the way I express myself in writing. I am tired of receiving low grades due to poor grammar. I will love to sit and write knowing that I have express myself well. . . . Many of my teachers encouraged me by telling how smart a student I am yet when I receive my papers they are comments like these "you have the content of an excellent paper however you need help in the way you present you ideas." . . . In writing, my assignments some times I tend to procrastinate. Although, I turn in my work in on time. Most times, I start an assignment but wait to the last moment to complete my tasks. However, I put time and effort in my writing even if it cost me some sleep.

In this letter, Audrey expresses deep concern about her written language skills and associated low grades; then Audrey admits to procrastinating and completing assignments at the last minute. Both points of information help to explain why Audrey was receiving negative responses (and mostly Cs) from her college teachers.

Audrey speaks and often writes a form of English that James Gee would identify as a non-dominant discourse. It is most evident in her spoken language, her ethnographic field notes, and in an oral story that Audrey told and later transcribed. The following excerpt comes from Audrey's transcribed story: "Out of all her other children you know um she tell me I'm special. You know even today as a grown woman mother says I'm her lucky child. I thank God, for a lot of things I done for myself was for her. . . ." In this transcript, there are two obvious nonstandard language forms: 1) "she tell me" and 2) "things I done for myself." These features of Audrey's spoken language appear sporadically (and probably in rule-governed patterns) in her spoken language; they are also partially evident in her written language, where they are likely to be viewed by Audrey's teachers as "writing errors" rather than as recognizable language patterns rooted in Audrey's sociocultural identity.

Audrey used the four-phase ethnographic research writing project that I describe above to write about a community to which she was deeply committed, a tenant patrol group in Tompkins Housing, where she now resides on a block not far from her childhood home. This project enabled Audrey to recognize and appreciate the differences between her oral and literate discourses, improving her academic writing in the process.

Audrey's Ethnography of Tenant
Patrol Volunteers in a Housing Project

Audrey approached her ethnographic research project with two related goals in mind: to create a positive image of the tenant patrol volunteers and to draw attention to the important services they render to their community. As Audrey later explains in her report, "The patrollers play an important role in the housing development. They take back their buildings from the drug dealers." As a volunteer patroller herself, Audrey was sensitive to other tenants' charges that patrollers are "snoops and gossips." Audrey wanted to rehabilitate the patrollers' image by creating a positive representation in her writing.

In the first lines of her two-page research proposal, Audrey articulates her aim as a writer and describes the community she will study:

> As a tenant in a housing project, I am convinced that the housing tenant patrol volunteers are not given the acknowledgement they deserved. They are provided with a phone for emergencies during patrol hours, a table with some chairs for some who can't stand for long and if petty cash is available, light refreshments will be provided. A jacket and hat is provided to let the visitors and residents see that the tenant patrol team is on duty. One night out of a year they go out for dinner at the community room for volunteer recognition day. This day is to recognize the patrollers and other staff who has labored though out the year.

As Audrey reiterates in her concluding paragraph, she wants the volunteer tenant patrollers "to be rewarded with more than just a recognition day" because, Audrey reasons, "they are a strong presence in their development and in their community and need to be recognized as such." With this clearly stated purpose in mind, Audrey set out to observe and interview her fellow tenants and volunteer patrollers in the Tompkins Housing Project of Bed-Stuy, Brooklyn.

Audrey began her research by writing descriptive field notes of her observations and interviews at Tompkins Housing. Below is an excerpt from Audrey's field notes:

> April 2000 It is 6:00pm Ms Louise is setting up the table. Here comes Ms everlyn and mantree. They are gathering around the table. They comes with-Hello's and small talk about the weather. Everlyn mentions Audrey you joining us tonight. I Respond by saying I'm here but not as a patroller. The convensatun Begins about me. They wanted to know why aren't I'm at school tonight. I shared with them about my assignment and they all appeared to welcome me as I gather my notes. It's 6:15pm He comes our First vistor for tonight he's greeted with hello then Ms Evelyn reaches for the pad She ask him to please sign in he Reply Im not a vister Im my sister Guess.

Audrey's field notes, as well as most of her other writing for this class, raise questions about how native English speaking writers from non-mainstream cultures acquire academic literacies.

As her college writing teacher, I encouraged and sometimes rather forcefully nudged Audrey to produce written texts that were in line with the expectations of the institutional environment in which we were both working. This had been Audrey's foremost concern at the beginning of the semester. In addition to the occasional appearance of spoken dialect forms, Audrey's academic writing exhibited frequent misspellings and punctuation errors, as well as some cohesion and coherence problems in her discourse. For Audrey, the challenge was to find some way to meet her teacher's (my) expectations and to avoid earning a low grade.

Although Audrey may have consciously learned very little about punctuation rules and formal written language during our fifteen-week semester together, her primary language remained intact as far as I could tell from her in-class spoken language and her free writing. However, what Audrey did change was her approach to writing and the "presentation" of her final drafts. By the end of the term, Audrey was handing in second and third drafts that conformed more closely to the academic language conventions and discourse forms associated with college writing. This improvement is evident in her ethnographic report, from which the following passage is excerpted:

> The tenant patrollers are in a sense security, the housing project does not have any security. However, because they are only volunteers they have no right to take matters into their own hands. They have to leave it up to the police for their own safety. . . . Although security is their first priority, they

play other roles also. They conduct clean-up campaigns, this is done among the children to promote cleaner grounds. It also serves as an incentive to get the children to be more involved in their communities. They are rewarded with McDonalds and around the holidays, along with other donations from other tenants, tenant patrol plan and supervise parties within the hallways for them. Another job duty is to condole. The tenant patrollers visit the sick and shut in and when a tenant passes away, they take up collections to help the family. They also help the senior citizens and the handicap in and out of the building.

This writing, which Audrey submitted on the last day of class, is markedly better than most of the writing that she handed in during the semester. I knew that Audrey could not (and perhaps would not wish to) dramatically alter her own primary language style; and I also knew she could not fully acquire a secondary style during such a short span of time. However, Audrey *could* develop her awareness of language and become something of a *bricoleur*, a person who learns language and literacy "by indirect observation rather than by reading, by watching rather than by . . . testing, . . . [and] by participation rather than instruction" (Goody 140). Engaged as she was in listening to everyday conversations, talking to informants, recording and reviewing spoken language, writing and reviewing her field notes, and then writing a more formal essay, Audrey had many opportunities to notice and to practice different language varieties and writing styles.

The improvement in Audrey's writing is evident in several final drafts that she handed in at the end of the semester. Audrey's later writing conforms more closely to the standardized language forms and written language conventions that are expected in college. Equally important, Audrey sharpened her ability to structure ideas and connect them meaningfully and logically within paragraphs and in longer discourse units. Audrey's improved writing resulted from her increased attention to language, from recording conversational forms and embedding excerpts as quotes in an academic essay, and from several newly acquired writing practices: starting earlier on assignments, conferencing with writing tutors, revising, proofreading, and getting others to read and proofread her drafts, both with her and for her. Further, because she expresses herself especially well in everyday conversation, Audrey was strongly positioned to profit from opportunities to interview people, to listen to and record conversations, and to conference with others about her written drafts.

By the end of the semester, Audrey had begun to combine her partial acquisition of academic language conventions with the use of strategies that helped compensate for what she did not know how to do, such as discussing her drafts with peers, teacher, or tutors and asking someone to help her with her editing. In the cover letter that she wrote for her end-of-term portfolio, Audrey explains,

I have many opportunities to get help from the tutors although JF and AS was forever on call. . . . I wanted to improve my writing skills. I've learned that writing can be enjoyable. . . . The most important skills I've learned was to grab the dictionary and use the required handbooks as needed. My spelling has improved and as I went over the many rules in grammar, I had found that many of my problems were right. . . .

As a writer, I still have some obstacles. But, I know that other writers have many challenges too. I have learn to revise and revise and let others help to edit my papers. . . .

At the end of the semester, Audrey earned a B as a final course grade. I awarded this grade on the basis of 1) her progress as a writer and 2) the quality of the final drafts in her end-of-term portfolio.

The six-page ethnographic report that Audrey completed presents an informative, coherent, and interesting portrait of tenant patrol volunteers and their work for the Tompkins Housing community. Her success with this project is due, in part, to Audrey's deeply felt commitment to her housing community and to her persuasive aim: improving the image of tenant patrol volunteers. In short, this was much more than an academic exercise for Audrey. There are clear descriptions of physical spaces, tenants, and volunteer patrollers, as well as summaries of interviews. However, Audrey's report lacks some features of the best ethnographic writing produced by the adult students I teach. Unlike many other students' reports, Audrey's has no references to primary or secondary sources and relatively few quotes from interviews; moreover, interpretation and analysis are far less evident than description, narration, and summary. Nonetheless, the final drafts and the cover letter in Audrey's portfolio are clear, purposeful, at times moving, at times humorous, and very often in conformance with the language conventions and discourse forms associated with "academic writing."

CONCLUSION

Although Audrey had specific goals in mind when she entered the course (to improve her academic language), she struggled throughout the semester. At mid-term, Audrey was by no means assured of a good grade for the course, yet she eventually earned a B. The ethnographic project, undertaken in the second half of the term, was key to her high course grade, although this was the most complex and challenging assignment of the entire semester.

For inexperienced writers, especially those in urban contexts, ethnographic writing presents both difficulties and opportunities: it is difficult because student writers at first cannot imagine what a finished ethnographic essay might look like; it provides opportunities because students are not

bound to a particular form and it enables students to capitalize on their existing urban literacies (rather than immediately be punished for them). As a
genre, ethnography is a hybrid, a mixture of different discourse structures,
purposes, and styles; it combines description, storytelling, historical narrative, linguistic analysis, and cultural analysis. In ethnography, a writer's style
can be plain, simple, and literal or decorative, elaborate, and metaphorical.
Clifford Geertz captures this complexity best by referring to ethnographic
writing as "blurred genres." Students can use a strongly subjective narrative
voice, with their inner experiences included in the essay; or they may express
themselves in a more public voice, with an objective orientation. Essay
arrangements can be episodic and chronological or thematic and topic-ori-
ented. Some student essays are mainly descriptive; others have a particular
aim or point of view or critical frame. And writing ethnographies, with all of
these options inherent in the genre, enables urban students to use the literacies that they already have as a way to improve the academic literacies they
seek to acquire.

Writing ethnographies encourages students to become conscious of
rhetorical options. As they write, students learn to ask questions: Can I use
"I"? Can I include my own experiences? How do I focus all of this information? How is the essay supposed to be organized? Do I have to have a thesis
statement? Should I change the names of the people I'm writing about? How
long should this essay be? Do I have to have a bibliography? These and many
other questions are generated not only by the writing process but also by reading other students' essays and professional authors' work. The experience of
reading ethnography can help students imagine communities that they might
choose to study. Titles of student essays are suggestive: My Name is John and
I'm an Alcoholic; Botanicas, Places for Cures; The Vermont Street Block
Association; The BMCC Learning Resource Center; Volunteer Services:
Behind Bars; NYPD Routine; A Profession of Cosmetology; Legal Techni-
cians' Job Problems.

Reading essays by students and professional authors also illustrates the
many different styles of writing that are available to urban writing students.
And, since we are learning about communities in our city, we also read pro-
fessional authors' writing about New York, including an excerpt from Edward
Rivera's memoir, *Family Installments*, Zora Neal Hurston's "Story in Harlem
Slang" (a fictionalized portrait of men talking together on street corners), and
Thomas Wolfe's "Only the Dead Know Brooklyn" (collected in Lopate).
Reading and writing about the city in which we live leaves us all with a
stronger sense of understanding, ownership, and, most important of all,
belonging. It also helps my students at the Center for Worker Education learn
to value their existing urban literacies while simultaneously acquiring academic literacies that will help them succeed in college and beyond.[4]

NOTES

1. Students who did not meet City College's admissions criteria could enter on a non-matriculated basis and later be admitted if they earned satisfactory grades.

2. The admissions standards for City College's Center for Worker Education have been equivalent to those of CUNY community colleges (but not CUNY senior colleges) since its inception. However, a recently instituted admissions policy for all CUNY senior colleges requires senior college applicants to pass the ACT exam before being admitted. As a program within City College, the Center for Worker Education will be affected dramatically by this policy.

3. Audrey's writing has not been edited.

4. I would like to thank Edward Quinn for making some helpful suggestions and "Audrey" for allowing me to quote her writing.

WORKS CITED

Bartholomae, David. "Writing with Teachers: A Conversation with Peter Elbow." *College Composition and Communication* 46 (1995): 62–71.

Chiseri-Strater, Elizabeth. *Academic Literacies: The Public and Private Discourse of University Students*. Portsmouth, NH: Boynton/Cook, 1991.

Chiseri-Strater, Elizabeth, and Bonnie Stone Sunstein. *FieldWorking: Reading and Writing Research*. Boston: Bedford/St. Martin's, 1997.

Cooper, Marilyn. "The Ecology of Writing." *College English* 48 (1986): 364–75.

Dean, Terry. "Multicultural Classrooms: Monocultural Teachers." *College Composition and Communication* 40 (1989): 23–37.

Doctorow, E. L. *The Book of Daniel.* New York: Random House, 1971.

Dorman, Joseph. *Arguing the World: The New York Intellectuals in Their Own Words*. New York: The Free Press, 2000.

Elbow, Peter. "Being a Writer vs. Being an Academic: A Conflict in Goals." *College Composition and Communication* 46 (1995): 72–83.

Gee, James Paul. "Literacy, Discourse, and Linguistics: Introduction and What is Literacy?" *Literacy: A Critical Sourcebook.* Ed. Ellen Cushman, Eugene R. Kintgen, Barry M. Kroll, and Mike Rose. Boston: Bedford/St. Martin's, 2001. 525–44.

Gleason, Barbara. "Connected Literacies of Adult Literacies: Ethnographies of Work in College Composition." *Multiple Literacies in the 21st Century*. Ed. Charles Bazerman, Brian Huot, and Beth Stroble. New York: Hampton Press, forthcoming.

———. "Returning Adults to the Mainstream: Toward a Curriculum for Diverse Student Writers." *Mainstreaming Basic Writers: Politics and Pedagogies of Access.* Ed. Gerri McNenny. Assoc. Ed. Sallyanne H. Fitzgerald. Mahwah, NJ: Lawrence Erlbaum, 2001. 121–44.

Goody, Jack. *The Domestication of the Savage Mind.* London: Cambridge UP, 1977.

Heath, Shirley Brice. *Ways with Words: Language, Life, and Work in Communities and Classrooms.* UK: Cambridge UP, 1983.

Kutz, Eleanor, Suzy Q. Groden, and Vivan Zamel. *The Discovery of Competence: Teaching and Learning with Diverse Student Writers.* Portsmouth, NH: Boynton/Cook/Heinemann, 1993.

Lavin, David E., and David Hyllegard. *Changing the Odds: Open Admissions and the Life Chances of the Disadvantaged.* New Haven: Yale UP, 1996.

Lopate, Phillip, ed. *Writing New York: A Literary Anthology.* New York: Library of America, 1998.

Lu, Min Zhan. "Conflict and Struggle: The Enemies or Preconditions of Basic Writing?" *College English* 54 (1992): 887–913.

Lytle, Susan. "Living Literacy: Rethinking Development in Adulthood." *Literacy: A Critical Sourcebook.* Ed. Ellen Cushman, Eugene R. Kintgen, Barry M. Kroll, and Mike Rose. Boston: Bedford/St. Martin's, 2001. 376–401.

Maher, Jane. *Mina P. Shaughnessy: Her Life and Work.* Urbana: NCTE, 1997.

Quinn, Edward. "Teaching Writing at the Center for Worker Education: A Short History." *The Compositor: CCNY English Department Newsletter* Feb. 1994. 1–3.

Rose, Mike. "Narrowing the Mind and the Page: Remedial Writers and Cognitive Reductionism." *College Composition and Communication* 39 (1988): 267–302.

Shaughnessy, Mina P. *Errors and Expectations: A Guide for the Teacher of Basic Writing.* New York: Oxford UP, 1977.

Traub, James. *City on a Hill: Testing the American Dream at City College.* Reading, MA: Addison Wesley, 1994.

CHAPTER THIRTEEN

TEACHING WRITING IN A CONTEXT OF PARTNERSHIP

Ann M. Feldman

Megan Bye, a student in a first-year writing class at the University of Illinois at Chicago (UIC), commented on her emerging sense of place during this course:

> I live in a suburb and take the train every day. When we started reading the book [*City Life: Urban Expectations in a New World*, by Witold Rybczynski] I'd begin to look out the window and see how the views changed from the suburbs to Chicago and then when we got really close to Chicago, there's all these really rundown buildings. I began to wonder . . . if that's where people lived and worked when they migrated here. I've been looking out the window differently since I read that book.

Megan's writing course, "A Tale of Too Many Cities: Globalization and the Metropolis," designed by teaching assistant David Dudenhoefer, examined urban issues from a wide variety of perspectives, using Chicago as a constant point of reference. Megan's comments suggest a growing awareness of the importance of history and context initiated by the reading, discussion, and writing occurring in her composition class.

First-year writing classes at UIC aim to heighten a student's sense of writing as a highly contextual and consequential activity, asking students to become interlocutors in ongoing public conversations. But just as we ask our students to understand writing as a contextual process, we too need to understand the *teaching* of writing as a situated process, taking into account its place in the newly emerging context of the engaged university that continually reinvents itself in reciprocal partnerships with its neighbors. As the boundaries of many urban universities are reconstituted in an effort to establish meaningful community partnerships, it makes sense to reexamine the teaching of writing in this newly emerging context.

In response to national and global issues as they are played out locally in its urban metropolitan areas, UIC has recently redefined itself through its Great Cities Initiative. The first-year writing program at UIC has begun developing partnerships with neighboring agencies and institutions, and these partnerships comprise the Writing Partners Program, which got its start as part of the Great Cities Initiative. In the Writing Partners Program, UIC's composition staff are released from teaching first-year writing classes and funded instead to work at a community agency or school on whatever projects are appropriate—writing grants, reports, or newsletters or developing a literacy program. These staff members then return to the writing classroom to design and teach "engaged" courses in which students learn, write, and, potentially, apply their knowledge in local urban settings.

In the first section of this chapter, "The Context of an Engaged University," I describe the development of the Great Cities Initiative and explain how a mission that supports fluid boundaries between the community and the university can provide a productive context for writing instruction. In the next section, "Establishing Writing Partnerships," I describe our current and ongoing partnership with Benito Juárez Community Academy, a high school in the neighboring community of Pilsen. In the last section, "Teaching and Assessing Writing in a Context of Partnership," I consider the challenging question of how to teach writing as a situated process and as a tool for consequential changes. Our assumptions about composition studies and community partnerships intersect, suggesting new ways to understand the impact of teaching and writing in highly reciprocal spaces.

THE CONTEXT OF AN ENGAGED UNIVERSITY

UIC opened its doors in 1946 as a two-year commuter school (an undergraduate division of the University of Illinois at Urbana-Champaign) but became an independent institution when ground was broken for its current site in 1963. Defining itself as an urban version of the land-grant institutions initiated with the Morrill Federal Land-Grant Act of 1862, UIC has struggled over how to fulfill what came to be known as its "urban mission." In "An Urban University and Its Academic Support Program: Teaching Basic Writing in the Context of an 'Urban Mission,'" Carol Severino traces the ways in which the trope "urban mission" has been used by universities to negotiate between excellence and remediation. UIC's urban mission, Severino reports, was reputed by some to be the result of a "deal" to provide services for the children of the former residents of displaced ethnic communities. Others recall that the previous Mayor Daley had promised a university for the children of the working classes. Historically, however, UIC faculty have been divided on the role of the university in its urban context—some have claimed that excellence could be achieved without attention to the school's urban location, and others have argued for a commitment to its current and former neighborhood residents.

In the early 1970s, UIC instituted the Educational Assistance Program (EAP), which recruited students from the largely African American communities on the near West Side and provided them with academic support. This program, modeled after the City University of New York's SEEK program, offered remedial composition courses and support in other subject areas for UIC's (then) mostly local student body. The EAP was one of UIC's first steps in the direction of an urban mission defined primarily by a process of "remediation," yet it was never very well supported by UIC's faculty and administration. Severino, now at the University of Iowa, taught in UIC's EAP program and tells of the persistent ambivalence between the university's commitment to its neighbors in the inner city and those who wanted a university of "excellence" undefined by its urban location. She describes how the university's ambivalence toward remedial education weakened the program and also weakened UIC's urban mission. However, it is unlikely that remedial education provided in the first year of college could overcome the students' unfamiliarity with academic work and the difficulty of being ill-prepared by the much-publicized Chicago City Schools prior to the reform efforts of the past two decades. Remediation is only one way to define a university's urban mission, and it often results in ivory-tower condescension rather than real reforms in urban communities.

The internal struggle between academic excellence and debt to its urban context continued as UIC merged with the University of Illinois Medical Center, thus becoming a Carnegie Class I Research University. For some time, UIC focused on the research efforts that would support its newfound status, ignoring its local urban context altogether. Yet while UIC's "remediation" urban mission was limited in its benefits to local Chicago communities, this push to excel in national research efforts also neglected UIC's real obligation to its neighbors altogether.

Eventually, UIC returned, under the leadership of Chancellor James Stukel, to the issue of its urban mission, redefining it in 1993 in terms of the Great Cities concept. The notion of an urban mission at UIC was reconceived in a more comprehensive way than before, connecting the university's traditional commitment to research, teaching, and service to the broader agenda of improving the quality of life in metropolitan Chicago. Initially, some faculty members expressed concern that this concept was little more than a public relations gesture, but over time it has taken hold and changed substantially the university's relationship with its surrounding communities. Now the metropolitan area of Chicago is seen by UIC faculty members as a rich resource, rather than merely as a site for required service. Engaged research depends on extended interactions and formal partnerships with local communities, communities that pose "questions and issues that represent opportunities for first-class research" (Wiewel and Broski, "Great Cities" 31).

UIC's Great Cities Initiative is based on notions of partnership and engagement, rather than the deficit relationship implied by the term *service*, which suggests that "the community, or society at large, had certain needs, and the university, as the home of experts, would fill these needs." In this earlier deficit model of service, researchers used the community as a "laboratory, with more or less compliant 'guinea pigs'" (Wiewel and Broski, "University Involvement" 16). The Great Cities Initiative, however, is based on a highly participatory view of partnership that "comprises literally hundreds of close relationships between urban communities and UIC's faculty, staff, and students built to help people and institutions face the issues and challenges of the city" (Perry). In the context of partnership, creating, applying, and disseminating knowledge depends as much on how community residents and agencies understand and analyze problems as it does on how academics understand and analyze them.

As a result of its Great Cities Initiative, UIC created the Great Cities Institute, which emerged in the context of this revised urban mission. The Great Cities Institute is an urban policy research center that draws together many existing campus programs and has influenced the university's research agenda. In addition, as a way of supporting multidisciplinary and applied research and outreach, the Great Cities Institute offers faculty seed grants and invites faculty to spend a year in residence at the Institute.

Perhaps the most innovative addition to the engaged landscape of the Great Cities Institute is the UIC Neighborhoods Initiative, which works in partnership with two adjacent neighborhoods—Pilsen, a Mexican American community located south of the campus, and an African American community, the Near West Side. The Neighborhoods Initiative, funded originally by the U.S. Department of Housing and Urban Development's Community Outreach Partnership Center, is now a well-established entity in the Chicago metropolitan area. It has developed an affordable housing consortium that improves the existing housing stock and facilitates new construction, provides technical assistance for business development, manages a healthcare clinic, offers training for nonprofit management and staff, and initiates school improvement programs. Built on a partnership model, the story of the Neighborhoods Initiative offers many lessons to those interested in working collaboratively in settings where power and politics reign. While many universities in urban settings target surrounding neighborhoods out of a self-interested desire to make the area safer for students and faculty, UIC wanted to demonstrate that the work of the Great Cities Institute was more than just an effort to improve public relations. Yet faculty members who conduct research in partnership with community agencies still struggle with the perceptions and realities of past political missteps taken by the university. Building partnerships takes time and involves both failures and successes.

As the role of the university changes in relation to its context, moving toward a more reciprocal relationship in developing, exchanging, and using knowledge, so the role of the writing course and the writing program must also change. Urban writing programs should no longer be viewed as providing only basic services required for success in university life. Instead the teaching of writing should be seen as parallel to the work of the urban university, contributing to, encouraging, and sustaining an education that will support students' critical and insightful participation in a democratic yet global society. Students in UIC's engaged writing classes enter a "learning atmosphere" with a strong sense that there is an increasingly dynamic connection between knowledge about writing and action-centered knowledge. Mary Walshok, who has tracked the changing role of knowledge production in engaged universities, argues that "knowledge needs connected to sustaining civic culture require critical thinking skills and familiarity with humanistic and intellectual knowledge sources as well as opportunities to participate in communities of discourse that can facilitate insight and understanding" (79). This engaged view of knowledge production goes far beyond what is typically seen as the goal of an undergraduate curriculum. Writing programs should place themselves squarely in the middle of this ongoing discussion, arguing for a substantial role in preparing students to participate in sustaining civic culture.

Not long ago, I spent a year as a scholar in residence at UIC's Great Cities Institute working to develop a conceptual framework for writing courses that would, first, offer students an opportunity to practice rhetorical inquiry into local urban institutions, and second, reflect UIC's expanded urban mission and its emerging identity as an engaged university. The courses that have been generated from this conceptual framework comprise the Writing Partners Program.

ESTABLISHING WRITING PARTNERSHIPS

The Writing Partners Program provides some of UIC's composition teachers with a paid stipend to work in community organizations. Those who successfully complete their community-based experiences become Writing Partners, and they bring to the writing classroom a firsthand understanding that urban issues are both academic topics and ongoing realities. Writing is viewed as a key activity in all of these settings, and students are asked to use writing to position themselves within these larger urban conversations. Seeing writing instruction as central to the work of an engaged university changes composition's role from providing an isolated skill to providing an intellectual lynchpin for the engaged academic work that will follow in subsequent years. The Writing Partners Program, and the composition classes we design as part of it, create a context in which to examine our changing understanding of service and its complex relationship with university and civic life; this program and its courses help us rethink how ideas of service might be reshaped so that students see engagement not as charitable giving but as the reciprocal structuring of knowledge and resources that benefit all participants. When students study writing as a way to promote both civic responsiveness and academic direction, first-year writing classes can no longer be characterized merely as isolated (or "basic") skills providers. And when we conceptualize our relationships with others as partnerships, we move from a one-way relationship of disseminating knowledge and charity to a two-way relationship in which knowledge and resources flow freely between the community and the university. The Writing Partners Program creates links among community agencies, writing instructors, and first-year writing students. When these links work, the flow of information, support, and activity is reciprocal: community agencies forward their own agendas, writing instructors broaden their professional and scholarly profiles, and students engage in writing activities in the context of urban social issues.

Each graduate student who teaches in our program takes English 555, a semester-long seminar in which Nancy Downs and I present the conceptual framework for UIC's writing program and guide teaching assistants through the process of designing detailed curricula that link graduate students' academic interests, writing instruction, and opportunities for writing that take advantage of our urban context.[1] On the one hand, the strong conceptual framework that emerges from our assumptions about writing and the nature of inquiry ensures that first-year writing students will have similar learning experiences across the more than one hundred sections we offer each semester. On the other hand, the fact that graduate students can develop courses that reflect their own scholarly and civic interests keeps our teaching faculty engaged and motivated.

This perspective on teaching writing as a social practice lays the groundwork for developing further links between UIC's writing program and the work of the Great Cities Institute. Even when we move beyond the idea of service as noblesse oblige, it is often connected only loosely to academic work through reflection, a term commonly defined as "thinking back on the experience." We have found, in planning the writing activities for our courses, that reflection as a cognitive practice has limited impact on the learning we expect in our writing classes (see Herzberg; Shutz and Gere). The notion of partnership, however, suggests a more complex view of how civic engagement might find its way into writing programs. Our concern for community engagement mirrors that of Judith Shapiro, cultural anthropologist and president of Barnard College, who characterizes the challenge from a social science perspective:

> Many undergraduates today demonstrate impressive levels of civic engagement in the form of community service. They serve meals in soup kitchens, work in homeless shelters, and staff AIDS hot lines. They work as interns in a variety of social agencies. Too few of them, however, are able to raise their eyes to the level of policy and social structure. They need the sociological imagination to see how their on-the-ground activities fit into a bigger picture, so that more of them can cross the bridge from serious moral commitment to effective political participation. (A68)

Our challenge in the writing program, then, is to ask students to see how writing is implicated in social situations and to respond in appropriate language and genres to answer the questions, "So what?" and "Who cares?" (Graff and Hoberek). As students develop research projects on, for example, the role of the Humanities in building community, they begin to see how, through writing, they can become active participants in academic disciplines and community institutions.

Our first partnership, with Mujeres Latinas en Acción, was established in 1997 through a Great Cities Seed Fund grant. Mujeres was founded in 1973 by women living in the Pilsen neighborhood of Chicago, and it serves the needs of more than six thousand Latinas and their families annually. As the only Latina-administered agency in Illinois, Mujeres is dedicated to providing comprehensive bilingual and culturally sensitive social services to Latina homelessness prevention, parent support, youth intervention, domestic violence, sexual assault, and Latina leadership. The grant, written with Cordelia Maloney and with support from Virginia Martinez, then Director of Mujeres, proposed that Tobi Jacobi, a poet and masters student in creative writing, work with Mujeres on fundraising and developing a newsletter. In addition, the grant purchased a computer for Mujeres and funded Keith Dorwick, then at UIC, to design a Web page so that Mujeres could provide information about their organization to other communities that might want to develop programs based on their model. But fledgling community-university partnerships are difficult to sustain, especially with small organizations that are stretched to the limits. Toward the end of our grant period, the Mujeres board precipitated a major change in leadership and our connections with the organization were lost. During the course of our partnership, however, Mujeres improved its basic grant template, upgraded its newsletter, and established e-mail and Web connectivity. Mujeres maintains ties with UIC's Neighborhoods Initiative, and the possibility exists that we will again place a graduate student with the agency and continue our relationship.

At UIC, Tobi Jacobi taught a required second-semester writing class with an emphasis on reaching out to the arts community, including Pilsen, where Mujeres is located. The final project for the course was a full proposal for an arts center that could fill unmet needs of ethnic communities, representing them more fully on the Chicago arts scene. The proposed arts center was to be located on the site of a small urban airport whose lease was just about up and which was the subject of many planning proposals for some sort of community use. As a result of her teaching and working with Mujeres, Jacobi (and Veronda Pitchford) produced a research manual called *The Road to Research: A Guide for Research and Resources at the University of Illinois at Chicago* that, among other things, helps students locate community-based resources in a variety of little-known libraries, museums, and archives around Chicago.

Another of UIC's partnerships began in 1999. While in residence at the Great Cities Institute, I encountered Connie Yowell, a faculty member in the College of Education who had been working at Benito Juárez High School on a five-year longitudinal research project analyzing the relationship between students' aspirations and whether or not they stayed in school. The student body of this school, the only public high school in Pilsen, is about 98 percent Mexican. Just over one-quarter of the students are first generation Americans and 94 percent come from low-income families. The graduation rate is 59 percent, and few of the graduates attend college after high school. The school, one of the most troubled in the city system (plagued by having five different principals in five years), has been going through a process of reconstitution.

UIC's first-year writing program has received grants to work toward a comprehensive partnership with Juárez that could include establishing a writing center staffed by UIC students, organizing mentoring relationships between college students and Juárez students, offering teachers support for writing instruction, and developing community-based support for parents. A Grant from the Center for Urban Educational Research, written in conjunction with Nancy Downs and Connie Yowell, allowed Dan Gonzalez, a writing teacher and graduate student, to spend a year working at Juárez assisting teachers with writing projects, tutoring, and advising students. Then Dan Gonzalez and I, along with a group of graduate students and writing instructors (Jennifer Cohen, Eva Bednarowicz, and Kevin Smith, as well as a student from another high school) continued this partnership with Benito Juárez High School by planning and carrying out an innovative summer program called High Velocity Summer.

Fourteen freshmen and sophomores from Benito Juárez High School participated in the High Velocity Summer Program, whose curriculum focused on the fields of science, medicine, and technology, and also required intensive writing and reading.[2] The Benito Juárez students attended workshop classes at UIC four days a week. In one project on technology, students used a moo-like software program to create virtual technology inventions that would help solve a specific problem in their community. This sort of work asked students to participate in a system of activities and to function as part of a team in which group goals helped each person achieve more writing than he or she would have been capable of doing in an isolated classroom setting. For example, Jose Garcia quickly learned the moo technology and created a time machine. The written description of the time machine was much harder for Jose to produce than its visual design, and it emerged only in response to questions from other members of the group and an intense collaborative effort. Interestingly, Jose's reason for creating the time machine was not to go into the future. He wanted to return to Mexico to see how his parents grew up—how they worked, how they danced together, how they brought water to their home. Several of us at UIC are continuing to work with the students from the summer program by creating communities of learning that link digital literacies with conventional communication literacies. In our work at Benito Juárez, we aim to help students see writing as a way to practice procedural activities—ones with consequences.

When we teach writing in a context of partnership, the loop is not closed until knowledge from specific projects informs the writing program curriculum at UIC. Several of us who work at Benito Juárez are designing writing courses on urban education that will ask first-year UIC students to consider some of the broader sociocultural contexts within which schools such as Benito Juárez exist and how identity formation at the high school and college level is influenced by school and home contexts. In this new course, students will read essays and documents of various kinds related to school reform, gentrification, neighborhood revitalization, and local culture and history to see how all of these issues create a context for schooling. We will supplement essays about these topics with written documents that played a role in this particular local context, such as grant applications and school policy statements. Since students at UIC often come from the city or surrounding suburbs and enter the local workforce after college, these writing classes promote a very real connection to local realities and professional as well as academic possibilities.

TEACHING AND ASSESSING WRITING IN A CONTEXT OF PARTNERSHIP

In a recent article in *College English*, Stephen Parks and Eli Goldblatt describe their university-wide writing program's efforts to move beyond traditional disciplinary boundaries, thereby engaging more fully with the communities surrounding Temple University. Housed in English, Temple's Institute for the Study of Literature, Literacy, and Culture offers a striking example of how universities can commit to reciprocal knowledge making, teaching, and learning with local schools and community agencies. In the conclusion to their article, though, the authors draw us back to the writing classroom by repeating a colleague's question that many of us have also heard: Won't all this community-based work distract us from our basic job of preparing students for the writing required in their college courses? (601).

I was asked a similar question during a site visit for the Urban University Portfolio Project. This three-year project, funded jointly by the Pew Charitable Trust and the American Association for Higher Education, focuses on how urban universities achieve success and represent themselves to the public. Six urban universities, including UIC, are developing Web-based portfolios to communicate their achievements and to illustrate how they assess them.[3] During this particular site visit, the project evaluators learned about UIC's Great Cities Initiative and our first-year writing program's focus on engaged writing courses. After many enthusiastic and supportive comments, one of the members of the project's review board asked, "But how do you know that the students' writing is improving?" I have come to understand that before asking whether or not students' writing has improved, one must examine the assumptions that drive a writing program's pedagogy. Further, one must examine how those assumptions fit or do not fit the university's mission or, more specifically, its vision for undergraduate studies.

In our first-year writing program at UIC, we assume that writing is a way of acting in the world, rather than just a way of demonstrating basic skills or achieved knowledge. With this assumption as our starting point, our pedagogical approach should take as its domain not only writing in the university, but also writing wherever it is used to take action. In our first required writing course, English 160, this assumption allows us to develop courses in which students are invited into ongoing conversations, particularly ones in which writing plays an important role. Rather than seeing "readings" as windows onto an issue, we ask students to consider a piece of writing through four interrelated rhetorical dimensions (context, genre, language, and consequences) as a way to situate the text and as a way for students to design their response to it. These four rhetorical dimensions, taken together, offer students a set of tools for analyzing texts on the one hand and creating texts on the other.

The second required first-year writing course at UIC, English 161, the one most commonly linked to partnership activities, builds on work done in the first semester to achieve a sense of active participation through writing. In this second course, students delve into an issue, such as urban education or the role of the arts in society, that has local and far-reaching consequences, that engages both academic and nonacademic communities, and that allows students the opportunity to develop a sense of working out a problem with peers in a research community. Students explore the textual practices or activities involved in making meaning in specific contexts or discourse communities, particularly local and perhaps even familiar ones. In this class we pay special attention to the ways in which contexts and possible consequences shape writing choices about genre and language.

Rather than seeing academic discourse as constituted in forms (the research report) deriving from static repositories of knowledge, the notion of "communities of practice" offers a dynamic relationship among a variety of participants. Described by Patricia Harkin as "lore," these relationships fight for dynamism against what others refer to as the mask of methodology. Students need to know how we make meaning in a variety of contexts. Rather than learn the form of the research paper, students should learn how we make meaning both inside and outside the academy everyday. In English 161, we ask students to understand how meaning is made in academic and nonacademic contexts, but most importantly we ask them to analyze how insiders might talk about a process that is hidden by the conventions of publication. We have two competing stories at work here: the story of the urban student who learns to write the research paper and absorbs the knowledge offered by the ivory tower versus the student who relies on her complex awareness of multiple contexts to negotiate learning to write. These stories mirror in some ways the historical relationship between urban universities and their surrounding communities. Wim Wiewel, who has directed the Great Cities Initiative and who was also the dean of the College of Urban Planning and Public Affairs at UIC, criticized *previous* relationships with neighboring communities in which universities saw their role as one in which they offered expertise and repaired deficits (Gilderbloom). By contrast, the Great Cities concept is based on partnership and a jointly driven conversation, not noblesse oblige. The teaching of writing as well must be a jointly driven conversation in which writing becomes a call to action and the writer is mindful of the practices that make action possible.

The sort of learning we aim for in UIC's writing program requires continuous conversation between composition instructors and how their teaching contributes to the writing program, general education classes, links to communicating across the curriculum, work in the major, and activities in the workplace. Because of the complexity of our goals, our social context, and our university's engaged mission, we have turned to rich assessment techniques such as portfolios, cover letters, focus groups, surveys, and context-sensitive rubrics for responding to students' papers. We are searching for ways to answer the big-picture questions we want to ask about our writing program.

How do students see the uses of writing for participating in important public conversations? How do they see writing as a way of representing themselves in more fluid and diverse contexts than previously conceived in high school or other settings? How does engaged writing change their awareness of the impact of context on genre and language? Like any other intellectual endeavor, assessment is a rhetorical activity. To the extent that we focus on evaluating writing out of context, we ignore the very important question of what it means to teach writing in a context of partnership.

NOTES

1. For a full description, see <www.uic.edu/portfolio/writing>.

2. The summer program is documented on the program's website at <www.uic.edu/depts/engl/hvsp>.

3. The UIC website can be found at <www.uic.edu/portfolio>, and the project's website is located at <www.imir.iupui.edu/portfolio>.

WORKS CITED

Gilderbloom, John I. "The Urban University in the Community: The Roles of Boards and Presidents." Occasional Paper No. 30. Association of Governing Boards of Universities and Colleges, 1996.

Graff, Gerald, and Andrew Hoberek. "Hiding It from the Kids (With Apologies to Simon and Garfunkel)." *College English* 62 (1999): 242–53.

Harkin, Patricia. "The Post-Disciplinary Politics of Lore." *Contending with Words: Composition and Rhetoric in a Postmodern Age.* Ed. Patricia Harkin and John Schilb. New York: MLA, 1991. 124–38.

Herzberg, Bruce. "Community Service and Critical Teaching." *College Composition and Communication* 45 (1994): 307–41.

Jacobi, Tobi, and Veronda Pitchford. *The Road to Research: A Guide for Research and Resources at the University of Illinois at Chicago.* Champaign, IL: Stipes, 1999.

Parks, Stephen, and Eli Goldblatt. "Writing Beyond the Curriculum: Fostering New Collaborations in Literacy." *College English* 62 (2000): 584–606.

Perry, David. Personal communication. 12 April 2000.

Severino, Carol. "An Urban University and Its Academic Support Program: Teaching Basic Writing in the Context of an 'Urban Mission.'" *Journal of Basic Writing* 15 (1996): 39–56.

Shapiro, Judith. "From Sociological Illiteracy to Sociological Imagination." *The Chronicle of Higher Education* 31 Mar. 2000: A68.

Shutz, Aaron, and Anne Ruggles Gere. "Service Learning and English Studies: Rethinking 'Public' Service." *College English* 60 (1998): 129–49.

Walshok, Mary Lindenstein. *Knowledge without Boundaries: What America's Universities Can Do for the Economy, the Workplace, and the Community.* San Francisco: Jossey-Bass, 1995.

Wiewel, Wim, and David Broski. "The Great Cities Institute: Dilemmas of Implementing the Urban Land Grant Mission." *Metropolitan Universities* 10 (1999): 29–38.

———. "University Involvement in the Community: Developing a Partnership Model." *Renaissance* 1 (1996): 16–23.

CHAPTER FOURTEEN

MOVING TO THE CITY

Redefining Literacy in the
Post–Civil Rights Era

Patrick Bruch

At a time when composition studies has been buoyed on a tide of rising institutional credibility, many writing teachers may have been puzzled to hear
Lester Faigley's comment, in his 1996 Chair's address to the Conference on
College Composition and Communication, that "it no longer seems like we
are riding the wave of history but instead are caught in a rip tide carrying us
away from where we want to go" ("Literacy" 32). But Faigley's comment
directs attention to an important reality that is easy to miss among composition's recent victories. When measured against the expectations regarding
social group mobility that many writing teachers have had for literacy
instruction, the strategies that have dominated the work of composition
studies over the past thirty years have been, as Tom Fox phrases it, "an
unqualifiable failure" (42). Specifically, composition studies has been unable
to respond adequately to the social inequities, such as institutionalized
racism, that both inspired and derived from the urbanization of the Civil
Rights movement in the 1960s. Yet we cannot simply step back into history
and return to past opportunities. Instead, as Faigley concludes in *Fragments
of Rationality,* the highly urbanized, post–Civil Rights context in which compositionists work today demands a new urban agenda for the teaching of
writing. But what kind of new urban agenda will it take for composition
studies to address effectively the social inequities of the twenty-first century
post–Civil Rights era?

Before we can begin to answer this question, we must first examine how our strategies for defining literacy instruction as a means to social mobility have backfired and carried us away from where we want to go. In what follows, I examine competing definitions of social mobility that accompanied the urbanization of social struggles in the 1960s and influenced the development of alternative urban agendas in the 1970s, and I consider the effects these definitions and agendas had on composition studies. I then discuss more recent post–Civil Rights contexts in which social group relations and definitions of mobility get written in and on urban spaces. Finally, I describe my own efforts to implement a writing pedagogy that involves students in redefining the nature and role of literacy in the process of social mobility.

MOVING TO THE CITY

> It was funny to see a town made: streets driven through; two rows of shade trees, hard and soft, planted; cellars dug and houses put up—regular Queen Anne style too, with stained glass—all at once. Dryfoos apologized for the streets because they were handmade; said they expected their street making machine Tuesday, and they intended to push things.
>
> —William Dean Howells

I begin my analysis of the forces that moved the Civil Rights struggle to the cities with this passage from William Dean Howells's 1889 novel *A Hazard of New Fortunes* because of its image of urban space as a social text that both writes about and gets written by our lives together. At the time that Howells wrote *A Hazard of New Fortunes,* urban space communicated the promise of the American Dream. In the city, people could step out of history and into an unlimited future, leaving the past behind and making of their lives whatever their individual imaginations could conjure and their personal capabilities accomplish. Though familiar today, this version of social mobility that is written through and on urban space strikes a discordant note. In the urban Minneapolis neighborhood in which I live, for example, specific spatial practices (ubiquitous "neighborhood alert" flyers and "THIS PROPERTY PRO-TECTED BY" alarm company lawn signs, as well as the window displays at the corner drug store exhorting neighbors, in red, white, and blue streamers, to "VOTE!") resist the effects of popular representations that picture urban space as a cage of fear, isolation, and apathy. These spatial practices seem to long for the past rather than the future. When we step into the shared space that speaks to us of our lives together, we want to recall the city of light and progress that Howells describes. Doing so is a way of dispensing with the dark city of deindustrialization, stubborn poverty, and the nagging fear that doing whatever we have been doing, only harder, will not transform the underlying causes of our urban problems.

Stark economic, political, and social disparities among neighboring urban communities have become the basis for popular representations of cities as spaces of uncomfortable confrontations between cultures of poverty and cultures of power. The flyers, lawn signs, and window displays that decorate our new urban landscape communicate a desire to transform these meanings that have dominated civic rhetorics and city spaces in the wake of the Civil Rights era. The challenge that faces compositionists today is to create forms of writing instruction that help students to critically negotiate debilitating definitions of urban space and group identity that inspire a retreat into a mythical past. Rather than allowing students to ignore or mythologize the challenges of social group equity that constitute life in twenty-first century cities, literacy learning can instead provide students with the tools necessary for positioning and repositioning their literacies and identities (at least in part) in response to those challenges.

The Civil Rights movement in the 1960s catalyzed unprecedented redefinitions of city spaces and social group identities. For composition studies, the most transformative aspects of the Civil Rights movement were the concentration of social struggles in America's cities and the resulting emergence of what sociologist Stephen Steinberg calls the "scholarship of confrontation," which was initially grounded in the written work of Civil Rights movement leaders, such as Martin Luther King, Malcolm X, Stokely Carmichael, and the Black Panther Party. This work confronted individualist ivory tower theories with real-world challenges of city life and social group justice. As these public confrontational rhetorics gained recognition, a new kind of academic scholarship emerged that confronted the individualist orientation of educational institutions and their elitist pursuit of objective knowledge that transcends history. For some scholars during this troubled time, transforming (rather than transcending) inequalities in the real world became the primary purpose of academic knowledge (Steinberg 68–106).

The scholarship of confrontation, both public and academic, expressed insights and energies that welled up from the depths of the Civil Rights struggle and carried that struggle out into city streets across America. Some of the main targets of this scholarship were definitions of social group mobility, popular in mainstream culture and media, that relied on individualist assumptions—for instance, that economic, political, and social justice could be achieved only through personal hard work and persistence. Instead, most Civil Rights activists argued that the inability of certain individuals (most of whom happened to be of color) to achieve social justice was not the result of widespread personal failings, but was the direct result of institutionalized racism. In their 1967 book *Black Power*, for example, Stokely Carmichael and Charles Hamilton explained that "while today, to whites, [the American Dream] may *seem* to include black people, it cannot do so by the very nature of this nation's political and economic system, which imposes institutional racism on the black masses if not upon every individual black" (51). For those involved in the Civil Rights movement, moving to the city and coming to see oppressive social group relations as institutionalized reshuffled the possibilities for social mobility, since the concept of institutionalized racism explained how group hierarchies were perpetuated without overtly discriminatory motivations.

While seeming to be inclusive by avoiding formal exclusions, institutions such as education actually enabled the upward mobility of dominant social groups at the expense of other groups through conventions that governed value judgments and terms of participation. And even with the implementation of Civil Rights policies enforcing nondiscrimination at the individual level, people of color continued to experience an inability to increase their social standing. These contradictions inherent in the individualist view of social mobility became more apparent with time, thus increasing the legitimacy of mobility theories that emphasized institutionalized racism.

But theories that explained social immobility as an institutional (rather than individual) problem were viewed as dangerous by many urban institutions, since the very foundations and structures of these organizations would have to be transformed if such theories were correct. Out of these fears emerged a powerful backlash movement that turned public attention away from institutionalized racism and returned it, as Steinberg explains, to a more complex individualist explanation of social immobility—the "culture of poverty" thesis. While the Black Power movement had identified institutional racism as the main obstacle to social mobility, the culture of poverty backlash against this redefinition explained group immobility as a product of individual efforts stunted and constrained by an urban culture of poverty that prevented both individuals and groups from competing in an open forum. Where confrontational rhetorics promoted education as a way of getting into urban social group relations and struggles, the culture of poverty view promoted education and public life as a way of getting out of the city, transcending its material impoverishment by abandoning its alleged cultural impoverishment. And this backlash view defined successful social mobility as the accommodation (rather than transformation) of existing dominant power structures, making compromise the only viable strategy for inclusion.

COMPOSITION STUDIES AND
SOCIAL MOBILITY IN THE 1960S AND 1970S

The rhetorics of confrontation and compromise that emerged from a relocation of the Civil Rights struggle to the streets of American cities were reflected in academic discourses of the 1960s and 1970s. Within composition studies, rhetorics of confrontation took the form of a critical reassessment of the relations between literacy, mobility, and city life, while rhetorics of compromise took the form of an uncritical accommodation of the dominant language (i.e., Standard English) that was viewed to be objectively correct and thus went unquestioned.

One of the earliest contributions to the confrontational rhetorics of social mobility in composition was James Sledd's sociolinguistic study, "Bi-Dialectalism: The Linguistics of White Supremacy," which challenged composition-ists who were concerned about urban issues to abandon individualist perspectives of social immobility and to view it instead as the result of institutionalized racism. Sledd explains that, for bidialectalists, "upward mobility, it is assumed, is the end of education, but white power will deny upward mobility to speakers of black English, who must therefore be made to talk white English in their contacts with the white world" (1309). Sledd argues that advocates of bidialectalism were playing into the widespread pop-ularity, among whites, of the culture of poverty perspective by concentrating their attention on transforming the individual cultural practices of the immo-bile rather than the institutionalized cultural practices that reinforce immo-bility. Rather than targeting African American culture, Sledd suggests, what needed to be transformed was the control over institutions exercised by "employers and labor leaders [who] dislike black faces but use black English as an excuse" for racist practices (1311). Through his confrontational rhetoric regarding composition's early urban agenda, Sledd helped prepare the profes-sion to include previously excluded urban voices and perspectives in the the-ory and practice of composition and literacy studies.

Further representative of this moment of confrontation is Geneva Smitherman's "'God Don't Never Change': Black English from a Black Per-spective." Drawing from the Black Power urban agenda of institutional trans-formation (while rejecting the dominant agenda of individual compromise), Smitherman extends Sledd's challenge to definitions of upward mobility. Like Sledd, Smitherman critiques bidialectalism as part of an "insidious design . . . to cut off Black students from they cultural roots" (833). Smitherman explains that the problem with bidialectalism is not its emphasis on upward mobility through language learning, but its definition of that mobility. Bidialectalism accommodates existing institutionalized languages and social group relations and is thus "perhaps, albeit subtly, racist because such goals involve only lat-eral moves and Black folks need (upward) vertical moves . . . *Up*, not sideways" (832). As the earlier Black Power advocates of the 1960s, such as Carmichael and Hamilton, had repeatedly argued, it was not so much that integration was an unattainable goal; rather, integration was undesirable because it either side-stepped the question of group mobility—ignoring questions of institutional power altogether—or else it falsely imagined that, at the group level, "a Black minority can bow its head and get whipped into a meaningful position of power" (51). As Smitherman explains, "what we mean when we sing, with Curtis Mayfield, 'We movin' on up'" (832) is very different from the individualized economic mobility promised by integrationist strategies like bidialectalism. Smitherman's (and Charmichael, Hamilton, and Sledd's) definition of upward mobility is rooted in the revision of group relations that can only come from recognizing how meanings and identities themselves are, at heart, mobile and thus dependent on institutional practices and subject to revision.

Where Sledd resists his own privilege and questions dominant definitions of mobility within a meritocracy that overemphasizes whiteness, Smitherman understands that only a full validation of Black Idiom can transform material and institutional structures through language. Confrontational rhetorics such as Sledd's and Smitherman's brought into composition studies new ways of confronting literacy that emphasized the social consequences of teaching and that represented literacy as a practice through which groups relate and enable mobility or suffer immobility. These rhetorics recognized that the definition of mobility that was motivating bidialectalism aligned teachers of writing with the culture of poverty perspective. As both Smitherman and Sledd argue, the trouble with bidialectalism was the sleight of hand through which it framed dominant literacies as themselves disconnected from, and as an antidote to, the group level immobility that those very literacies cemented in place. Within composition studies, then, the influence of the culture of poverty perspective was felt most strongly in compromise rhetorics that encouraged students to accommodate existing institutional power formations and individualized definitions of mobility, rather than inviting students into city life through the study of how social relations are constructed and transformed through language use.

In contrast to Smitherman's and Sledd's confrontational rhetorics, by the mid 1970s many compositionists had forgotten the lessons of Civil Rights activists, once again defining social mobility in narrow economic and individualist terms. This new urban agenda (similar in many ways to the culture of poverty backlash against confrontational Black Power rhetorics) was defined by individual access to the American Dream of privatized material prosperity. Partly characteristic of this rhetoric of accommodation and compromise is Mina Shaughnessy's *Errors and Expectations*, the most widely known urban literacy text of the time. Shaughnessy begins this book by framing her students as attending college to achieve individual mainstream mobility. The central factor constraining her students' mobility was, for Shaughnessy, that their language practices did not permit them "to be read without prejudice" (6). Such a view is striking in that it dismisses the essential insight of earlier confrontational rhetorics—that is, that supposedly "neutral" institutional practices actually reinforce social prejudice—and it situates Shaughnessy, at least initially, within the individualist (accommodating, compromising) culture of poverty perspective of social mobility.

For Steinberg, the distinguishing characteristic of the culture of poverty perspective is that it "shift[s] the onus of responsibility for America's greatest crime away from powerful institutions that *could* make a difference onto individuals who have been rendered powerless by these very institutions" (135). While Shaughnessy does incorporate this perspective into certain aspects of *Errors and Expectations,* taken as a whole the book seems to straddle the eras and the perspectives of confrontation and backlash. The urban agenda that Shaughnessy offers compositionists seeks to reinterpret the tensions between cultural validation and social mobility that were potently redefining urban space and group relations. Like the confrontational scholars advocating group mobility through a redefinition of literacy, Shaughnessy expresses concern for the cultural and political factors that influence how written products get interpreted by audiences and institutions. But, like the early bidialectalists, she also views dominant group practices as an inalterable social fact. In the end, despite its mix of perspectives, Shaughnessy's influential urban agenda for composition studies ultimately frames the politics of mobility within a liberal vocabulary that promotes lateral movement within group hierarchies by emphasizing spatio-economic mobility through the individual appropriation of privileged institutional power structures.

As Smitherman, Sledd, and many others have argued, placing the responsibility on individual students to appropriate discursive and ideological standards—standards that are "read without prejudice" because all agree to disguise or deny those standards' inherent prejudice—is to demand that students abandon identities and practices that dominant groups are prejudiced *against* and assimilate identities and practices that dominant groups are prejudiced *toward.* Locking groups in existing institutional hierarchies, such a view continues to work against the redefinition it seeks to make possible, namely a redefinition of what it means to be white or black or brown or red or yellow in the United States.

POST–CIVIL RIGHTS RHETORICS
AND CULTURAL STUDIES PEDAGOGIES

In previous sections, I have argued that the public and academic rhetorics of the 1960s Civil Rights era were supplanted in many ways by the backlash compromise rhetorics of the 1970s post–Civil Rights era. While both urban life and composition studies have evolved significantly over the past thirty or forty years, some of the same problematics that defined the competing rhetorics of the 1960s and 1970s persist even today. Jerry Herron identifies my former home town, Detroit, Michigan, as "the most representative city in America" of the post–Civil Rights era (9). Through its role in narratives of urban decline, Detroit aligns racialized urban suffering with the culture of poverty perspective. In an interview on *Prime Time Live,* Detroit's long-time mayor, Coleman Young, pointed out that people love to attack Detroit in subtle and not so subtle ways because "to attack Detroit is to attack Black" ("Detroit's Agony"). Herron explains what makes Detroit representative in a way that unpacks Young's insight: ubiquitous representational attacks against cities (i.e., nonwhite civic spaces) by suburban, privileged forces "preserve for us the belief that our culture does not carry within it those seeds of death, which are come to such terrible fruition [t]here" (27). Representations and popular perceptions of cities often "attack Black" as a way of responding to the urban experience that distinguishes the post–Civil Rights era—the experience of being accused of white privilege that results from institutionalized racism. These latest variations of the culture of poverty perspective respond to charges of institutionalized racism by shifting the focus from group relations and social mobility back to an individualist stance.

In Minneapolis, where I presently live and work, racial group dynamics are being transformed from the black/white oppositions characteristic of the Civil Rights era to a more global problematic characteristic of the twenty-first century post–Civil Rights era. Here the traditional struggles among Anglo-European majorities and Native American and African American minorities are being transformed by large numbers of Vietnamese, Hmong, Eritrean, and Somali immigrants. Two recent local incidents embody for me how the old challenges of social mobility are being redefined in light of a new global urban agenda.

The first example is an election-eve newspaper advertisement in the Minneapolis *Star-Tribune* in which Renee LaVoi, a candidate for the Minneapolis School Board, offered a thinly veiled attack on nonwhite immigrant cultures that introduce into American culture and American schools what she referred to as "Africa's heathen practices." Her statements explicitly construct minority global cultures as the cause of social ills ranging from violence to poverty, and they must be quoted at length to be believed. According to this representative of the Republican Party, coming to the city schools of Minneapolis, people

> find Americans who are far from God, who pierce their bodies with rings, . . . who tattoo their bodies and paint their hair. . . . They find Americans exposing their bodies immodestly, wearing as little clothing as possible. They find adultery and sexual immorality running rampant. They find Americans mesmerized and enthralled in front of televisions, and video games filled with violence and cruelty.

They find many of these people personally involved in violent acts, tak-ing pleasure in killing for no purpose. They find kids feeding off of music glorifying death and murder and other kids joining gangs which act out those very scenarios. They find Americans listening, even in church, to rock music with an African-style throbbing drum beat. They find Americans turning increasingly to witch craft, even featuring occult call in lines on tele-vision. They find a trend toward powerful women who sometimes need to compensate for lazy, unmotivated, drunken adulterous men.

America has voluntarily chosen to trade places with Africa. She has adopted all of Africa's heathen practices.

It is only a matter of time before America experiences starvation, poverty, plagues, horrible sickness, and every kind of misery known to mankind. (B5)

Although her apocalyptic claims may seem outlandish, what most strikes me about this advertisement is how it demonstrates the flexibility of the culture of poverty perspective for claiming to "fix" the meanings of and relations between dominant and subordinate groups. This culture of poverty theory, which once "explained" why African Americans were unable to improve their social standing in the 1960s, easily transforms into a theory that "explains" why global cultures are unable to improve their social standing in the twenty-first century.

Another version of the culture of poverty thesis has also emerged in the post–Civil Rights era, a version that emphasizes the pleasures of diversity while avoiding attention to the relations of power that immobilize group identities and stabilize hierarchies of difference. An example of this new way of responding to the problem of social mobility comes from a recent advertis-ing campaign for a restaurant in a trendy Minneapolis neighborhood called Uptown. Uptown is a youthful, punky neighborhood that features high rents and hot styles. Uptown allows privileged classes to experience "safe" tastes of various subcultural dark sides. One restaurant, Chino Latino, offers an upscale pastiche of cooking from "all the world's hotspots." A recent billboard adver-tises that the mix of Asian, Latin American, and new-world food is "as exotic as food gets without using the dog"; another ad jokes, "Don't know what to order? Ask your cab driver." These callous references to Third World poverty and ethnic stereotypes invite highly mobile "identity tourists" into a rhetoric that turns recognizing and validating group differences into a way of livening up the "bland" culture of whiteness.

Michael Omi has argued that the post–Civil Rights era is distinguished by the racialization of whiteness—the heightened awareness of race that has cut whiteness adrift from its moorings on an island of comfortable invisibility and forced white people to grapple with the freefloating mobility of their own identity, especially their vulnerability to the charge of being global oppressors

(181). In each of the two examples discussed above, whiteness is a central theme in which dominant culture is represented as mobile and Other cultures are fixed. In LaVoi's newspaper ad, dominant culture's upward mobility is hindered by infection from the static culture of poverty that keeps minority cultures down. In the Chino Latino ads, dominant cultures gain social cachet (and thus mobility) by temporarily participating in "risky" and exciting subcultural practices while, of course, never losing sight of their own dominance. Responding to rhetorics of mobility that call white identity into question, these urban rhetorics reinscribe white dominance (and ensure white mobility) by stabilizing the degraded position of nonwhite cultures.

These examples illustrate the backlash against the confrontational rhetorics of the 1960s that offered institutionalized racism as the cause of social immobility for minority cultures. Faced with the threat of losing the privileges of unilateral mobility, the mainstream cultural identity of whiteness has struggled to maintain its dominance through civic discourses that locate Others in an immobile culture of poverty (see hooks). Thus, the only way for these Other cultures to gain mobility (if we go by these examples) is to denounce their own static cultures and assimilate into dominant white culture, that is, the only culture that is mobile in any meaningful way. The challenge for compositionists with an urban mission in the twenty-first century, however, is to teach representational practices that do *not* immobilize some by defining social mobility as assimilation rather than transformation. In this effort to transform our disciplinary practices, we must continue to critique "culture of poverty" perspectives of social mobility and explore the kinds of mobility that literacy instruction enables.

Over the past ten years, my understanding of an urban agenda for composition studies has developed out of my attraction to and frustrations with the resources of cultural studies for responding to the social immobility that is caused by liberal individualism. I am attracted by cultural studies' explicitly confrontational rhetoric and its participatory agenda. James Berlin suggests that cultural studies was the urban literacy of the 1980s and early 1990s, a literacy defined around "cultivation of the students' ability to critique the cultural narratives of others and construct in their place narratives more adequate to the complexities of [current] historical conditions" (266).

But instead of transforming institutionalized values and criteria, the composition pedagogies that emerged from cultural studies tended to replace one expert discourse (e.g., rhetorics of clarity and objectivity) with the equally expert (and thus equally oppressive) discourse of academic critique. Frank Farmer points out that because it is an expert discourse, critique can easily alienate those it is intended to liberate (187). For urban students, this alienating posture often makes the critical literacy being offered seem distant, located in a space of privilege that is removed from urban realities.

Another problem with cultural studies composition pedagogies is that they lack a viable alternative to the individualist rhetoric of hope. For urban and suburban students, and for the public at large, schooling is often rooted in a larger narrative of education as a means to transcend their vulnerability to the social ills associated with city life. In classroom practice, cultural studies composition pedagogies replace a naive investment in transcendence with a jaded investment in irony—seeing through culture and rhetoric to an oppressive reality, students are tempted to give up totally on the prospects of redefining social mobility. In this sense, literacy instruction may be "critical" yet still serve to reinforce the retreat from city life and the progressive politics of social mobility.

Recently, writing teachers concerned with urban literacy have responded to these concerns by developing pedagogies that place their emphasis on textual and cultural production. Pedagogies based on theories of "urban" and "community" literacies in composition studies ask students to construct texts that enact alternatives to the injustices that critique uncovers. While compositionists addressing urban literacies have tended to focus on inner cities, the project of an urban agenda for composition studies must be broader than a focus on inner city students and the problems they present for composition studies. The danger is that a focus on inner city language practices alone will represent social group immobility as a problem that resides *within* inner city cultures and practices, reinscribing a culture of poverty perspective. In fact, the roots of inner city immobility lie outside of the inner city itself, and a meaningful engagement with social immobility must include an urban agenda for those teaching, learning, and living in suburban and privileged urban spaces. The focus, then, should be less about how inner city residents can use language to free themselves and more about how privileged persons (city residents or otherwise) can use language to create better social relationships.

TOWARD A POST–CIVIL RIGHTS
URBAN AGENDA FOR COMPOSITION

An urban composition pedagogy that responds to the concerns I have raised in this chapter must go beyond asking privileged students to write *about* group relations of difference that characterize city life and move instead toward asking them to see their writing and others' writing as working both *in* and *on* those relations. This goal demands a redefinition of mobility through literacy that would undermine the grounds for "attack Black" rhetorics and challenge the culture of poverty thesis that ignores forces such as institutionalized racism. While the culture of poverty thesis understands groups as fixed and mobility as individual, a definition of mobility grounded in city life understands groups as relational and pursues the mobility of all groups in relation to others.

I have responded to some of the concerns raised in this essay by designing a community action first-year composition class within the General College at the University of Minnesota. The General College has a transfer mission. The approximately 950 freshman we admit each fall do not meet the admission criteria of the University of Minnesota, Twin Cities. The purpose of the General College is to prepare these students for "upward mobility" into the degree-granting colleges of the University of Minnesota. All students participate in the writing component of this preparation, designed to help them develop practices for success in the university. The two primary goals of the course I have designed are, first, to help students use literacy to pursue the mobility they want, and second, to help them reflect critically on writing in ways that make them rethink social group relations. Specifically, I hope that all of my students (especially those from privileged spaces and cultures) come to see their own writing in terms of three insights: first, that individuals effect meaning as members of groups; second, that groups have meaning through their relations to each other; and third, that language is a key medium through which relations are made and maintained. With these three insights, students can better learn the tools to critically challenge the roles of language and writing in shaping how they interact with others. Applying these insights to their own writing means fundamentally redefining literacy in terms of group relations.

In order to create opportunities for students to begin redefining literacy according to these insights, my students work with several Twin Cities nonprofit organizations that need volunteers to help them pursue community action work through innovative literacy practices. Of the options I make available, two are afterschool programs for inner city youth. In one, children write and produce their own TV shows about community issues. The other is a community youth choir where children write, perform, and record music. Other options include working with a nonprofit organization that helps immigrants develop conversational English skills and working in a daytime drop-in center for homeless people where the primary function of workers is to listen. Students are introduced to these options for community involvement on the first day of class, and they rank their preferences of where they would like to work. They are assigned in groups of three or four to a specific agency where they work two hours per week for the remainder of the semester. The work the students do in each case is the work of the agency. Students who work with the youth choir, for example, lead small group sessions, sing, and supervise children as they create, practice, and perform music.

The innovative literacy practices used in these nonprofit organizations, combined with the traditional academic literacy practices used in my classroom, enact the theme of urban literacies. They bring together diverse ways of being and seeing and the power relations that attend them. The community work my students do is complemented by class readings and writing assignments designed to help them develop and apply a vocabulary for critically assessing the relations between competing literacies. In addition to helping students become more critical of how social issues such as opportunity and access are represented, the course is designed to encourage students to loosen their definitions of social mobility through language and begin working with others to redefine literacy in particular contexts.

Through course readings, including authors such as James Baldwin, Roberto Unger, and Cornel West, students develop a relational perspective on language. Baldwin's "If Black English Isn't a Language, Tell Me What Is?" for example, argues in word and form that language use has been defined by and for white dominance, but it also provides a key terrain for resisting and transforming such dominance. And Unger and West, in *The Future of American Progressivism*, challenge readers to consider the institutional and structural transformations of group relations necessary to make good on the American promise of self-determination. Such readings offer critical frameworks for students to use as they interpret work practices in community agencies whose own privileged discourse about social mobility actually contests mainstream discourse. Thus, my pedagogy encourages students to question definitions of literacy that emphasize individually accommodating status quo social group hierarchies. I hope that my students will begin to explore literacy as a contextual practice for redefining the meanings of groups such as homeless people, inner city youth, and white college students, as well as the relations of power among these groups.

I try to accomplish some of these goals through assignments that ask students to document and analyze communicative practices and how they relate to each other. For example, one assignment asks students to compare various ways of representing and understanding an issue of significance in a particular setting. For many students, the real life context for thinking helps bring to life ideas about history and power from course readings, and some students quickly achieve critical distance from currently valued definitions of literacy and mobility. Many of these students spend the term honing literate practices for accomplishing relational goals rather than autonomy from others. The most inspiring to me begin to see writing in school as embedded in an institution and also as a way of engaging and working to transform institutionalized expectations about communication. These students are able to use their writing to question the institutionalized group relations built into academic expectations for writing. Mark, an African American student, exemplifies the critical reflectiveness I have in mind with his sophisticated idea that "by me writing this paper in this way, I am communicating my thoughts about communication to you, but yet a lot of people may not see it this way at first." Steven, another student of color, offers a less flexible interpretation of what conventions mean for writers, arguing that through literacy and communication "you can fight the hard battle to survive, but if you try to reform the society, you will be slammed down so hard it will crush you for life."

But students such as Steven and Mark, working largely from outside the privileged discourse, obviously cannot alone transform that discourse or its institutional functions. Timothy Barnett has recently pointed out that privatized definitions of mobility and literacy that attend the culture of poverty thesis have long been promoted by white unwillingness to question what he calls the "white ground" of social life. As Barnett argues, "[I]f the only route to economic and social power was through the language of the majority, this language would have been looked on by many who did not speak it as necessary, despite the individual and community identities that may have been compromised if the home language were to be lost" (26). Barnett emphasizes the consequences of white unwillingness to reflect on how we institutionalize group relations through practices such as literacy. From this perspective, a major part of the legacy of educational underservice to nonwhite students has been the collective inability or unwillingness to critically challenge white students' senses of the roles and functions of literacy. Barnett argues that rather than reinforcing the culture of poverty perspectives that have historically operated for white people as an ideological bulwark defending institutionalized racism, writing classes can be, in part at least, places in which whites begin questioning the purposes of literacy and the need for the linguistic and cultural compromises they have historically demanded. This questioning is essential to an urban writing pedagogy in the post–Civil Rights era. It is much more common today than in the past among informed white composition teachers. But it is extraordinarily rare among white students and in the white public.

Many white students respond with angst to assignments that ask them to reflect on group relations of power and how communication reinforces and resists those group relations. Michelle, for example, begins her paper with the idea that in her experience, the perspectives that people bring to communication make all the difference. She clarifies that "rather than trying to save others" through volunteering, "much better communication can be established if a volunteer stops trying to save the people they are working with but only concentrates on establishing a meaningful trusting relationship." The paper goes on to describe several examples of communicative challenges that she, as a white suburban female, encountered in her efforts to establish trust, using these examples as a foundation for imagining better communicative practices. She describes conflicts and miscommunication with parents of children participating in an afterschool program and a general sense of mistrust between volunteers and parents. She concludes that the barrier to good communication is "privilege," and explains,

> Even though America is supposed to be a society in which all are equal, many people still hold the belief that Caucasians are more privileged than minorities. I believe that this belief is the one thing that keeps us, the volunteers, from the communication we would like to have with the community. Although the thought never crossed my mind that I was "privileged" I can see where the adults in the community are coming from. This was and is the barrier to good communication. It is not so much the children of the community, but the adults who believe that we as volunteers feel that we are superior. Imagine the negative vibes we as . . . Caucasians give off to a predominantly African American society.

The combination in Michelle's paper of defensiveness and recognition of responsibility is typical of what it looks like when white students of good will start reflecting on how others understand them. This is the writing of a privileged person beginning to question her own position as it relates to others and beginning to think about what it might look like to work with others on redefining the relationships between positions.

I read Michelle's choice of the bureaucratic term *Caucasians* rather than the oppositional term *white* as reflecting a defensive gesture to distance herself from critical discourses addressing institutionalized racism. Extending the defensive posture, when Michelle argues, "I believe that this belief is the one thing that keeps us . . . from the communication we would like to have," she seems to suggest that what obstructs trust is not a history of privilege but the "belief that Caucasians are more privileged." If that were the case, all that would be necessary would be for all sides, especially nonwhite people, to stop believing that whites "feel that we are superior." Such a view represents privilege as a myth, dismissing questions of institutionalized group power.

But I see more than simple defensiveness working in Michelle's discussion. Michelle sees herself and her own perceptions and practices as being caught up in the situation, too. When she says that she "can see where the adults in the community are coming from," she recognizes that beliefs-in-context are the seeds of actions and practices and that the parents in the community are not the only ones whose beliefs about privilege shape relationships. For Michelle, if thoughts about their own privilege have never crossed white people's minds, as they had not crossed hers, then "imagine the negative vibes we . . . give off." Inherent in this conclusion is a potent insight into the purposes of literacy. If literacy is, in part, about the vibes we give off, then a good literacy is one that avoids giving the negative vibe of unreflectiveness. While I do not want to exaggerate my sense of Michelle's present posture toward white privilege, I do think that a goal such as communicating responsiveness to others' perceptions can lead privileged students such as Michelle, over time, to learn about privilege and appreciate the ways in which privilege affects institutions and the vibes groups give off in and through them.

Michelle is beginning to explore a relational approach to literacy. Trying to "see where the adults in the community are coming from" means trying to see herself as others read her in a particular context. Rather than simply accomplishing the goal of seeing as others see, the real value of this work is in recognizing that her actions and the contexts in which they are read are ways of implementing group dynamics of power. Recognizing that she was sending negative vibes as a member of a social group, Michelle begins to reflect on how she has participated in, and how she might resist, communicating a completely unreflective posture toward questions of privilege. Of course, Michelle's response as it stands is not a radical rethinking of her relations to others in light of questions of institutionalized power. But the kinds of shifts in thinking that are needed are, I think, more gradual than sudden.

Michelle concludes her paper with what seems at first a throwaway hope that "volunteers and people in the community can come together and may all have the innocence of children." My initial reaction was to see her as relinquishing agency from herself and others and assigning miscommunication and unequal power to the status of unfortunate but inalterable realities. But at such points, one advantage of a pedagogy rooted in relationships in the urban community takes shape. For their final projects in my class, students are assigned to work with people in their community site to write texts that serve the community and that implement insights into communication that they have developed. Michelle's encounter with the concept of privilege as an obstacle to meaningful, trusting relationships led her to a final project in which she composed a text that would "step in the direction towards trusting relationships." She recognized that dealing with privilege—both the community's belief that "we feel that we are superior" and the "negative vibe we are sending" when we do not think about privilege—was essential to "break the stereotypes on both ends and establish solid relationships." Michelle worked with people in her site to rhetorically reverse the spotlight and, rather than focusing on those the volunteers were trying to serve, she decided to tell the stories of the volunteers. She asked parents and children what they would like to know about the program and the people involved, and she created a series of short biographies that tried to address concerns regarding backgrounds and motivations. Rather than an "attack Black" response to questions of privilege, this final project transforms the way that communication is often structured by white privilege. Positioning the parents in the community as the primary audience and trying to respond to their concerns, Michelle's text begins the process of redefining literacy around renegotiating relationships.

CONCLUSION

The key problems I have highlighted in this chapter revolve around an ongoing legacy of attacking attention to institutional racism rather than attacking institutional racism itself. Within composition studies, efforts to use literacy to undo the consequences of institutional racism have tended to reinforce the culture of poverty thesis, distracting white attention from how institutions such as education are defined in the first place. In this context, a major challenge to our profession is to teach writing as participating in changing what writing means. Cities are spaces in which experiments with transforming institutional racism, social group relations, and literacy are already underway. One strategy for an urban pedagogy of writing is to position student writers as participants in these context-based alternatives to dominant notions of literacy and mobility. Writing as urban citizens, students can begin to redefine literacy as a practice of struggling for better relationships and thus begin to contest the dominant "attack Black" response to the politics of mobility.

WORKS CITED

Baldwin, James. *The Price of the Ticket*. New York: St. Martin's, 1985.

Barnet, Timothy. "Reading 'Whiteness' in English Studies." *College English* 63 (2000): 9–37.

Berlin, James. "Literacy, Pedagogy, and English Studies: Postmodern Connections." *Critical Literacy: Politics, Praxis, and the Postmodern*. Ed. Colin Lankshear and Peter McLaren. Albany: SUNY Press, 1993. 247–70.

Carmichael, Stokely, and Charles Hamilton. *Black Power: The Politics of Liberation in America*. New York: Random House, 1967.

"Detroit's Agony." *Prime Time Live*. ABC. 8 Nov. 1990.

Faigley, Lester. *Fragments of Rationality: Postmodernity and the Subject of Composition*. Pittsburgh: U of Pittsburgh P, 1992.

—. "Literacy After the Revolution." *College Composition and Communication* 48 (1997): 30–43.

Farmer, Frank. "Dialogue and Critique: Bahktin and the Cultural Studies Writing Classroom." *College Composition and Communication* 49 (1998): 186–207.

Fox, Tom. "Standards and Access." *Journal of Basic Writing* 12 (1993): 37–44.

Herron, Jerry. *Afterculture: Detroit and the Humiliation of History*. Detroit: Wayne State UP, 1993.

hooks, bell. *Black Looks: Race and Representation*. Boston: South End, 1992.

Howells, William Dean. *A Hazard of New Fortunes*. New York: Boni and Liveright, 1889.

LaVoi, Renee. "A Vote for Renee LaVoi is a Vote for Morality." Paid Advertisement. *Minneapolis Star Tribune* 1 November 1999: B5.

Omi, Michael. "Racialization in the Post-Civil Rights Era." *Mapping Multiculturalism*. Ed. Avery Gordon and Christopher Newfield. Minneapolis: U of Minnesota P, 1996. 178–86.

Shaughnessy, Mina. *Errors and Expectations: A Guide for the Teacher of Basic Writing*. New York : Oxford UP, 1977.

Sledd, James. "Bi-Dialectalism: The Linguistics of White Supremacy." *English Journal* 58 (1969): 1307–15, 1329.

Smitherman, Geneva. "'God Don't Never Change': Black English from a Black Perspective." *College English* 34 (1973): 828–33.

Steinberg, Stephen. *Turning Back: The Retreat from Racial Justice in American Thought and Social Policy*. Boston: Beacon, 1995.

Unger, Roberto Mangabeira, and Cornel West. *The Future of American Progressivism: An Initiative for Political and Economic Reform*. Boston: Beacon, 1998.

CONTRIBUTORS

Tracey Baker is Associate Professor of English at the University of Alabama at Birmingham, where she serves as Director of the English Resource Center and teaches courses in composition and professional writing. She is co-author of *Writing and Synthesis: A Multi-Cultural Approach* and has published articles and reviews in *Journal of Basic Writing, The Writing Lab Newsletter, Journal of Business and Technical Communication, Journal of Advanced Composition,* and *Teaching English in the Two-Year College.*

Patrick Bruch is Assistant Professor of Writing Studies and Co-Director of the Writing Program, General College at the University of Minnesota, Twin Cities. He is co-editor of *Cities, Cultures, Conversations* and has published articles on the social dynamics of teaching writing in journals including *Rhetoric Review, Journal of Advanced Composition,* and *Basic Writing e-Journal.* He would like to thank the Office of the Vice President for Research at the University of Minnesota for support of his current work on the past, present, and future of struggles over literacy for equality.

Daniel Collins is Assistant Professor of English at Manhattan College, where he teaches a variety of composition courses. Recent publications include an essay entitled "Audience in Afrocentric Rhetoric: Promoting Human Agency and Social Change" in the collection *Alternative Rhetorics: Challenges to the Rhetorical Tradition* and a co-authored essay with Robert Sutton, "Rhetoric as Commitment: Ethics and Everyday Life," in *Teaching English in the Two-Year College.*

Elizabeth Ervin is Associate Professor of English and a participating faculty member in the women's study minor at the University of North Carolina at

Wilmington. Her teaching and research interests deal mainly with public and local literacies, rhetoric and cultural studies, and pedagogy; she has published several articles and chapters on these subjects as well as a textbook, *Public Literacy*. Ervin has participated in and coordinated a number of service learning projects in the Wilmington area and received several grants to pursue research related to civic rhetoric. She is perpetually investigating the ways in which our most humane and civic ideals for language can enhance the quality of our lives and the lives of those around us.

Ann Feldman, Associate Professor of English and Associate Vice Chancellor for Academic Affairs at the University of Illinois at Chicago, is interested in how identity, inquiry, and disciplinarity interact. For the past five years, she directed the First-Year Writing program at UIC and is now responsible for developing writing instruction campus wide. She has written two textbooks: *Writing and Learning in the Disciplines* and *In Context* (with Nancy Downs and Ellen McManus).

Linda Flower, Professor of Rhetoric at Carnegie Mellon University and Director of the Carnegie Mellon Center for University Outreach, is the author of numerous publications including *The Construction of Negotiated Meaning: A Social Cognitive Theory of Writing, Problem-Solving Strategies for Writing in College and Community,* and most recently, *Learning to Rival: A Literate Practice for Intercultural Inquiry* (with Elenore Long and Lorraine Higgins). She has twice won the Richard Braddock Award and is Co-Founder and President of the Board of the Community Literacy Center in Pittsburgh.

Lynee Lewis Gaillet is Associate Professor of Composition and Rhetoric and Director of Lower Division Studies at Georgia State University. She has published *Scottish Rhetoric and Its Influence* as well as numerous articles in journals including *Rhetoric Review, Composition Studies, Issues in Writing, Rhetoric Society Quarterly,* and *The Journal of Teaching Writing.*

Barbara Gleason is Associate Professor at the City College of New York, where she teaches in the English Department and at the Center for Worker Education. She has published several essays on basic writing, teaching returning adults, and writing course curriculum. She has co-edited, with Mark Wiley and Louise Wetherbee Phelps, *Composition in Four Keys: Inquiring Into a Field: Nature, Art, Science, and Politics* (Mayfield 1995) and, with Faun Bernbach Evans and Mark Wiley, *Cultural Tapestry: Readings for Pluralistic Society* (Harper Collins 1992).

Jeffrey Grabill is Associate Professor in the Department of American Thought and Language at Michigan State University. He works at the intersection of professional and technical writing, rhetorical theory, and literacy theory and focuses on the literate and technological practices of citizens, users, students, and other such people within non-academic institutions. Grabill has written *Community Literacy Programs and the Politics of Change* (SUNY, 2001) and has won awards for articles published in *College Composition and Communication, Technical Communication Quarterly,* and *Computers and Composition.*

Van Hillard is Assistant Professor of the Practice of Rhetoric at Duke University, where he directs the First-Year Writing Program. He has written about public art and memory, the civic geography of city parks, and the rhetoric of architecture. Recently, he directed a three-year project in "Moral Deliberation, Disagreement, and Community," sponsored by the William and Flora Hewlett Foundation, and is at work co-directing a project in rhetorical and civic education in conjunction with Duke University's Center for Documentary Studies.

Krista Hiser has taught writing in many San Francisco contexts, including homeless shelters, employment agencies, libraries, and San Francisco State University. She served as Writing Coordinator for "Socrates in the City," a college level seminar sponsored by San Francisco State University and taught at community-based centers serving low-income residents in the city. Hiser also served as Program Assistant for the Conference on College Composition and Communication in 2001.

David Jolliffe is Professor of English at DePaul University. From 1997 to 2001, he served as Director of the First-Year Program, a sequence of four sets of courses designed to introduce incoming students to experiential leaning, seminar inquiry, academic writing, and quantitative reasoning. His most recent book is *Inquiry and Genre: Writing to Learn in College,* published in 1998 by Allyn and Bacon.

Peggy Jolly is Associate Professor of English and Director of Freshman English/Developmental Studies at the University of Alabama at Birmingham. She is the author of several composition textbooks and articles focusing on composition and technology, developmental writing, and writing assessment. Jolly is also the recipient of several grants funding distance-learning courses at UAB.

Richard Marback is Associate Professor of English at Wayne State University. He teaches courses on cultural studies, the history of rhetoric, rhetorical theory, and writing pedagogy in the graduate program in rhetoric and com-position. His publications include *Plato's Dream of Sophistry* and a co-edited text entitled *Cities, Cultures, Conversations,* along with several articles about the urban context of Detroit, theories and practices of literacy, and students' rights to their own language. Marback is currently involved in a long-term research project on the intersections of city space, racial identity formation, and rhetorical practices in contemporary American cities.

Paula Mathieu is Assistant Professor of English at Boston College. Her work has appeared in *Rhetoric Review* and *Works and Days.* She has co-writ-ten articles with various colleagues for *Theorizing Composition: A Critical Sourcebook of Theory and Scholarship in Contemporary Composition Studies, The Relevance of English,* and *By Any Other Name: Writing Groups Inside and Out-side the Classroom* and has co-edited a collection entitled *Beyond English, Inc.: Corporatization and Curricula in the 21st Century* (Boynton Cook/Heine-mann). Mathieu serves as a member of the North American Street Newspa-per Association.

Bruce McComiskey is Associate Professor of English at the University of Alabama at Birmingham. His work has appeared in such journals as *Teaching English in the Two-Year College, Philosophy and Rhetoric, Business Communica-tion Quarterly, Rhetoric Review, Composition Forum,* and *Rhetoric Society Quar-terly.* In 1997, he won the James L. Kinneavy Award for his essay "Social-Process Rhetorical Inquiry," published in the *Journal of Advanced Composition.* His most recent publications include *Teaching Composition as a Social Process* (Utah State UP, 2000) and *Gorgias and the New Sophistic Rhetoric* (Southern Illinois UP, 2001).

Marilyn McKinney, Professor of Literacy Education at the University of Nevada, Las Vegas, serves as Co-Director of the Southern Nevada Writing Project. She has also worked as Elementary Coordinator of the Urban Teach-ing Partnership Program, a year-long, field-based, post-baccalaureate pro-gram developed to prepare individuals to teach in urban schools. She has pub-lished several articles on reading and writing assessment, writing portfolios, and literacy.

Ed Nagelhout is Assistant Professor of English at Indiana University-Pur-due University, Indianapolis, where he teaches in the Writing Program and is helping to develop a new literacy track for English majors. He has published articles in journals including *Technical Communication Quarterly, Journal of Technical Writing and Communication,* and *Business Communication Quarterly* as well as chapters focusing on interdisciplinary writing. While Assistant Professor and Co-Director of Business Writing at the University of Nevada, Las Vegas, Nagelhout received a university-sponsored planning initiative award (with Jeff Jablonski) for developing a business writing curriculum extending into the Las Vegas community.

Cynthia Ryan is Assistant Professor of English at the University of Alabama at Birmingham, where she teaches courses in rhetoric and composition and professional writing. Her work is published in journals including *Composition Forum, Issues in Writing, Journal of American Periodicals, Journal of Business Communication,* and *Journal of Medical Humanities,* and she is completing a book focusing on the politics of breast cancer discourse in popular periodicals.

Susan Swan, a doctoral candidate in rhetoric at Carnegie Mellon University, serves as Research Assistant in the Center for University Outreach and teaches a variety of courses in composition. She received the E. Murry Award for Outstanding Graduate Work at Southern Illinois University. Her current research interests include community-based problem solving, workplace literacy, and service learning.

INDEX